Profitable
Direct
Marketing

Profitable Direct Marketing

How to start, improve, or expand
any direct marketing operation...
plus 11 detailed case studies of
prominent direct marketing companies.

Jim Kobs
President
Kobs & Brady Advertising, Inc.
Chicago, Illinois

NTC Business Books
a division of National Textbook Company • Lincolnwood Illinois U.S.A.

1988 Printing

Published by NTC Business Books, an imprint
of National Textbook Company, 4255 West Touhy Avenue,
Lincolnwood, Illinois 60646-1975 U.S.A.
Manufactured in the United States of America.
Library of Congress Catalog Card Number: 79-53509

8 9 0 ML 0 9 8 7 6 5 4

Dedicated to Nadine,
for her understanding and patience.
And to Karen, Ken, and Kathleen,
who missed a couple of vacations
while Dad was pounding his typewriter.

Contents

Part I   How to Start a Direct Marketing Program

1   A New Marketing Discipline . . . .
Direct marketing today. Direct marketing in the year 2000.
What's really different about direct marketing? From the consumer's viewpoint. From the advertiser's viewpoint. Can your
firm benefit from direct marketing? The last word on a new
marketing discipline.

2   Launching a New Direct Marketing Program . . . . . .
Basic questions to consider. The effect on your dealers, dis-
tributors, or sales force. Ten essentials for long-range profits.
The last word on launching a new program.

3   Selecting Products and Services . . . .
The "four plus one" formula for product selection. The appeal
of a service. Product decisions to consider. The life cycle of a
product. The last word on product selection.

4   Proven Direct Response Offers . . . .
Relate the offer to your objective. Case study of a consumer
mailing offer. Case study of a business mailing offer. Most-
popular consumer and business offers. Presenting your offer
most effectively. Checklist of 99 proven direct response offers.

Foreword

It was great news to everyone in direct marketing when word got around that Jim Kobs was writing a book on profitable direct marketing. No one is more qualified to write on this subject than Jim Kobs. As one of the field's most creative people, with so much personal involvement in so many outstanding direct marketing programs, he is in a unique position to combine the talents of a great writer with the knowledge which comes only through direct involvement in the creation, execution—and most important—the evaluation of both direct marketing successes and failures.

Jim's willingness to share his experiences with others is an important step forward in the education of both the newcomer with an interest in direct marketing and the "old pro" who knows you can never learn enough about this rapidly developing method of marketing.

One of the most important things you quickly learn when you get involved in direct marketing is that, while there are no hard and fast rules, the route to success is usually paved with the stones of others' experience. Those who move forward with the fewest failures take the time to carefully study the experiences of others.

It is easy to become awed by the much publicized stories of innovative entrepreneurs who have scored impressive direct marketing successes through application of unique promotion methods. Unfortunately, too little publicity has been given the thousands who tried unique, unproved methods and quickly failed.

Certainly direct marketing is an area for unconventional approaches. But such innovation comes *after* building a sound foundation through the application of time-tested basics. And you'll find these basics laid out for you in easily understood fashion in this book.

But Jim Kobs has gone one step further and carefully researched a series of representative case histories showing how companies big and small have developed successful direct marketing programs. His detailed presentation of these success stories not only makes for interesting reading but underscores the importance of fundamentals in developing profitable direct marketing programs.

One caution: this is not a book to just read and then cast aside. It is a continuing reference source to which you will want to return time and again to refresh yourself on the basics of direct marketing. In my own seminar work, I've been surprised at how often I find successful direct marketing executives in the audience. When I talk with them personally, they comment as if with one voice about their continuing need to "brush up on the basics."

So consider yourself privileged to have this highly readable book at your beck and call whenever a review of the elements of profitable direct marketing can help you solve a pressing problem or smooth off the rough edges of an important project.

Dick Hodgson
Author, *Direct Mail and Mail Order Handbook*

Preface

Somewhere in America there's a bright, young college student who's destined for a career in direct marketing. But right now, he or she probably doesn't even know what direct marketing is. For it hasn't gained as much recognition yet in academic circles as it has in the business world.

After getting a degree, the student will decide upon a career in advertising. Chances are, the glamour of general advertising will have the most appeal for our job-seeker. Somewhere along the line, however, he or she will be exposed to direct marketing, discover it's a different type of advertising that's totally measurable, and get "hooked" on it.

I should know because it happened pretty much like that for me. Despite taking Jack Maguire's direct mail course at the University of Illinois, I never thought of it as a career. And even when I went to work for Jack Thompson at the Rylander Company as a direct mail copywriter, it was only to collect enough experience so I could get a job with a general ad agency.

But I got hooked on direct mail and mail order enough to want to stick with it. And I've been fortunate to be involved during its greatest growth period, a period during which the whole field has become known as *direct marketing*. It's a term so new that some of the industry leaders are still wrestling with its official definition. But this new-found name has gone a long way toward encompassing the growing scope of this marketing discipline—and toward making it more palatable to everyone from top corporation executives to career-minded students.

During my own career, I've been fortunate to meet and work with some of the direct marketing giants of yesterday, today, and tomorrow. I can still remember the thrill of going to my first Direct Mail/Marketing Association convention and meeting the real greats I'd heard so much about. People like Henry Hoke, Sr., John Caples, Ed Mayer, Pete Hoke, and Dick Hodgson.

But it's been equally thrilling to speak at some of the DMMA Educational Foundation Institutes and meet the direct marketing pros of tomorrow. To see these young students get turned on by a marketing method that's testable and accountable. To watch them discover that even though some of their professors may have questioned the economic contribution of advertising, there is one type of advertising that definitely pulls its own weight—and then some.

It's smart, young, questioning people like these who are helping to make direct marketing an even more efficient and productive marketing system. Hopefully, this book will also play a small role in doing that.

The book has been planned and structured to have something for everyone. Newcomers to direct marketing will probably find the first section most valuable. It covers the basic questions to consider in launching a new program, selecting a product or service, creating an effective offer, testing different facets of your program, and developing a multi-media plan.

Those experienced practitioners who already know the basics will probably find the second section more helpful. It deals with improving an already successful direct marketing program and shows how to boost results with advanced ideas for creative effectiveness, management, marketing, and fulfillment.

Industrial direct marketing is one of the fastest-growing areas of the business. And while many of the suggestions throughout the book can be applied to this area, there's a separate chapter dealing with this important subject. It explains how industrial direct marketing can be used to get sales leads, make direct sales, and reinforce the sales effort.

But whether you're a newcomer or practitioner, involved with consumer or industrial direct marketing, the most important part of the book may well be the case history section. The eleven case studies have been carefully chosen to reflect the broad scope of direct marketing today. They reinforce the basics by showing actual applications. And they give you an insight into the advanced techniques being used by some of the most successful direct marketing firms around.

Perhaps most important, they're *not* just "sunshine success stories." The case studies deal with the real world of direct marketing, complete with the challenges, setbacks, and problems we all face. Most of them concentrate on a relatively short two- to four-year period and present an in-depth look at the firm's marketing strategies and execution.

Throughout the entire book, I've tried to go a step beyond most others by not merely telling you about something, but also providing examples. You see how to write a mini marketing plan, develop a test matrix, take the risk out of a new product development program, and apply an RFM formula to maximize repeat sales from customers. In the same vein, there are more than 125 illustrations, charts, and graphs to amplify the text.

I've also tried to avoid handing down hard-and-fast rules like tablets from the mountaintop. While you will find various lists of numbered techniques, please consider them as guiding principles that can be adapted to fit your own marketing situation or break new ground.

In total, writing *Profitable Direct Marketing* has been a tremendous experience. It brought back fond memories of client programs I was involved with. It gave me new insights into some specialized areas. And it helped me put into perspective a lot of things that make direct marketing such an exciting and fast-growing area. I sincerely hope you get as much out of reading the book as I did in writing it.

Jim Kobs

Acknowledgments

"Now you're an author," my editor, Mel Brisk, said when I dropped the completed manuscript on his desk. But I wouldn't be, if it weren't for the help of many people. The first is Mel himself, publisher of Crain Books, who provided some valuable suggestions and guided this would-be author through his first book.

Special thanks go to Pete Hoke, whose *Direct Marketing* magazine and recorded cassettes were invaluable in my research. Also, thanks to the "insiders" whose comments are found at the end of each case study; their cooperation is typical of the willingness to share information that has always characterized this field.

Thanks, too, to Bonnie Rodriguez at DMMA who provided valuable background information. To Campaign Communications Institute of America, Inc. (CCI), for providing the telephone sales scripts included in the A. B. Dick chapter. And to people whose opinions I valued enough to ask them to review certain chapters or sections: Frank Daniels for his thoughts on creativity; Jim Bernard on industrial direct marketing; and Florence Leighton on foreign direct marketing. Likewise to Professor Ken Mangun, who exposed the case studies to his direct marketing classes at Roosevelt University.

I'm not sure how much the typing of the manuscript had to do with their job changes, but I did have three different secretaries involved in getting these more than 100,000 words down on paper: Nikki Alban, who typed the early parts of the book; Susan Yantis, who finished the original manuscript; and Mary Ellen Guy, who made the painstaking final corrections. Randy Howell also did a great job in assembling the many illustrations.

Finally, thanks go out to all the fellow workers and colleagues who helped me build the knowledge and experience this book represents. While I've had the opportunity to work with and for some fine people, I'm especially grateful that I had the opportunity to be associated with Bob Stone for many years. And more recently, with Tom Brady. Many others, who I equally respect, are quoted throughout the text.

J. K.

1

A New Marketing Discipline

In 1923, the great advertising pioneer Claude Hopkins called it *scientific advertising*. Through the years others have called it *mail order* or *direct mail* or *direct response*. Today it's called *direct marketing*.

Regardless of the nomenclature, this sales technique has suddenly caught the fancy of everyone from one-man entrepreneurs to bottom-line executives in giant corporations. And the buying public has echoed its enthusiasm by responding with orders and dollars.

Maybe that's why it's been described as the marketing revolution of the seventies. And why some observers predict it will become the tidal wave of the eighties. This is why the American business community has embraced this "new" distribution channel for selling direct to the consumer. And why large and small companies alike have employed direct marketing to generate sales leads and reduce selling costs. And why it continues to grow at an almost astounding rate with no slowdown in sight.

Of course, it didn't really happen overnight. The basic techniques have been around for more than half a century. They've been used successfully, but quietly, by scores of firms. Yet, the spurt in direct marketing interest has been so dramatic in the past five years that the term *revolution* is probably justified.

Direct marketing today

When a business is growing as rapidly as direct marketing, it is to be expected that some confusion on semantics will occur. Everyone has his own favorite way of defining things. But here's how to distinguish between direct marketing and some of the other terms to which we referred earlier.

Direct mail is simply an advertising medium, like magazines or television, except that it uses the mail to deliver its message. That message can have a wide variety of objectives, from making a sale to changing opinions or providing information.

Mail order is a way of doing business. It is a distribution channel in which the customer's order is received by mail or phone and delivered through the mails or a similar direct-to-the-buyer shipment method. Of course, the order can be solicited by any advertising medium.

Direct response is an advertising technique. This is a specialized type of advertising that solicits an immediate action or response. The action requested might be an order, an inquiry, or even a store visit.

Direct marketing is a term that embraces all of the above—direct mail, mail order, and direct response. Direct marketing uses media to deliver the message; it calls for action on the part of the message recipient; and it often provides its own distribution channel. Direct marketing, however, is also a method of promotion that can be employed with traditional distribution channels, such as providing leads for a sales force. While there are many more elaborate definitions floating around, I prefer to define it simply as: *Direct marketing is getting your ad message direct to the customer or prospect to produce some type of immediate action.*

The two key words are *direct* and *action*. This is because direct marketing is really the straightest line between the advertiser and the action he wants the consumer or businessman to take. You take your message direct to the customer or prospect, and you direct him to take a specific action.

Dollar volumes and percentages document growth

What does that "action" add up to in consumer purchases? Here are some key figures from the *Fact Book on Direct Response Marketing* (Direct Mail/Marketing Association, 1978):

- Direct marketing now accounts for 12 to 15 percent of all consumer purchases.
- An estimated 1.6 billion mail order transactions were made in 1976.
- Annual sales of goods and services through direct marketing in 1978 were $82 billion.

Direct marketing is not only big, it's growing rapidly. U.S. census figures show that, for a recent five-year period, sales of mail order houses grew 22 percent faster than general merchandise sales through retail stores. In some product categories, mail order sales are growing at a rate almost double the increases stores are posting.

How much do advertisers spend to make these increases happen? Direct mail gets the largest share of direct marketing expenditures. In 1970, $2.8 billion was spent on direct mail advertising. By 1976, direct mail dollar volume had topped $6 billion and represented about 15 percent of all advertising dollars.

Other media not only get their share of direct marketing expenditures but have also shown strong growth. Mail order expenditures in magazines, for example, increased from $58.8 million in 1971 to $86.2 million in 1977. Newspaper preprints of all types have more than doubled—from 8 billion in 1970 to 20 billion in 1977. Moreover, television direct response has soared from $22 million in 1969 to an estimated $340 million in 1977.

The explosion of product categories

When you mention direct marketing, it is natural to think of a few product and service categories which represent extensive volume. Yet the variety of products and services promoted via direct marketing is truly broad.

One of the most complete lists of successful mail order businesses is given in

Julian Simon's book, *How to Start and Operate a Mail Order Business* (McGraw-Hill, 1976). Simon discusses and provides examples of business types that range from selling food and drink to homes and home furnishings (see Exhibit 1).

Exhibit 1. Types of mail order businesses.

Food and drink—meat, cheese, fruit, health foods, and gourmet items
Smoking materials—cigars, pipes, and tobacco
Health and medical products—vitamins, prescription drugs, hearing aids, and diets
Cosmetic and beauty aids
Clothing—ready-to-wear apparel, special size clothing, hosiery, shoes, uniforms, and outdoor clothing
Jewelry—diamonds, rings, and watches
Autos, boats and accessories—auto parts, seat covers, polishing cloths, and boating accessories
Magazine subscriptions
Books—single volumes, sets, and clubs
Correspondence schools—self-improvement, technical, and career courses
Information services—stock market advice, newsletters, and directories
Phonograph records
Photography—cameras and equipment, film processing
Garden supplies, plants and seeds
Hobbies—guns, fishing tackle, leatherwork, musical instruments, stamps, coins and crafts
Art—supplies, prints, collectibles
Toys
Printing—stationery, greeting cards, office forms, collection aids
Money—loans-by-mail, insurance
Home business equipment and supplies
Business to businesses—office equipment and supplies, sales training materials, building maintenance supplies
Homes and home furnishings—land, furniture, house plants
General merchandise—cameras, cookware, drills, and so on

Source: *How to Start and Operate a Mail Order Business* by Julian Simon, published by McGraw-Hill.

While the scope of direct marketing is very broad, the sales figures and results are equally impressive. Here are a few examples of direct marketing's contribution for selected product and service categories:

- Approximately 11 percent of all records and tapes in the United States are sold via direct marketing with a volume of $368 million.
- About 70 percent of all magazine subscriptions are sold by mail and account for $1.2 billion in annual sales.
- Oil companies do an estimated $210 million in annual sales of merchandise to their credit card customers.
- About one-fifth of all film processing is done by mail with an annual volume of $335 million.

- Premiums of $1.8 billion were paid in 1977 for all kinds of insurance bought through the mail.
- In 1976, nonprofit organizations (religious, educational, charitable, and public interest) raised $13 billion through the mail, or 33 percent of their total contributions.
- Sales of book clubs and mail order book offers now exceed the book store total by $118 million. Over 100 book clubs are currently operating in the United States, and the three largest each have over 1 million members.

Major corporations now using direct marketing

Firms using direct marketing can be classified in two broad categories: those who use it as their primary distribution and selling method; and those who are not primarily in direct marketing, but do use it for certain divisions, subsidiaries, or marketing situations.

The first category includes some old-line mail order firms that have been around for years as well as newcomers who have built "kitchen table" success stories. I regard the giants in the field as those doing $100 million or more in annual sales. This includes firms like Colonial Penn Insurance, Doubleday & Company, Fingerhut Corporation, Franklin Mint, National Liberty Corp., and New Process.

The second category is somewhat harder to identify. It consists primarily of medium-size to large corporations, namely, the "blue chips." Most of these have entered direct marketing in the past five to ten years—some by acquisition, others by developing new businesses. Some sell under their own name; others under the name of a subsidiary. Some have entire divisions devoted to direct marketing; others integrate direct marketing techniques into their total marketing program, such as lead-getting programs for the sales force.

Despite the identification problem, more than half the nation's top 50 companies are known to be in direct marketing. Chances are the same percentage holds true for the entire Fortune 500 list. The way direct marketing is growing, it's safe to say that the balance of these industry leaders are probably thinking about or investigating this technique.

A representative list of Fortune 500 companies engaged in direct marketing reads like a "Who's Who of American Business" (see Exhibit 2). Some of the largest direct marketing subsidiaries include Columbia House, Time-Life Books, and RCA Music Service. And, of course, there are the "big three" catalog giants—Sears, Montgomery Ward, and J. C. Penney. Wards alone had total catalog sales of about $1 billion in 1977, which was 22 percent of their total sales volume.

Contributing factors for the growth

Everyone has his or her pet theories to explain the explosive growth of direct marketing. While it's possible to make a rather lengthy list of contributing factors, I think the following list encompasses the main ones:

1. *Changing lifestyles.* There's been a steady increase in working women. Women now hold about 40 percent of all U.S. jobs, and, in families with school-age children, half of the mothers are working outside of the home today. As a result, less

Exhibit 2. Representative list of Fortune 500 companies engaged in direct marketing.

Avon Products	W. R. Grace	Pitney-Bowes
A.T.&T.	Hewlett-Packard	Shell Oil
Bell & Howell	Honeywell	Sperry Rand
Boise Cascade	IBM	Polaroid
CBS	Kraftco	Standard Oil (Cal.)
R. R. Donnelley	Macmillan	Standard Oil (Ind.)
Dart Industries	Mobil Oil	Sun Oil
General Foods	McGraw-Hill	3M
General Mills	NCR	Time Inc.
General Motors	New York Times	Times Mirror

time is left for conventional shopping. Coupled with this is a growing trend toward more leisure-time interests and activities. Consumers are no longer content with being full-time purchasing agents.

2. *Decline and cost of personal selling.* A lot has been written about the growing cost of personal sales calls, which has jumped to over $96 per call (see Exhibit 3). This rise primarily affects industrial marketing. A corresponding decline in personal selling at the retail level has occurred. The trend to self-service discount stores has eliminated scores of salespeople, and those remaining are often uninformed and indifferent.

Exhibit 3. Cost of an industrial sales call, 1942–1977.

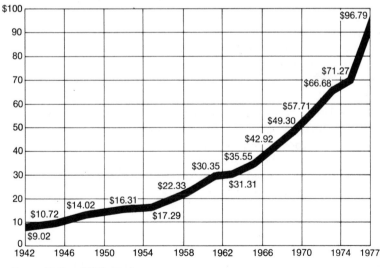

Source: McGraw-Hill Research.

3. *Technological communication advances.* The growth of the computer has made direct marketing an even more exact science today than ever before. Com-

puters provide tremendous list selectivity and personalization for direct mail. Technological changes have also made print media more selective and efficient. Finally, the computer plays a key role in generating meaningful result reports, while computer modeling enables sophisticated direct marketers to examine dozens of options and select the optimum media mix.

4. *Consumer credit.* The availability of credit has made possible the sale of bigger-ticket items that would never have been considered for direct marketing years ago. For the most part, the direct marketer has not even had to worry about carrying his or her own paper, thanks to the boom in credit cards. In 1977, Master Charge and BankAmericard (now Visa) alone had over 91 million cards outstanding, while oil companies accounted for 133 million. The addition of travel-and-entertainment cards, plus retail store and miscellaneous cards, bring the total "plastic" outstanding to a whopping 586 million.

5. *Growing income and education levels.* Most direct marketing activity is not geared to selling the necessities of food, clothing, and shelter. It's directed toward what some have called *marginal luxuries.* And a population with growing income and rising educational levels is better able to appreciate and afford these items.

Direct marketing in the year 2000

When a field is growing as rapidly as direct marketing is, the odds are that growth will continue, at least over the near term. But what about the long term? One would naturally expect those engaged in direct marketing to believe the outlook is good. So, in the hope of getting a somewhat more objective viewpoint, let's look to some outsiders. Let's see what top executives of general advertising agencies have predicted.

Joseph Daly, chairman of Doyle Dane Bernbach, recently said, "We conservatively believe that the increase for the direct marketing industry will be 50 percent in the next five-year period."

Edward N. Ney, president of Young & Rubican, was recently asked by *Advertising Age* about the future of the advertising business. He was quoted as saying, "Direct marketing, direct response will be the biggest growth area in the next twenty-five years."

Finally, the late Andrew Kershaw, chairman of Ogilvy & Mather has said, "When you wake up ten years from now, you will find direct marketing is beginning to take over. If you choose direct marketing, you will be entering the most vital segment of the economy for the next fifty years."

So, whether you look ahead five years, twenty-five years, or fifty years, direct marketing appears to have a pretty rosy future.

What the future might be like

It's always fun to try to predict the future. Especially in a dynamic field that's bound to get a lot of technological attention. I'm not sure how good my crystal ball is, but here are some of the things that I think will have an impact on direct marketing in the year 2000.

Electronic mail transmission is bound to affect the U.S. Postal Service and mail delivery as we know it today. My own feeling is that it will have more impact on personal communication than on advertising mail. But the mechanism should create some interesting opportunities in the latter area as well.

Two-way TV communication has been "just over the horizon" for a number of years now and is finally being test marketed. Columbus, Ohio, was selected by Warner Communications for an elaborate test of its QUBE cable TV system. Imagine a customer viewing your commercial and simply pushing a few buttons to place an order or get more information. It's happening now and early results are encouraging.

Customized catalogs could allow the advertiser to change items or pages to tailor the merchandise selection to different list segments, geographical areas, or a customer's past purchase record. Also, non-impact printing offers the promise of adding personalization throughout a catalog, thanks to computer-regulated ink jets that can imprint personalized messages on-press at extremely high speeds.

National retailers can be expected to increase in number. More and more retailers are starting catalog operations outside their traditional trading areas. As this trend continues, you can expect them to put more expansion dollars into direct marketing or nonstore retailing and less into brick-and-mortar stores.

Dual integrated marketing should also grow as direct marketing techniques are incorporated into regular advertising and traditional distribution channels. You can expect to see more ads and mailings that offer the consumer a choice of ordering direct or picking up the product at a nearby retailer. The result: a more efficient total marketing plan.

Finally, one more major factor will play a key role in the year 2000's direct marketing efforts, the *human element*. The direct marketing field has been developed by creative executives who recognize important changes in the marketplace, adapt them to their own selling situation, and produce improved results. And that's one thing I *don't* expect to change, regardless of how much progress we make in technological developments.

What's really different about direct marketing?

A few years ago, I was describing direct marketing to a group of advertising students. When I finished, one of the students said, "Direct marketing uses the same media as general advertising. It uses the same type of words and pictures to convey the message. So what's really different about it?"

At the time, I may not have had a very good answer. But I've thought about it quite a bit since then. And I think there are four key factors that set direct marketing apart.

Advertising and selling combined

General advertising transmits ideas about products and services. But the actual sale of those products and services happens somewhere else—in a retail store or another person-to-person selling situation. Direct marketing, on the other hand, combines the advertising and sales function into a single ad, mailing, or commercial.

One result of this combining, of avoiding a separate sales function is that a larger percentage of gross sales income is spent on advertising. James McLane, formerly in charge of the direct marketing group at General Mills, cited this as one of the factors that attracted his firm. He said, "General Mills is a company that spends between 3 and 4 percent of sales on advertising. We looked at the mail order field and the direct mail field and saw that people were spending anywhere from 10 to 20 percent of sales on advertising. This kind of leverage against sales by advertising was impressive and interesting to us indeed."

Built-in result feedback

Inherent in direct marketing's appeal is its self-measurement. The reply cards, coupons, and phone calls that come back—the inquiries, orders, and payments—give you an opportunity to measure virtually every element of your marketing program.

DMMA president Bob DeLay recently explained this effect as follows: "Every next move is based upon feedback—the instant replay—available from the marketplace." As a result, direct marketing is the most scientific method of advertising. You can find out which creative approach motivates the most people; if a computer letter is better than a printed one; whether a premium is cost effective; or, whether a particular list or publication delivers an acceptable selling cost. In short, you know what's producing and what isn't.

Service concept adds value to products

Les Wunderman of Wunderman, Ricotta & Kline gets the credit for advancing this concept. He recently said, "I believe direct marketing has the unique ability to convert products to services and satisfactions. It's built into the way we sell."

For example, the sale of individual books at retail can become a book club when offered by mail. Likewise, a magazine: Buy one at the newsstand and you're buying a product. But a year's subscription, delivered to your door, is a service. Even a direct marketing merchandise offer becomes something of a service by offering convenient monthly terms or a free home trial.

Action oriented for impulse sales

Various studies have shown that the majority of retail sales are planned purchases. Direct marketers know that most customers aren't sitting home waiting for an attractive ad or mailing to land in their lap. So direct marketers concentrate their efforts on stimulating unplanned purchases or impulse sales. And everything they do is geared toward making it as easy as possible for the prospect to place an immediate order.

Here's how Tom Brady, senior vice-president of Kobs & Brady Advertising explains the difference: "Basically, the general advertiser attempts to build brand or name awareness—*image,* if you will—so that when a customer is ready to buy, he or she will be favorably inclined toward the advertiser's product. Thus, the general advertiser may have to wait months or even years before the full effects of today's ad dollars are realized.

"The direct response advertiser, on the other hand, wants to sell his product *right now!* And he uses all the salesmanship techniques at his command to persuade the reader to act immediately."

Add up these unique characteristics and I think you'll see why I like to describe direct marketing as a new marketing discipline. It requires a special discipline, in many specialized areas that we'll be discussing throughout this book, to maximize revenue and profits.

From the consumer's viewpoint

Why they like shopping by mail

The amount of research that's been done on why consumers purchase by mail is relatively limited, and those studies that have been done are often difficult to compare because questions are not standardized. Despite these limitations, let's look at two research studies that bring out some interesting comparisons.

The first was done some years ago by *Better Homes & Gardens* to measure reader attitudes and buying habits from its mail order shopping section. Readers were asked: "Why do you purchase items by mail?" The responses (in percentages) came out as follows:

Can't find items elsewhere 33%
Convenience 27%
Fun 7%
Price 5%
Better quality 1%
Other 1%
Don't purchase items through the mail 32%
(Note that total exceeds 100 because of rounding.)

The second study was done more recently by a leading direct marketing catalog house and was limited to its own customer list. One question asked: "Why do you buy from (firm name)?" Here's how the answers (in percentages) came out:

Convenience 49%
Items not found elsewhere 37%
Variety 16%
Price 14%
Service 12%
Desirability for gifts or personal use 11%
Quality 10%
Other (e.g., free gifts, utility of items) 10%
(Note that total exceeds 100 because of multiple answers.)

While there are some obvious differences in the figures, the similarities are worth noting. Both studies put "convenience" and "can't find elsewhere" at the top of the list. While the latter points out the importance of offering items that are not readily available at retail, I suspect that many of the items consumers had in mind *were* available at retail. But the consumer was not aware of them and a direct marketing ad or catalog was needed to bring them to his or her attention.

Moreover, in both studies, price and quality were rated much lower. It should be mentioned, however, that the merchandise most commonly found in this magazine's shopping section and this particular catalog tends to be low-priced. Direct marketers offering more expensive or upscale merchandise might find these factors are more important with their customers.

The convenience of armchair shopping

What about that convenience cited by consumers? If one thinks about it, convenience actually covers two broad areas. First, avoiding some of the problems and frustrations of retail shopping. Second, the particular benefits that are common to direct marketing, such as free trials and delivery to the home.

John L. Blair, president of New Process Company, believes that convenience has played an important role in the growth of his mail order clothing firm. He recently commented to stockholders, "In the opinion of many knowledgeable retailers, the newest (and perhaps the most exciting) era of mail order selling is just dawning. Ever-higher gas prices, the eternal problem of finding a parking space, the incomplete stocks, the indifferent clerks—these reasons and many more are causing increasing numbers of people to forsake lengthy and time-consuming shopping excursions. Instead they seem to prefer the convenience of shopping by mail, at their leisure, in the comfort of their living room."

Balanced against these direct marketing advantages, the major drawback for many consumers has been the inability to "touch and feel" an item before ordering. But Martin Baier, vice-president and marketing director of Old American Insurance Company, is among those who believe that even this negative factor is gradually becoming less important. Baier reasons that today's consumer is a more self-reliant purchaser. He or she has been made so out of necessity, by the trend toward discount stores and the decline of personal selling. And it's this growing self-reliance, he feels, that makes a consumer more likely to shop on his or her own from a catalog, ad, or mailing.

From the advertiser's viewpoint

Five inherent advantages

Through the years I have had the opportunity of talking to and working with many large advertisers who were exploring direct marketing for the first time. Of all the advantages the field offers, these five are the ones that seem to be most universally significant.

1. *Establishment of a separate and substantial profit center.* It's no surprise that the profit motive heads the list. Many firms reach the point of near saturation through existing channels and believe they must explore new areas to maintain their growth. What may be a surprise is that direct marketing often provides the opportunity for higher profit percentages than other distribution channels.

One reason for this has been called *profit dynamics.* When the manufacturer is selling through traditional channels, the firm may gross only about 50 percent of the retail sales dollars its items generate. Therefore, it takes a substantial increase in sales for the manufacturer's profits to increase dramatically. With direct marketing, by contrast, 100 percent of the retail sales dollars usually accrue to the manufacturer. The manufacturer is not sharing profits with distributors. And even a relatively small increase in results or response rates has a much more dynamic effect on the firm's bottom line.

2. *The advantage of controlled distribution.* General advertisers often spend many months in filling the distribution pipeline. Much of their marketing effort is directed toward moving the product along from various wholesalers through distributors to the retail shelf. Because the advertiser doesn't control the distribution, getting enough shelf or display space becomes very important.

In direct marketing, the product usually moves directly from the manufacturer to the consumer. You control the distribution. You decide when and where to move out your product, what market segments to go after, how much advertising support the product should have in the marketplace. And the whole process is geared toward making things happen much faster.

3. *Projectable financial investments.* Just as you control the distribution, you also control the risk. All direct marketing expenditures are measurable and projectable. Based on studying your test results, you should know what to expect in the way of total revenues, payments, and returns. You know what to anticipate for every media investment. And again, through testing, you know exactly what to expect from a price increase or what a free gift will do to your variable costs. Besides the controllable risk, direct marketing businesses tend to have a good cash flow and are usually not labor intensive.

4. *Maximizes market penetration.* Direct marketing offers the opportunity to "fill the gaps" in an existing distribution system. It's an excellent way of reaching into unrepresented markets where you lack a sales force or retail distribution. (In some cases, the people in such markets may already be pre-sold on your product or service by the national advertising you've done.) You may also maximize market penetration by developing new products and services that for one reason or another don't result in profitable sales through other channels. Direct marketing and retail distribution may even be used simultaneously to allow customers to purchase in the manner most convenient to them.

5. *Total marketing accountability.* This is what it all adds up to. You improve the return-on-investment of your advertising budget because you know exactly what results are produced. Your advertising dollars are no longer an unmeasurable expense item. They not only pay their own way—in terms of traceable responses and orders—they provide self-funding ad exposures to those who see your ad or mailing but don't respond.

Can your firm benefit from direct marketing?

It's tempting to suggest that direct marketing makes sense for everyone. Fact is, it doesn't. There have been some notable failures: where the product concept wasn't sound, where advertisers didn't want to believe their test figures, or where direct marketing simply didn't fit a particular marketing situation.

Factors to help you decide

In his *Advertising Age* column on direct marketing, Bob Stone recently interviewed Robert Kestnbaum, who heads the consulting firm of R. Kestnbaum & Company. The title of the article is "Should Mass Marketers Go into Direct Marketing?" Two of the key questions that were posed, along with Kestnbaum's replies, are given here:

Q: What criteria do you establish to determine whether it is advisable to use direct marketing?

A: Basically, I like to see an important reason for a company to consider this form of marketing. Examples of such reasons would be (1) a unique product or service for which other distribution channels are unsatisfactory, too expensive, or unavailable; (2) a market where the best prospects have some highly recognizable or definable characteristic and where lists or other media can be found to match this characteristic, and (3) a product that needs to be fully and carefully explained.

Q: What types of merchandise are suited to direct marketing?

A: The range of merchandise and services that can be sold by direct marketing appears to be almost unlimited. I hesitate to assign any restrictions. Direct marketing thrives on products (1) that have poor retail distribution, (2) for which the purchase decision is difficult by reason of multiplicity of brands and models to choose from or the need to have a full explanation of the product or service, or (3) for which the impulse factor and ease of purchase are dominant factors.

A ton of sound advice is evident in those answers. Other questions to think about include: What resources does your firm have for starting a direct marketing operation? Do you, for example, have a substantial customer mailing list? Or, can you perhaps build one easily and inexpensively by using product warranty cards or inserts in your retail packages? Perhaps your resources include particular manufacturing skills, editorial expertise, or a strong consumer identity with a particular product area.

The conclusion, I think, is a rather obvious one: The more resources you can bring to bear on a direct marketing program, the more sense it makes. And the more likely it will work.

How to cash in on it

If you're still unsure whether direct marketing is logical for your operation, let's look at what I call the "big opportunity areas." These are areas in which direct marketing is already being used successfully by numerous other firms.

Opportunity 1. Use direct marketing as an alternate distribution method for specific products, types of customers, or geographic areas. Perhaps your small accounts can be sold more cost efficiently via direct marketing. Or, perhaps your distribution method fits your present product line like a glove—except for one type of product you've been holding back on. Hewlett-Packard's pocket calculator line is a good example of this situation. (You'll find it discussed in chapter 11.)

Opportunity 2. Use lead generation systems to lower the growing cost of personal sales calls. We've already considered the rapid rise in selling costs. There's not much argument that a good sales force will close more sales if they're working qualified leads. (A concrete example is provided by the case history of Lanier Business Products in chapter 15.)

Opportunity 3. Use direct marketing to test or expand into new product and service concepts. You may have a great idea for a new product, but it's too expensive to launch through traditional channels, or even to "tool up" and manufacture it until you're sure the market is viable. You can often test a product or service concept less expensively with direct marketing, sometimes without even having the product finalized. A prime example is the Montgomery Ward Auto Club (which you'll read about in chapter 16).

Opportunity 4. Use a specialized program to maximize profits on aftermarket sales. In some firms, aftermarket sales account for 50 percent or more of total revenue. Regardless of the percentage, if you can handle them economically, these sales can be quite profitable. But that might call for a specialized marketing approach, like the A. B. Dick Company's program described in chapter 20.

Opportunity 5. Use direct marketing techniques to improve the performance of your regular advertising. Some common offers used in direct response, such as a free gift, can be applied to many sales promotion programs. You can even design tests to find out which gift is strongest. Or simply use some type of "send for" offer to measure the readership of your ads. Many direct marketing techniques can successfully be transferred to general advertising. You'll find these techniques discussed and explained in the following chapters.

The last word on a new marketing discipline

In my experience, it's very difficult for a direct marketing program to be successful unless it has a firm commitment from top management. So many details and different ways of doing things unique to direct marketing exist that top level support is virtually essential. You will need the cooperation of others in the organization, and it certainly helps if they know that management is behind the program and wants to see it succeed.

It takes a lot of people to make something happen. This is especially true in a medium-sized or large organization. One person who has the main responsibility for the direct marketing program should be in charge. While this person doesn't necessarily have to be full-time at the outset, he or she should be a person who is able to oversee and coordinate the many elements in this new and exciting marketing discipline.

2

Launching a New Direct Marketing Program

Let's assume you've made the decision to go into direct marketing. Or at least to investigate it. You understand what's different about it. You appreciate the advantages it offers. You think your firm can benefit from direct marketing. So now you're ready to wrestle with some of the basic, but important, questions almost every direct marketer before you has faced in launching a new program. You want to know what major problems to anticipate. What essential factors have to be covered in planning a successful program. And finally, how to get started.

Basic questions to consider

Not necessarily in order of importance—because they're all equally important—here are some key questions to ask yourself. (And if you don't ask them, your management probably will.)

Do we have a sound concept for direct marketing?

It is surprising how many firms decide to go into direct marketing simply because their executives see others selling a similar product or service via direct marketing. And because direct marketing is considered a "hot growth area" in many management circles, they decide it's the thing to do. But a good marketing person does more than that. He or she studies the direct marketing competition to see how well they're covering the market. He or she tries to find opportunities either to improve on what the competition is doing or to zero in on areas they seem to be overlooking. And in so doing he or she tries to develop a unique concept or idea for his or her direct marketing program.

Is the profit potential big enough to justify the test investment?

Very few direct marketing programs show a profit on the initial test. This is primarily because of the start-up expenses for finished art and production, plus the premium one pays for small-run printing of a mailing package or a regional test in a magazine. But most firms are willing to make the test investment if the down-the-road profit potential is substantial enough. So you should look at what the competition is doing and make some profit and loss projections. It's difficult to come up with precise figures until you make a test and get actual experience under your belt. Use the best estimates you can arrive at and look at what your direct marketing sales volume and profit picture might be a couple years after the test.

Will direct marketing hurt our image?

Many firms spend a lot of advertising dollars to build a modern, high-quality image. And their management is concerned that direct marketing can hurt that image because they still associate it with hard-sell mailing packages and tiny mail order ads jammed with type. Those types of direct marketing are still around. But today they're overshadowed by sophisticated catalogs, large tastefully done ads, and attractive full-color mailings. So, if you set high standards for your direct marketing efforts as you do for your other advertising, there's no reason for it to hurt your image. And I've seen consumer research results to prove it.

Do we need professional help?

Having spent most of my career with a direct marketing agency, I may not be totally objective about this one. I do think professional help is important, whether you go to a direct marketing ad agency or add an experienced direct marketing person to your staff. There are so many details and intricacies in direct marketing that professional help is essential to ensure a sound test program that will provide some definite answers. I guess I've seen too many examples of firms that tried to do it themselves or went to a general ad agency which had no real direct marketing experience. Not only is their test usually unsuccessful, they don't find out how well they *might* have done with a properly constructed direct marketing test.

Should we use our own firm name?

This question is often asked because a firm is concerned about one of two things: direct marketing's effect on their image (a subject we've already covered) or its effect on their dealers, distributors, or sales force (a subject we'll cover later). The assumption is that going out under a different firm name or brand name will allow them to enjoy "plus" business from direct marketing, without detracting from their existing business.

The main thing that's overlooked here is the value of their well-established name in establishing a direct marketing profit center. Yes, you can launch a successful program under a new unknown name. But that unknown name is going to seriously depress results. That happened to a Fortune 500 company that recently tested a consumer merchandise offer two ways. Half of the test mailing went out under its well-established firm name; the other half offered the same merchandise with the identical mailing package except that it was sent under an unfamiliar name. The test using the well-known name pulled 91 percent better! And I've heard of other tests where the well-known name has made an even greater difference.

If this isn't reason enough to go with your own firm name, it's also a fallacy to assume that your dealers, distributors, or sales force won't eventually discover your direct marketing effort regardless of what name you use. And by using an unknown name you may actually be deprived of some of the extra sales that will otherwise accrue to your normal distribution channels.

The effect on your dealers, distributors, or sales force

Looking back on my experience in helping a variety of firms launch a new direct marketing program, this has got to be number one on their list of major concerns. The normal reaction is that direct marketing will hurt other channels of distribution, that it will take sales away from a firm's dealers, distributors, or sales force. Or, even if it doesn't hurt these sales channels, executives know it will produce a very negative reaction from those involved. A typical dealer, for example, is concerned first with his or her own sales. So, if the dealer *thinks* direct marketing is going to rob him or her of sales, the company will surely hear about it.

Four often overlooked facts

Dealer reactions like this either overlook or ignore four key facts:

1. A percentage of any audience or group of prospects prefers to shop and buy by mail. The reasons for this were covered in chapter 1. But various studies have shown that 25 percent to 35 percent of consumers fall into this category. If you don't offer them an opportunity to buy by mail, there's a good chance they'll do so from a competitor.

2. Any direct marketing effort has a very high "failure rate." A direct marketing space ad will usually get less than 1 percent of the audience to respond. A mailing package can prove very profitable, even though only 2 percent of the audience respond. That's a 98 percent "failure rate." This means that if you make a mailing of one million pieces, 980,000 people will not respond or order by mail.

3. The direct marketing budget provides bonus advertising impressions at no extra cost. Most of those 980,000 people will receive an advertising impression, just as they do from a firm's regular radio, TV, magazine, or newspaper advertising. Research shows that 75 percent of all consumer mailings are at least opened and glanced at, and about half of these are read thoroughly. Applying these percentages to our example, we find that 750,000 people will open and glance at the mailing, probably at least noting the advertiser's name and registering an impression of the product being offered. Of these people, 375,000 will read the mailing thoroughly, and, in the process, they'll absorb a good amount of your advertising message. Best of all, if the 20,000 who do respond by mail make the mailing profitable, all these bonus advertising impressions cost you nothing.

4. A portion of your audience will buy through regular distribution channels. Just as there are those who prefer to shop and buy by mail, there is another even larger group that prefers to see a product first-hand or prefers to buy through a salesperson. Even if a direct marketing ad or mailing doesn't suggest it, some of those 375,000 readers in our example will seek out a dealer, distributor, or salesperson who has the product. This is what I like to call the "echo response"

of direct marketing. We understandably devote most of our attention to the direct response in the form of order cards and coupons and often forget the echo responses that accrue to other distribution channels.

The positive effect of direct marketing

All the available evidence I have seen points to the fact that direct marketing enhances other distribution channels. Let's look at some of that evidence. Here's the experience of Bob Kestnbaum, a highly respected direct marketing consultant, who has recently worked with three major marketers who entered direct marketing. Bob reports:

> In one case, Nielson data showed a significant increase in the company's retail share of market at the same time that it began selling substantial amounts of merchandise by mail.
>
> In the second case, the company's retail sales force continued to report major increases in retail sales at times when large-scale mailings took place.
>
> In the third situation, where the same company has an extensive chain of retail stores and a large mail order catalog, the company has proved that one-third of the retail purchases are pre-shopped in the catalog, e.g., that the customer has made the purchase decision by reading the catalog and then has gone to a store to pick up the item.

The case of Polaroid

When Polaroid gingerly approached direct marketing in the 1960s, the company put together a syndicated mailing package selling a complete Polaroid camera outfit for $99.95. Because of company concern that their dealers might feel the company was competing with them, the camera being offered was a "blind" model created just for direct marketing. Polaroid took one of its popular existing cameras, put a new face plate on it, and gave it a different model number.

Direct marketing sales of this special camera outfit totalled millions of dollars. But there was an unexpected side effect. Each time Polaroid dropped a million pieces of mail at $175 per thousand, they were increasing their ad budget by $175,000. And many customers walked into Polaroid dealers with the mailing in hand to buy the camera outfit. The alert retailers realized they couldn't give the customer that model, but they had a full line of Polaroid cameras to trade the customer up or down. And whether the cameras were sold by mail or by dealers, the retailers benefited from the highly profitable film aftermarket.

The case of the book industry

There are currently over 100 book clubs in the United States. But mail order clubs have been around for some time. The two majors—Book of the Month and Literary Guild—go back to the late '20s. Naturally, bookstore owners were concerned that clubs would steal their sales and put them out of business.

It is difficult to come up with a historical comparison between bookstore sales and book club sales from the time clubs were started because industry figures were not then broken down on that basis. Since 1971, however, total book sales have been growing at almost the same rate as book club sales: a 43.4 percent growth rate for all book sales versus a 49.5 percent rate for book club sales (see Exhibit 4).

Exhibit 4. Book sales (millions of dollars).

	1971	1972	1973	1974	1975	1976	Percent Increase from 1971
All book sales...	$2,917.8	$3,017.8	$3,213.6	$3,569.9	$3,850.7	$4,185.2	43.4
Book club sales.	$ 229.5	$ 240.5	$ 262.4	$ 283.6	$ 303.4	$ 343.1	49.5

Source: Association of American Publishers.

While book retailers naturally feared clubs at the outset, their feelings have changed considerably. When asked whether book clubs have a positive or negative effect on retail sales, Linda Kahn of McGraw-Hill reported, "Definitely positive. It took years for bookstores to overcome the negative feeling, but they definitely have. Actually, clubs spur sales despite the lower prices of the offers. Remember, there are many people who would never join clubs and actually prefer to purchase from an outlet. Keep in mind that clubs—whether Book of the Month or Literary Guild—send people into bookstores, and this traffic is what we're after. Once they're in the store, we can take care of them."

The case of a leading insurance company

A few years ago, a well-known insurance firm began extensive testing of direct marketing to sell various policies *by mail.* Executives were naturally concerned about the reaction from their own agents. So they first assured the agents that direct mail solicitations would not be continued if they took business away from the agents. They then asked a professional research center to conduct a series of tests to measure the effect of their direct marketing efforts.

The research reports showed that one test after another produced similar results:

For a mailing soliciting auto insurance sales, two carefully matched groups of prospects were set up. One group was mailed. The other wasn't. Agent sales in the same areas were tracked, and it was found that the mailed group produced 29 percent more *agent sales* than the non-mailed group.

Two groups of 100,000 prospects were matched as identically as possible. Only one group received a direct mail solicitation on life insurance. But life insurance sales by agents were tracked to both groups. Forty-five days after the mailing, agents' life insurance sales to the mailed group were *double* the agent sales to the non-mailed group.

A similar test was set up on a small loan program. Total agent loans to the mailed group were 26 percent greater than to the group that did not get the mailing.

All these results are for agent sales only. And this "plus" business written by the agents was in addition to the significant revenue the firm produced on direct-by-mail responses.

The case of two companies with their own retail stores

Heath Company, which sells electronic Heathkits, has substantial mail order sales and a growing group of over 45 retail stores. The company's experience has been that, when they open a new retail outlet, mail order sales fall off in that area for six months to a year. After that, mail order sales in the area resume their normal level, and the store provides additional sales.

LeeWards, a division of General Mills, has also found that dual distribution makes sense. The division has over two million mail order customers and 30 retail stores. For those who prefer to shop at retail, store locations are listed in the firm's mail order catalog. What happens? According to Lee Anderson, former president of LeeWards, "Each time we distribute a new catalog for direct sales to the consumer, we get a substantial bulge in sales at our retail stores."

How to neutralize negative reactions

This evidence certainly indicates that direct marketing enhances sales through other distribution channels. The initial reaction of your dealers, distributors, and sales force, however, is still likely to be negative.

You can usually minimize or neutralize that reaction if you *inform* them and get them involved. Tell them that you're testing direct marketing. They're going to find out about it anyway, so you might as well explain it your way. Assure them that it should help rather than hurt their own sales results.

Try to find a way to involve them in the program. Some firms pay their salespeople a token commission on orders generated through direct marketing. Though the major thrust of your direct marketing effort should be toward producing orders by mail, you can mention that the products are available through other sources. Or, in the case of a direct mail program, you might offer each dealer a small quantity of mailings to send out in his or her own area. Most won't take advantage of the offer, but at least you've made an effort to get them involved.

Ten essentials for long-range profits

In embarking on a new direct marketing program, you naturally want to build substantial sales and profits as soon as possible. But direct marketing should be looked upon as more than a one-shot program. It should be viewed as a distribution channel that can provide steady growth in the years ahead. With that thought in mind, let's consider ten essentials that not only will help pay immediate dividends, but also will lay the groundwork for long-term direct marketing success.

1. Develop a master financial plan

Success in direct marketing begins with the numbers end of the business. You must determine proper selling prices with adequate markups. You have to establish test budgets that are adequate to provide projectable results and know what your true breakeven points are on those tests. While it is not imperative, you can also develop cash-flow charts to project your peak investments and payout points.

Most large firms entering direct marketing like to develop a five-year profit-and-loss projection. If this is done before the first test, the projection naturally has to be based on some assumptions. But it provides an indication of what can be expected. And, after the initial test, the five-year plan can be revised to substitute actual test results for the assumptions.

Most management financial experts like to work with direct marketing programs. They know that sales and expense forecasts can be based on actual test results. And they like the idea of expanding a program step by step with an opportunity to review results and see if the program is on target at each stage. This provides a built-in safety factor because plans can be changed or altered as necessary.

The appendix of this book includes a handy worksheet that can be used for planning profitable mailings, and the same type of mathematics applies to print and broadcast media.

2. Select products or services suitable for direct marketing

While you may have an extensive product line for other distribution channels, it's not necessarily true that all products will be suited to direct marketing. I know of one large industrial company that had hundreds of products in its line. A new product that was ideally suited to direct marketing was used for an initial test. It produced very satisfactory sales and profits for many years. But a number of the company's other industrial products were later offered via direct marketing, and none of the others did nearly as well.

Chapter 3 will go into more detail on product selection, but naturally you want to consider products that represent good quality, have broad appeal, and can be offered to the consumer as a sound value. It's nice to have a product or service that has a built-in repeat business factor, such as office supplies that are consumed or an insurance policy that will be renewed year after year.

3. Make your offer irresistible

Some direct marketing newcomers are shocked to learn that the offer can make more difference in results than the copy that tells your story, the graphics that display your product, and the format you use for your ad or mailing. The offer is one of the most important factors for direct marketing success. It will be covered in depth in chapter 4. For now, let's just say that the development of the offer or proposition you make to the customer deserves your best thinking. Your goal is to come up with an offer so appealing it's hard to resist.

4. Use lists or media that zero in on your best prospect

Even a good product or service with a strong offer has little chance of success if your message doesn't get to the right prospects. In media selection and planning, your first job is to select the mailing lists, magazines, newspapers, or broadcast buys that are most likely to deliver the prospects you want. A general rule of thumb is that if you start with the best—and they don't pay out—your direct marketing effort doesn't have much potential.

Given some initial success, your second media job is to test enough different mailing lists, publications, or broadcast stations to determine how big a universe you can successfully sell. To a major degree, the potential profitability of your direct marketing program will be determined by the number and size of the lists and publications that will pay out for you. Chapter 6 is devoted entirely to the media most widely used for direct marketing.

5. Choose formats that fit your story and objective

Almost every medium offers a wide variety of formats. Your direct mail efforts can range from an inexpensive two-color self-mailer to a 9 × 12 mailing package or a catalog with a hundred or more pages. Likewise, in print advertising, you can choose a small space ad, run a two-page, full-color spread with a bind-in card, or use a newspaper insert. Even on television, common spot lengths range from 30 seconds to 2 minutes.

Which format you use depends on several factors. You'll want to consider how much copy and how many illustrations you'll need to adequately tell your story. You'll want to keep your objective in mind. If you're soliciting inquiries rather than orders, you normally need a less-elaborate format because your goal is to tell only enough of the story to whet the readers' appetite for more information. And your audience is also important. Do you want a mailing package that will stand out among the many other mailings on a businessperson's desk, or is it designed for leisurely reading by the consumer at home?

6. Create advertising that sells

Unlike general advertising, the creative aspect of direct marketing usually is not intended to inform, entertain, or build brand awareness. The objective is to sell, to get an order or have the consumer take some other specific action. There's a lot more to the selling process than just combining nice-sounding words and pretty pictures.

Think about the creative strategy. Try to come up with a ''big idea'' you want to get across in each ad or mailing. Then get an experienced direct response writer to prepare copy that captures the prospect's attention, weaves a strong selling story, and calls for action. And don't be reluctant to use long copy. It often takes a lot of copy to get people to order a product, sight unseen, by mail. And, if it's sufficiently well written to hold their interest, prospects will read long copy.

Graphics are also an important part of the creative-selling process. Their job is to capture on paper the excitement of your product and the benefits of your proposition. Graphics should be in character with your firm's image, the nature of the product being offered, and the profiles of the markets being reached.

7. Plan for prompt fulfillment

If your creative effort is effective, prospects will often order on impulse and look forward enthusiastically to getting the product. But that enthusiasm can die quickly if it takes four to six weeks to get product delivery or get a response to an inquiry.

A good fulfillment program must be designed to handle orders promptly and economically. Many companies who enter direct marketing have a shipping operation that is geared to handle large orders, such as those from a wholesaler or dealer. And it's usually difficult for them to efficiently handle smaller volume orders for consumers. Fortunately, there are some organizations that specialize in direct marketing fulfillment who can be used at least until the proper internal capability is developed. The fulfillment operation is also responsible for capturing and recording the information needed for analyzing results.

8. Set up an R&D budget for testing

Your testing budget is like the research and development budget for a manufacturing firm. Whether your program is a brand new one or one that's been going on for years, you never stop testing. This is simply because there are always new things to try, new things to learn, new ways to improve response.

The bulk of your testing budget should be directed to testing the big things that can lead to a major improvement in results. Just as a manufacturer's R&D department is often measured by how many new products it develops, the success of your testing program can be measured by how many breakthroughs you produce. Chapter 5 goes into more detail on testing, including the major areas where your testing should be concentrated.

9. Analyze results carefully

Direct marketing tests are often quite complicated with many different things being tested simultaneously. So you have to do more than just count the orders to see how a test comes out. Result reports should be studied, analyzed, and interpreted, taking into account the front-end response (orders or inquiries), the back-end results (conversions, pay-ups, and returned goods), and the lower costs anticipated for a roll-out. Part of the job of analyzing results entails recommending the specific action that should be taken. Where you have some proven success, you would naturally recommend expanding the test to a bigger universe.

10. Maximize customer value through repeat sales

If you look at the broad spectrum of products and services sold via direct marketing, you find that very few operations have become big simply by making a single sale to each customer. The classic formula for direct marketing success is to build a list of satisfied customers and then go back to them for repeat sales.

In some cases, you can sell your customers more of the same product, such as the renewal of a magazine subscription. In other cases, you can sell them accessories, supplies, or similar or related products.

It makes sense to have a structured program for getting repeat sales. Mail your customer list frequently. Use every customer contact opportunity to increase sales, such as including package inserts with your shipments. Have your customers help you find more like them by establishing a referral program in which they send in the names and addresses of friends who might be interested in your product or service.

For a direct marketing firm, the customer list you build becomes your greatest asset. If you send an identical mailing to a list of good prospects and a list of your customers, it's not unusual for the customer list to respond three to six times as well. In other words, a mailing that pulls a 1 percent response from prospects can pull a 3 to 6 percent response from customers. And, because your mailing cost per piece is about the same to either group, you don't have to be a super mathematician to figure out that the customer mailings will be much more profitable.

The last word on launching a new program

It takes more than just a "good idea" to launch a new direct marketing program. There's a lot to think about. To help you sort out and organize your thinking, I strongly recommend you put your plan on paper. Your written plan doesn't have to be elaborate. But it should cover such things as the concept, rationale, market segment, competition, proposed operation, and problem areas. Following is an example of such plan. It's one of a series of new product ideas considered by George Collins, vice-president of Encyclopaedia Britannica.

Famous American Buildings direct marketing plan

1. *Concept.* To develop a series of kit models of important historical buildings and market them as fun and educational projects for kids eight to fourteen. Each kit would include an informative booklet that adds insight into the construction and history of the building. Completed models would be freestanding and suitable for use as school projects or home decorations.

2. *Rationale.* The popularity of model car, train, and boat kits has enjoyed a long history. Blocks and other building sets are also favorites of young children. In recent years the "build-it-yourself" idea has even been successfully applied to the fad interests of monsters and superheroes. But none of the large model companies has developed historical buildings as kits for young people.

3. *Market segment.* Famous American Buildings kits could have a broadbased appeal. Young boys represent the major market, though many girls might also be interested. The series is a natural to offer to Britannica's house list. The offer would fit many child-oriented magazines, and a lot of suitable mailing lists are available.

4. *Competition.* A few manufacturers produce assemble-yourself replicas of historical buildings. They are made of heavy paperboard and are priced from $1.25 to $4.00 each. They range from historical buildings like Independence Hall to more modern buildings like Chicago's Art Institute. All have been offered as individual kits, primarily through gift stores and hobby shops.

5. *Proposed operation.* Famous American Buildings would be offered as a continuity series with a new kit being shipped monthly. Each shipment would include an attractive booklet on that building. There would probably be from 12 to 16 kits in the series. Kits would be priced at about $2.98 each plus shipping and handling with the introductory kit being offered at a reduced price.

6. *Problem areas.* The product development expense could be substantial. Perhaps an arrangement could be made with a manufacturer to buy enough of an existing product to make testing the concept possible. If the test were successful, the rest of the kits could be developed.

3

Selecting Products and Services

Most things about direct marketing are pretty logical; some persons even call it scientific. You study audience demographics. You assemble your costs. You analyze test results. And you make decisions in an impartial, logical way.

But when it comes to choosing a product or service for direct marketing, perhaps selecting the most appealing of dozens of possibilities, there's something more to it. The best way I can think of to describe that "something more" is a combination of instinct and creativity.

Can any product or service be sold through direct marketing? Technically, I guess it can. But from a practical standpoint, a product can do well at retail and just "so-so" in direct response. Or be just fair at retail and be a big winner in mail order. Picking those big winners is where instinct comes into play.

The "four plus one" formula for product selection

I've had the pleasure of working with only a few people that have a true instinct for picking and developing merchandise suitable for direct marketing. And most of them have trouble explaining exactly why they select one item or reject another. Bob Stone discovered this a few years ago when he did an *Advertising Age* column on the subject, but he still managed to suggest some helpful guidelines.

With Stone's article as a guide, I've developed a formula to help you select products suitable for direct marketing. It's no substitute for that magic intuition. But, if you aren't fortunate enough to be blessed with it, this list should be of help in evaluating products.

1. *Broad appeal.* Always look for an item that has universality or widespread appeal. That appeal can be to broad-scale lists and markets—something that virtually every man, woman, or household can use. Or it can have broad appeal to specific market segments which can be reached cost-efficiently. Such as a book on engineering where you can direct your ads and mailings to engineers with very little waste circulation.

2. *Unusual features in the basic product.* Because of the growth of discount stores and self-service, little or no salesmanship is left at the retail level today. So, unusual features may not have much appeal unless the browsing consumer discovers them. But in direct marketing, those same unusual features can be highlighted

with glamorous photography and skillful copy. So look for something different or unique that can be built up, that can create desire, that can get the consumer to order now.

3. *Not readily available this way.* This might seem like a catchall point because there are so many different situations it covers. But it zeroes in on one of the main things a good direct marketing offer can have going for it. Namely, that it's not easy to find the same product, offered the same way, somewhere else. For example:

- The product is a direct marketing exclusive—you won't find it in stores. Like a product you manufacture yourself or one made especially for you.

- Or it's not readily available at retail at this price. Because you can offer a bargain by selling direct.

- Or it's not usually available as a complete package. Like a movie camera outfit complete with camera, projector, film, movie lights, carrying case, and screen. Sure, camera dealers offer all these items, but they don't usually merchandise them as a complete outfit.

It's important to realize here that you can often build this uniqueness into a product by adding extras or accessories. Years ago, in selling a blender by mail, I felt it needed something to make it more attractive. So I developed a deck of blender recipe cards that could be included with the product. We tested with and without this inexpensive addition and found it increased response 32 percent.

4. *Proper price and profit margins.* The starting point for any product or service being sold by mail is the right price. Most direct marketers require at least a three-time product markup. For example, if you're selling a home appliance for $29.95, your product cost should be around $10.00. Publishers usually work on a greater markup. Catalog firms, which spread out their promotion costs over a large number of products, can often get by with less than a three-time markup.

Naturally, in establishing the price for a new product, you'll want to consider your market and what's being charged for competitive products, making sure, of course, that you have sufficient margin for your offer to be profitable. Rather than make an arbitrary pricing decision, many direct marketing firms will do price testing on new products.

Bob Stone wisely points out that the price must *appear* to be the right price to the prospect you're going after. He or she must perceive your price as being a definite value. And that perception will vary depending upon the item, the type of person, and the point in time. For example, let's say you are selling men's ties. A price of $3.00 might represent a good value to a blue collar worker, but connote poor quality to a businessman.

Plus—The dream element. One person who has that instinct for picking products is Sam Josefowitz, the legendary European mail order consultant. At a recent international direct marketing conference, he was asked what he looks for in a mail order item. Josefowitz replied, "I look to products with a dream element. An exerciser, for example, which promotes the dream fulfillment of a better figure without putting forth much effort." It's interesting to note that just such an item has recently been successful here in the United States. It's a pedal exerciser that was promoted as a means to pedal your way to a better figure, while watching television!

There's an alternative to the dream element that can be equally important. I call it is the *story* element. Does the product have an interesting or appealing story behind it? Such as how it was discovered accidentally. Or how some new technology developed for the space program was adapted to an everyday household product. Such a germ of a story, placed in the hands of an experienced copywriter, can often blossom into a spellbinding selling message.

To see how the "four plus one" formula really works, let's try applying it to a basic direct marketing product, a set of kitchen knives. Discovery House in Westport, Connecticut, successfully sold a set of knives by mail for many years.

First, the product had broad appeal. Every household uses kitchen knives. Second, there were some unusual features in the product. The knives were made with chrome molybdenum steel which requires less sharpening. Third, the set of four knives offered by Discovery House was not readily available at retail the same way it was offered by mail, because the firm threw in a convenient, hanging wall rack for the knives. Fourth, the profit margin was sufficient for them to sell at an attractive price of $19.95.

Finally, if you study the Discovery House mailing package, you discover it has both a dream element and a story element. Many homemakers would like to have a complete set of knives that seldom need sharpening so they'll always have the right knife for each cutting chore. And there's a story behind the product of how Hal Gelston, founder of Discovery House, discovered the knives on a trip to the Orient.

The appeal of a service

In recent years, one of the key changes in our lifestyle is what economists call the trend from a manufacturing-oriented economy to a service-oriented one. A much larger share of the typically affluent consumer's budget goes for services today—from appliance and car repair to health services to having someone maintain their house and lawn.

The same trend is affecting direct marketing. Many successful offers are built around products that are readily available at retail. But in direct marketing, those same products are turned into a service. Take, for example, the fact that the great majority of records are sold by mail under a club or continuity plan. The consumer is really buying more than a product. He or she is buying a convenient service that includes reviewing hundreds of new records, offering the most appropriate ones on a set schedule with return privileges, and shipping them automatically right to the home with the privilege of paying for them later.

Some successful direct marketing services are not readily available at retail. One is the popular World of Beauty Club, which offers women a chance to sample a wide variety of cosmetic products at bargain prices. Or a computerized horoscope, which is individually prepared from the information each customer provides on the order form. Other direct marketing computer services range from personalized children's books to investment advice.

Product decisions to consider

In selecting and refining the product for your direct marketing offer, there are many things to think about. We will cover the major decisions many firms wrestle with and then some of the details involved in product planning.

Existing products, new ones, or variations?

Let's assume you already have a successful product line being sold through other distribution channels and you're trying to decide what product or products to use for your initial direct marketing offer. First, it's usually wise to start with the same type of products your firm is already familiar with, not go into an entirely new product area. This way, you're building on the product knowledge, strength, and consumer reputation you already have.

One large blue chip company that entered direct marketing a few years ago didn't follow this principle. The firm launched an entire new product line for direct marketing. One major problem during the first few years was developing the product expertise to know what types of products to offer at what price points. The problem was sufficiently serious that it almost caused the entire direct marketing program to fail before it got off the ground.

An existing proven product is normally your best bet. But, if it's important to minimize dealer reactions to your direct marketing offer, you can use an alternative product that permits a "blind" offer. An example is a camera where you change the face plate design or color and give it a different model number. Ordinarily it is relatively inexpensive to make such changes.

New product development just for direct marketing, on the other hand, can be quite expensive. It's usually more practical to try to launch or test a new direct marketing program with existing products. Once you've established an ongoing program, with a substantial number of members or customers, it's easier to justify the expense of new product development.

A couple of other considerations, however, are relevant. The product you're offering through retail may not be priced at the ideal level for direct marketing. For instance, you may want to develop a higher-priced or deluxe version of the same item.

In direct marketing, you usually don't have the same physical limitations as might be expected in retail product development. Let's say you've developed an inexpensive kit to help children learn to tell time. The kit includes a book, a clock with movable hands, and punch-out numbers. For retail, it would be essential to have all components fit together in a box or see-through bag for display purposes. And you would probably need colorful graphics on the package to show the product in use and do a selling job. In direct marketing, your main concern is that the product is easy to ship. So the same three components can be put in a shipping carton without a self-contained package. And, because your ad or mailing will do the main selling job, a colorful package is not essential.

One-step or two-step?

A one-step offer is the approach to be used when your ad or mailing aims for an immediate sale. This contrasts with a two-step offer where your ad or mailing is designed simply to produce an inquiry (the first step), and that inquiry is followed up to produce the sale (the second step). Naturally, the inquiries can be followed up any way you choose—by a salesperson, a series of mailings, or a telephone sales contact. Generally you're better off to go with a one-step offer, especially on lower-priced products. But sometimes a product is too expensive or too complicated to be directed right for the order, for example, a home-study course or an encyclopedia set. While some encyclopedias have been sold successfully by mail, most require a two-step offer with a high-powered sales force to produce maximum sales.

Sometimes media limitations require you to use a combination of the one-step and two-step offers. You might have a complicated product that can be sold successfully with an elaborate mailing package. But, in space advertising where you're normally limited to a page or spread ad, you may not be able to tell enough of the story to do an effective selling job. You might be forced to use a one-step method in the mail and a two-step method in space advertising.

Continuity or series?

Many advantages exist in a continuity product plan in which you ship the product in continuous installments. But they can only be enjoyed if the product or service is suited to a continuity, such as a series of books or records.

If the product is of this type, the very nature of a continuity makes repeat sales to the same customer almost automatic. You also benefit from a larger unit of sale to the average customer. If the product and value you offer are good, the average customer might accept six to eight shipments before dropping out of the program. And, if the program sells for $5.00 a shipment, that brings your average order up to the $30.00 to $40.00 range.

Start a catalog?

A catalog provides still other product considerations. First of all, every catalog item doesn't have to have the broad appeal of items offered by themselves. A catalog is more like a department store with something for everyone. Although all the products might be selected to serve a particular interest, such as a catalog of tools, some items will appeal to some customers and some to others.

Launching a full-scale catalog operation, however, can be expensive. Not only must you come up with enough products to offer a wide selection, your development expense for art and production can be substantial. Many direct marketing firms start with a smaller catalog and expand it in stages. Or some develop winning items through individual mailings and then use them as a nucleus to start a catalog.

Other product details

Finally, other product details to consider in your direct marketing offer are:
- Do we offer a choice of sizes? (If so, how does this affect inventory needs?)
- Should we offer a choice of colors? (Or do we want to adopt Henry Ford's famous stance: You can have any color so long as it's black?)
- Can the items be personalized? (Personalization usually enhances the sale of a mail order item.)
- Is the product relatively lightweight and easy to ship?
- Can you include any necessary accessories (like batteries or film) so the product will be ready to use when it's received?
- What will it cost to refurbish or restore returned goods to salable condition?

The life cycle of a product

It's nice to dream about a new product that can be successfully tested and then promoted year after year with steady growth. It's nice. But it's not too realistic because the marketplace is a dynamic one with constant changes in everything from consumer tastes to the competitive environment.

The accompanying chart shows the life cycle of a typical direct marketing product. The process takes a product through various stages from testing, to growth, maturation, saturation, and decline. The cycle assumes that maturation will come during the third year and estimates the percentage of total sales that might be expected from each stage of the life cycle (see Exhibit 5). The ideal situation is to be able to bring on tested new products at the time old ones are beginning to decline.

Exhibit 5. Life cycle of a product.

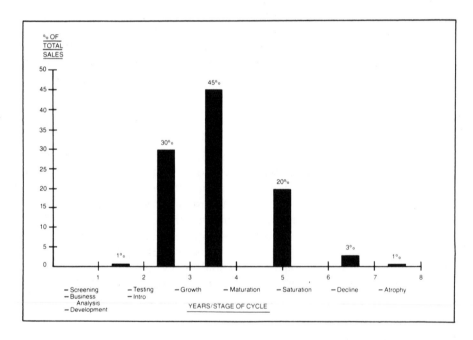

Source: Developed for the Direct Mail/Marketing Association by Maxwell Sroge Company, Inc.

The last word on product selection

It should be noted that life cycles sometimes repeat themselves. One insurance company I know has sold the same basic types of policies by mail for over thirty years. The firm has a couple of old standby policies that do very well for a few years, then seem to reach the saturation point. So management rests them, while promoting other policies, and then recycles the original policies a few years later.

If a product seems to be wearing out, don't give up on it. Just put it on the "back burner" for a while and test it periodically to see if it can be revived.

4

Proven Direct Response Offers

Probably the most misunderstood concept in direct marketing is the offer. I've known persons who have been in the business for years but didn't really understand how to structure an offer. Some have made what they thought were very insignificant changes in an offer, and their response dropped 35 percent or more.

Yet the offer is one of the simplest and most dramatic ways to improve results. If the average direct marketer spent as much time testing, refining, and fine tuning his or her offer as editing and polishing a piece of direct response copy, the bottom line would look a lot better.

But let's start with the basics. What is the offer? It's simply your proposition to the prospect or customer, what you will give the customer in return for taking the action your mailing or ad asks him or her to take.

What does the offer include? Your product or service, the price and payment terms under which the customer can get it, any incentives you're willing to throw in (like a free gift), and any specific conditions attached to the offer. Sometimes the offer includes free literature or booklets as a first step toward selling the actual product or service.

Why is the offer important? Because the right offer can sell almost anything. Because it can mean the difference between the success and failure of a promotion. Because it can make a successful promotion dramatically more successful! I've seen rather simple changes in offers that have improved results on the same product or service by 25 percent, 50 percent, and 100 percent.

Relate the offer to your objective

The first step in planning an offer is to think about your objective. Are you trying to get orders by mail? Produce more sales leads? Sell subscriptions? Raise funds? If your efforts are designed to produce any type of immediate response, the offer should be carefully planned to help you accomplish that objective.

The more attractive you can afford to make your offer, the better your response will be. So your goal is to come up with the most attractive offer you can afford, one that will melt away human inertia and get people into action now. Please note that I didn't say the most attractive offer possible. I said the most attractive offer you can afford.

Before you get the impression that all good offers are expensive ones, let's spend a minute on the economics of the offer. Without going into great detail, I think it's important for you to realize that your advertising program includes both fixed costs and variable costs. Let's take direct mail as an example. Fixed costs are basic expenses like postage, list rental, and production of a given mailing package. Variable costs change according to the number of responses you get, such as merchandise, free gifts, and fulfillment.

You can usually "sweeten" your offer and make it more attractive without increasing your fixed costs. On the other hand, the cost of an incentive (like a free gift) normally has to be applied to all orders. If a $1.00 free gift improves your results from 10 to 13 orders per thousand, you incur the free gift cost for all 13 orders, not just the 3 additional orders. So how does your profit come out? It depends on such things as your gross margin per order, what you spend on the gift, and how much it improves your response.

Let me just point out that the best or most successful offer is not necessarily the one that will be most expensive for you. Even if you do increase your cost, by throwing in an incentive like a free gift, your objective is to increase response more than enough to offset the added cost involved, so your cost per order or cost per inquiry is lower than it was without the free gift. If you plan your offers carefully with budget in mind, that's exactly the way they can turn out.

Basic offers to relieve risk

Two basic offers have become real standbys. Both are designed to reduce the risk of ordering a product by mail.

Free trial. If mail order advertisers suddenly had to standardize all their efforts on one offer, this would no doubt be their choice! Down through the years, it's proved to be effective time after time. Probably first used by book publishers, today it's also the favorite marketing tool for selling merchandise by mail.

When you think about it as a customer, you can recognize that the free trial offer is almost essential for mail order buying. You're dealing with a firm by mail, someone you probably don't know, and who is located hundreds of miles away. You've seen an attractive piece of printed literature, but you haven't had the opportunity to see a "live" product before buying, as you normally do in a retail store. So the free trial offer relieves the fear that you might get stuck. The advertiser is willing to let you try his product before he gets your money!

If your product or service is suited to a free trial offer, you'll want to think carefully about how long the trial period should be. Most trial periods are 10 or 15 days. But the trial period should fit the particular product or service being offered. How long will it take the prospect to be sold on your merchandise? If you don't allow enough time, you tend to force a "no" decision. On the other hand, allowing too much time can permit procrastination to set in and enthusiasm to wear off. Here are some guidelines to follow:

- Ten days is plenty of time to examine and make a decision about most book and merchandise offers.

- A trial period of 15 days or more may be necessary for a product that entails a habit pattern. In selling cigars by mail, for example, you want the cigar smoker to acquire the habit of smoking your brand.

- If you are selling something more complicated, such as a foreign language course, 30 days may be more appropriate. Where personal effort is required, a longer trial period is usually warranted.

Naturally, a trial offer will result in some returned goods from persons who decide for one reason or another not to keep the merchandise. This group will generally average 10 to 15 percent of those who accept the offer. But a trial offer will normally produce about *twice* as many orders as a money-back guarantee! So even with the added cost of shipping and processing the returned goods, the free trial offer should pay out better.

One word of caution: The free trial offer is so common to most direct marketing promotions that it's easy for the copywriter to take it for granted and not play it up enough. This was dramatically borne out by a research study for Amoco Oil Company. The research disclosed that many of the firm's charge card customers, who had been exposed to a number of free trial offers from the company, didn't actually realize that the products were being offered on such an attractive basis. So future promotions were designed to play up the "no-risk trial offer" more strongly.

Money-back guarantee. This is an offer that has worked pretty well for Sears, Roebuck & Company. For over 80 years Sears has guaranteed satisfaction on every item ordered from the company's giant mail order catalog. Today, Sears still uses valuable catalog space to play up their guarantee. And the technique has been duplicated by scores of mail order firms, large and small alike.

If for some good reason you can't use a free trial offer, the money-back guarantee is the next best thing. The main difference is that you are asking the customer to pay part or all of the purchase price *before* you let the customer try your product.

This can be used to your advantage. Because the customer has already paid, inertia is on your side when he or she gets the merchandise. Unless the customer's really unhappy with the product, it's unlikely that he or she will take the time and effort to send it back. As a result, you can afford to be more generous with a guarantee period than with a free trial period.

Price and payment options

Price is an important part of the offer that's already been covered in the previous chapter. So let's concentrate on the payment options that go along with it.

Cash with order. This is the basic payment option used with a money-back guarantee. It's also commonly offered with a choice of other payment options. Incentives (such as saving the postage and handling charge) are often used to encourage the customer to send a check or money order when he or she orders.

Your credit and collection problems are minimized with this option. If you offer *only* cash terms, however, your response will be substantially lower. Because you are asking the customers to come up with the full price immediately, they may delay ordering until they're in a better cash position. And, of course, some people are reluctant to send any payment until they've seen the merchandise.

Bill me later. This is the basic payment option used with free trial offers. The bill is usually enclosed with the merchandise or follows a few days later. And it calls for a single payment. Because no front-end payment is required by the customer, it's easier for him or her to respond immediately, even on an impulse purchase.

Despite the fact that "bill me later" provides some collection and bad debt problems, it is usually one of the most profitable payment arrangements to offer. And these problems can be minimized by checking credit before you ship.

Installment terms. This payment option works like the one above, except that it usually involves a higher selling price with installment terms set up to keep the payments around $10.00 to $20.00 per month. Installment terms are almost essential to selling big ticket items by mail to the consumer. Terms usually produce an even better response than "bill me," because the customer knows that he or she won't have to come up with the full purchase price at one time.

Charge card privileges. This payment option offers the customer the same advantages of "bill me later" and installment plans, but the seller doesn't have to carry the credit. It can be used with bank cards (Visa and Master Charge), travel-and-entertainment cards (such as Diner's Club and American Express), and specialized cards (like those issued by the oil companies or large retailers). The bank cards are usually preferred for consumer offers. The travel-and-entertainment cards are preferred for selling to business and professional people.

C.O.D. This is the U.S. Postal Service acronym for cash on delivery. The letter carrier collects on delivery of the package. It's not widely used today because of the added cost and effort required to handle C.O.D. orders.

Sometimes there is a good reason for offering the customer only one of these payment options. But, in most cases, it's best to provide a choice of two or more payment terms. Such as a choice of installment terms or cash. Or bill me, charge cards, and cash. Some customers traditionally buy on a cash basis, while others prefer some type of delayed payment or installment billing. Giving them a choice makes it easy for both types to take advantage of your offer.

Case study of a consumer mailing offer

In talking about the offer at direct marketing workshops and seminars, I've learned that it's much easier for someone to grasp the concept when they can see how it applies to an actual mailing sample.

The mailing package we'll analyze is one used a few years ago by the firm of Haverhill's. It's selling a product known as the Townley Desk Central, a desk set with a number of built-in accessories. The complete mailing included a 6 × 9 outer envelope, a two-page letter, a two-color brochure illustrating the product actual size, and a combination order form and envelope.

In analyzing the offer, I'd like you to take a few minutes to read the letter and the order form (see Exhibits 6, 7, and 8). These two pieces contain all the details of the offer. It isn't necessary to see the brochure. There are six parts of the Haverhill's offer to look for.

Exhibit 6. Haverhill's letter (first page).

haverhill's

584 WASHINGTON STREET, SAN FRANCISCO, CALIFORNIA 94111

Dear Customer:

YOU HAVE ATTAINED SUCCESS IN YOUR BUSINESS OR PROFESSION AND HAVE
REACHED A POINT IN YOUR CAREER WHEN THE BEST "TOOLS" AND THE BEST
SETTING ARE NOT A LUXURY, BUT A NECESSITY.
That is why you may wish to add an extra measure of efficiency and
enjoyment to the spot where you spend most of your working hours, with:

Townley Desk Central

THIS EXTREMELY USEFUL UNIT IS "ALL BUSINESS" AND STURDILY HANDSOME.
You've probably seen many fanciful desk accesories — combination
intercoms, TV's, coffee-makers and phone loudspeakers! You need a
special course of instruction to operate some of them, and you might
have to be willing to give up a third of your desk space to accomodate them.

IF YOU TAKE A DIM VIEW OF SUCH BUSY CREATIONS, YOU WILL APPRECIATE THE
TOWNLEY AS MUCH AS WE DO. This black-and-walnut, chrome-trimmed beauty
has everything you look for in an executive working desk set:

- TWO FINELY CRAFTED SLIMLINE BALLPOINT PENS
  One red, and one blue, in chrome swivel holders.

- AN EXCELLENT CLOCK
  with luminous face and bell or radio/alarm.

- A REVOLVING PERPETUAL CALENDAR
  with easy-to-read white-on-black numerals and letters.

- A GENEROUS SPACE FOR NOTE PAPER
  with paper supplied.

- A POWERFUL 8-TRANSISTOR BATTERY AM RADIO
  with 2 1/2" speaker and radio/alarm.

THE RADIO IS EXCEPTIONALLY SELECTIVE,
with clear, static-free tone, that can easily be heard even at low
volume (without disturbing others.) You may operate it (off/on) in the
usual manner, but you can also set it to be switched on by the alarm
clock . . . automatically.

I DON'T CALL THIS AN ALARM CLOCK/RADIO
because that would imply rousing a sleeper — certainly an unlikely
event at your desk! But, it can remind you of a favorite news program,
jog your memory about an important phone call, or call your attention
to those "must-not-forget" things in your business day.

THE TOWNLEY DELIVERS WHAT IT PROMISES!
It doesn't play tapes or records . . . won't answer phone calls when
you are away . . . and it contains no hidden safe to store your valuables!
IT IS A PRACTICAL DESK ACCESSORY THAT WILL PROMPTLY BECOME INDISPENSABLE
TO YOU. YOU WILL USE IT EVERY DAY, AND YOU WILL BE PROUD TO OWN IT.

Exhibit 7. Haverhill's letter (second page).

```
AND IT'S BEAUTIFUL!
JUST HAVE A LOOK AT THE ATTACHED COLOR PICTURE OF THE TOWNLEY - ACTUAL SIZE!
It's finished in black pebble crushed vinyl, with simulated walnut panels
on three sides and framing the speaker - and the entire unit discreetly
chrome trimmed.

GO AHEAD . . . CUT ALONG THE DOTTED LINE AND PLACE IT ON YOUR DESK!
Doesn't it look great? Doesn't it look as though it belongs on the desk
of a busy executive? And, although it's designed with the executive and
professional in mind, its clean good looks and usefulness make it a
perfect accessory at home too. Your wife will be flattered to have one
in her study or on her kitchen counter . . . for messages, weather re-
ports, notes, time, etc. And it's great at bedside too!

But, it is primarily an executive unit and a real working aid. Therefore,
consider the Townley in two ways:

            1. AS AN IDEAL GIFT TO YOURSELF
               and a sensible addition to your work scene. Not
               a gimmicky conversation piece, but a dignified
               tool — useful and attractive.

            2. AS A "BUSINESS GIFT" THAT SPEAKS ELOQUENTLY
               OF YOUR TASTE AND THOUGHTFULNESS,
               and of your regard for the fortunate recipient.
               (We giftwrap and ship direct, if you wish, and
               can also include your gift card.)

A BONUS FOR PROMPTNESS:
For your prompt order (see order/envelope) we will engrave YOUR NAME,
OR ANY NAME YOU PREFER, on a special BRUSHED CHROME PLAQUE which we'll
mount on the Townley. It makes the Townley a bit more personal, and may
even protect it from the acquisitive designs of others!

THE TOWNLEY IS MODESTLY PRICED.
As a gift to yourself, or a favorite friend or co-worker, the Townley
is priced at just $39.95. It's a lot of desk-top usefulness and good looks
for a reasonable sum.

HAVERHILL'S CLEAR-AS-A-BELL GUARANTEE GOES WITH IT.
You must be satisfied or you may return the Townley within two weeks for
full credit or refund — no questions asked. Even with the personalized
plaque we'll accept its return. That's how sure we are that you will
approve of the Townley.

Sounds good? It is! Order the Townley Desk Central today and see for
yourself. I know you will be pleased you did.

                                   Sincerely yours,


                                   Gerardo Joffe, President



PS: PLEASE REMEMBER: The personalized brushed
    chrome name plaque is A BONUS FOR PROMPTNESS.
    Take advantage of this and order right away.
```

Exhibit 8. Haverhill's envelope/order form.

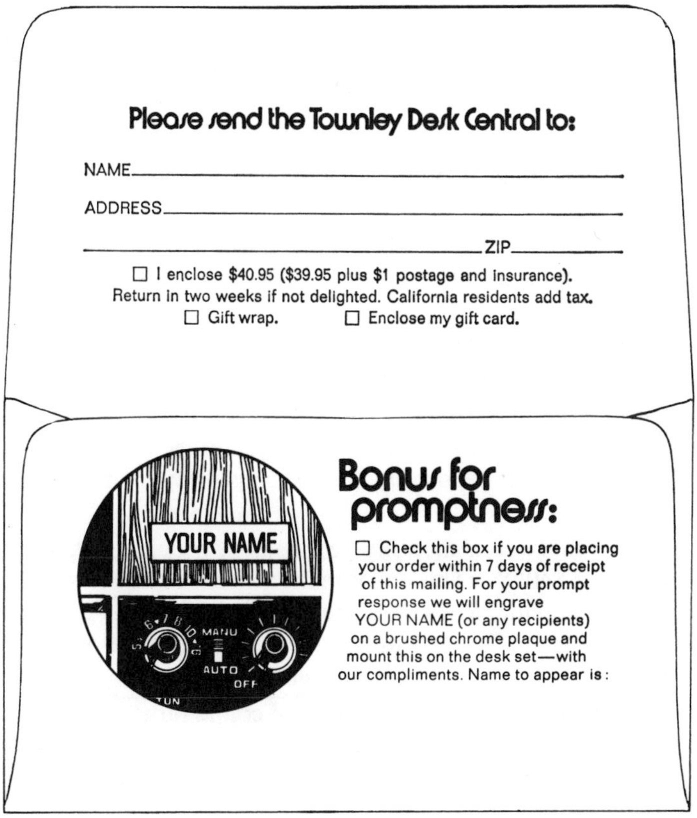

Please send the Townley Desk Central to:

NAME____________________

ADDRESS____________________

____________________ ZIP________

☐ I enclose $40.95 ($39.95 plus $1 postage and insurance). Return in two weeks if not delighted. California residents add tax.

☐ Gift wrap. ☐ Enclose my gift card.

Bonus for promptness:

☐ Check this box if you are placing your order within 7 days of receipt of this mailing. For your prompt response we will engrave YOUR NAME (or any recipients) on a brushed chrome plaque and mount this on the desk set—with our compliments. Name to appear is:

Now that you've studied the letter and order form, jot down what you think are the six parts of this Haverhill's offer. To refresh your memory of our earlier definition, remember that the offer includes the product or service, the price and payment terms, and any incentives thrown in.

1. ____________________

2. ____________________

3. ____________________

4. ____________________

5. ____________________

6. ____________________

Compare your answers with those shown at the bottom of the next page. Those six parts comprise the exact proposition that Haverhill's is making to the customer, what they are offering the customer in return for an order.

Now let's do some brainstorming to see how this offer can be improved. Pretend for a moment that you're the advertising manager of Haverhill's. Your job is to improve this offer, and you have an unlimited budget. What else could you do or throw in to make the offer more attractive to the customer? You call in your ad agency people or direct marketing consultant and have a brainstorming session. Here are some of the ideas that might come out of such a meeting, along with appropriate comments:

1. Offer a quantity discount. (Could be a good way to encourage quantity orders as a business gift.)

2. Free year's supply of note paper. (This might make sense because many desk accessories take an odd-size paper which is difficult to obtain at an office supply store.)

3. Include an extra set of batteries. (This idea could be negative. It reminds the customer that batteries will wear out and must be replaced. Unlike the case of the note paper, standard sizes are readily available for replacement.)

4. Offer a free trial instead of the money-back guarantee that requires cash with order. (That's a good one! Probably the best single way to improve response on this offer.)

5. Let the customer make four monthly payments of roughly $10.00 each instead of one payment of $40.95. (This could make sense, because low monthly terms are important when selling consumer products. Another way to accomplish the same thing would be to let the customer put the purchase on a charge card, many of which have built-in installment terms.)

6. Offer the Townley Desk Central in a choice of colors rather than just black with walnut trim. (The black and walnut combination is probably good for business offices, but other color choices might be important to sell the product for at-home use.)

7. Give a free Cadillac with every purchase. (Every brainstorming meeting comes up with at least one wild idea like this! There's no doubt a free Cadillac would improve response substantially, but . . . .)

8. Include personalized note paper with the customer's name imprinted. (This might add some appeal to the offer, although the name plaque already provides personalization.)

9. Offer a full-year guarantee on the product. (This makes sense, especially with a product whose brand name is unfamiliar. The customer may hesitate to order if

---

Answers for Haverhill's case study

Here are the six parts of the Haverhill's offer:

1. Product—Townley Desk Central.
2. Price—$39.95 plus $1.00 for postage and insurance.
3. Terms—customer must send cash with order.
4. Free gift for promptness—personalized name plaque.
5. Two-week guarantee of satisfaction.
6. Gift service—free wrapping and shipping of gift orders.

he or she thinks it will be difficult to get the product serviced locally.)

10. Provide a discount to encourage the customer to send cash with the order. (If we add other ordering options like a free trial, monthly payment terms, or charge cards, this discount would be logical. Many mail order firms add a postage and handling charge on credit orders, but they pay postage and handling on cash orders.)

Case study of a business mailing offer

As we did with the Haverhill's example in the consumer area, let's look at an actual business mailing. The following letter was used by Eastman Kodak's incentive marketing division. The letter was sent to advertising managers who can use Kodak cameras for their premium or incentive programs. Take a few minutes to read the letter (Exhibit 9) and analyze the offer.

Exhibit 9. Kodak letter.

EASTMAN KODAK COMPANY
1901 WEST 22ND STREET
OAK BROOK ILLINOIS 60521

HOME OFFICE
ROCHESTER NEW YORK 14650

TELEPHONE
AREA CODE 312   654 5300

The Kodak name is well known around the world. Over the years Kodak products have earned fame for quality and dependability. The brand name KODAK helps to sell your products faster, no matter what you plan to promote or how you plan to promote it.

Kodak's national advertising, telling millions of consumers about the "world's most gifted cameras", helps to sell your promotion. When you choose a Kodak premium, Kodak printed and television advertising, direct mail, and displays promote the appeal of all products--movie and still--to your customers.

I am enclosing our Kodak Premium Catalog to provide you with further information on the products and services available to our premium customers. Our complete line of still and movie cameras and projectors is available for sales incentive programs and dealer loaders, and our special "Kodak HAWKEYE" line is available for the previously mentioned functions as well as self-liquidators. Our new fulfillment program offers a complete service package--from factory to consumer--and allows you to concentrate on promoting your goods and services with no inventory investment or handling worries.

May I have the opportunity to work with you in planning your next promotion.

Yours very truly,

Tom Hackett

TFHackett:CP
Enc.

INCENTIVE MARKETING REPRESENTATIVE

Kodak

In this case I won't keep you guessing about what the offer is. It's a "nothing offer." I purposely use it as an example because it's typical of a lot of business or industrial mail I've seen. Someone decides to do a mailing without giving any thought to the offer.

If the objective of this particular mailing was just to send out some literature, that's fine. But if it was designed to produce an immediate response, no offer was made to help accomplish that objective. How could it be improved? What could you do or throw in to make it an interesting offer to the advertising managers who received this letter?

Let's have another brainstorming session. Here are some ideas that might come out of such a session, along with appropriate comments:

1. Offer a camera as a free gift. (Because an incentive program usually produces a fairly good-size order, we should be able to afford to give one camera away to the ad manager. It's an easy way to familiarize the manager with product features, quality, and so on.)

2. Provide free promotion planning service. (This is a logical offer. Most people are lazy or busy or both. So you offer to help them do their job and show them how to plan an effective promotion using Kodak cameras. It could spark their interest.)

3. Offer free advertising support literature. (Like the idea above, this could be helpful to a busy advertising manager who must come up with a complete premium program. If he or she buys a camera for a traffic-building program, we could offer to provide free store posters or window banners and let the manager request samples of them.)

4. Give the manager a quantity discount. (Chances are Kodak already has a quantity discount for premium buyers, so this offer would be easy to make.)

5. Offer a free Kodak premium catalog. (If the objective is to provide sales leads, this idea is a natural! Instead of enclosing the catalog with the letter, as Kodak did, ask the prospect to request it.)

6. Provide drop shipping service to premium users. (Judging from the letter, this is apparently something Kodak will do, and it can be an appealing benefit to the prospect.)

7. Offer free film. (That's an idea with a lot of possibilities. We could offer the ad manager a roll of film to give away with every premium camera purchased. Or, provide free film for the salespeople to demonstrate the camera to retailers and help get good display space for their promotion. Or, just give the ad manager a year's supply of his or her favorite film to get an inquiry.)

8. Make it a "your choice" offer. The ad manager requests information on the type of premium program he or she is most interested in—a sales incentive program, dealer loader, self-liquidator, and so on. (These are all common types of incentive programs. By offering information on each type, we show that we have one or more Kodak cameras suitable for each objective.)

9. Offer a free price list. (This is not a very exciting offer in itself. Maybe it could be combined with one of the other offers, such as a free catalog and price list.)

10. Offer to send case histories of actual promotions using Kodak cameras as premiums. (Sounds good! If you were an ad manager considering the use of Kodak cameras, you would probably like to know what other marketers have done with them and how their promotions worked out.)

Most-popular consumer and business offers

When you sit down to make a list of direct response offers and their variations, it's amazing how many you can come up with. I know, because I did it. And I came up with 99 proven direct response offers. A complete description of all these tested and successful propositions is in the appendix, and a handy checklist is at the end of this chapter.

With the exception of the basic offers and payment options we've already covered, the 99 offers fit rather nicely into 11 categories. In reviewing them, keep in mind that most of these offers are used to get an order rather than an inquiry. Not all of them are suitable for all types of products. Some can best be used on their own, while others can be readily combined into one master offer.

1. Free gift offers

The number of ways you can offer a free gift is only limited by your own imagination. Some of the most popular offers include a gift just for inquiring or requesting more information, a gift for agreeing to *try* the product (which the customer is usually allowed to keep even if he or she sends the merchandise back), a gift for *buying* your product or service, or a gift related to the amount of the customer's order.

With a catalog operation, for example, you can use a free-gift offer to help upgrade your average order. Let's say your average order has been $8.00. You might offer a free gift for any order of $10.00 or more. Or you might offer gifts of varying value: an inexpensive gift for orders under $10.00; a better gift for orders running between $10.00 and $20.00; and a deluxe gift for orders over $20.00.

Others in this category include multiple free gifts, mystery gifts, and "your choice" of free gifts. Be careful with the "your choice" offer. It sounds logical. But every time I've tested it, a single gift comes out better than giving people a choice of two or three different gifts.

Care should also be taken in selecting the right gift. I've seen some gift offers that have pulled two or three times better than others! There's no absolute rule of thumb for what percentage of the merchandise selling price you should spend on a free gift. An inexpensive gift will sometimes produce a better net profit than an expensive one. Or vice versa.

Beware of gifts so appealing that they overshadow the merchandise or attract bad credit risks. Likewise, if gifts are used to get inquiries, a gift that's too appealing can have a negative effect on closures. If possible, make a test and find out which gift does best for your market and your product or service.

When you are planning a gift offer for the business market, the only real difference to consider is how it affects the business purchase.

Some advertisers believe that a free gift or premium should be related to the business product they are selling. On the other hand, one large business mailer I know has literally built his business on premium offers. The firm tries to select premiums that can be used either at the office or at home. Such as a high-intensity desk lamp. This appeals to the larceny of some prospects. They know they can take the premium home if they wish, and still justify the purchase as a sound business decision.

Perhaps the best example of how successful gift offers can be is Fingerhut Corporation's marketing efforts. The company tested one gift and found it improved results. So a second gift offer was added to the same mailing and the firm did even better. At last count, Fingerhut was up to four free gifts for a single order!

2. Other free offers

The word "free" has a lot of magic to it. And it's been used to develop a variety of proven offers. Most of them in this category are designed for lead-getting situations, especially in the business market where the usual objective is to get an inquiry for a salesperson to follow up. It's important to realize that your offer can control both the quantity and quality of inquiries you receive.

If you want a good *quantity* of leads, make your offer as generous as possible. The more you promise to send or give away, the more leads you will get. But this tends to lower the *quality* of leads. On the other hand, if you want a fewer number of better-qualified inquiries, make your offer less generous. And you'll get less leads. Inquiries themselves are easy to get. You have to know what kind of inquiries you want before you finalize your offer.

The more-generous types of lead-getting offers include free gifts, free information, a free catalog, or a free booklet. Catalog offers can be very appealing. Especially in the business market. Many business or industrial catalogs are used as buying guides. They are reviewed, studied, and often filed for future reference.

A free booklet is one of the best ways to establish your company's expertise and know-how about the specific problems of the industry you serve. Such a booklet need not be elaborate in terms of size or illustrations. The key factor is the information it contains. That information should include some down-to-earth helpful material, not just a straight commercial for your product or service. If possible, it helps to have the booklet written by an outside authority whose name is known and respected. And it should be played up prominently in your ad or mailing package, so the reader quickly sees he or she can send for it without obligation.

The real value of a booklet or fact kit like this is to provide a "door opener" for the salesperson. It gives the salesperson an excuse or reason for a sales call—the chance to deliver the booklet, get acquainted with the prospect, and see how to help solve the prospect's problem. In many cases it will get the salesperson in to see a key person or decision maker, where ordinarily he or she would be asked to see the purchasing agent. The prospect gets the booklet he or she wants, and the salesperson gets a few minutes of valuable time which might otherwise be very hard to get.

Other free offers that tend to produce more-qualified inquiries include a free survey, free estimate, or free demonstration. The latter is valuable for business equipment that has to be demonstrated to be fully appreciated. The offer's appeal depends largely on the equipment itself. The demonstration of a revolutionary new product obviously is going to be more appealing than one that's been around for years.

Perhaps the most qualified free offer of all is one I call "send me a salesperson." Anyone who responds is probably a highly qualified prospect, who is either ready to order or seriously considering it.

The actual wording of your offer will probably be a little more discreet than "send me a salesperson." You might ask the prospect to fill out a reply card that says, "Have your sales representative phone me for an appointment." Or you might provide space for the prospect to suggest the best time for the salesperson to call. On the other hand, if you are offering free literature or additional information that will not be delivered by a salesperson, this can also be an appealing offer. Many businesspeople may want to learn more about your product or service without getting buttonholed by a salesperson. So by all means play up the fact that "no salesperson will call" or "we'll send free literature by mail."

3. Discount offers

Everyone loves a bargain. And that's what makes discount offers work. Some of the most popular types include a cash discount, a quantity or volume discount, and an early-bird discount.

One form widely used for direct response is the short-term introductory offer. An example of this technique is, "Try 10 weeks of the *Wall Street Journal* for only $5.38." Most mail order insurance companies have built their business by getting new policyholders with an offer like "30 days of accident protection for 25¢." These offers work because they break down human inertia by making the introductory offer easy to accept. This substantially increases the initial response.

To be truly successful, however, you must be able to convert such respondents to a long-term sale. You need to sell a year's subscription or get that policyholder to pay the regular premium to continue his or her coverage after the 30 days are up. If your proposition is a good value and you have a strong follow-up mailing series, it's not unusual to get conversions of 30 to 40 percent.

Another type of discount is the refund certificate. Technically, it's a delayed discount. You might ask a prospect to send $1.00 for your catalog and tell him or her you'll include a $1.00 refund coupon good on the first order. I've seen this offer work very effectively because it can not only increase your front-end response, it can also improve your back-end results— the number who order once they get the catalog. A refund certificate is like an uncashed check. It's difficult to resist the urge to cash it in.

In general, discount offers are most effective when your product or service has a well-established value. And they should be tested carefully. In most cases, a discount offer will *not* do as well as an attractive free gift with the same value.

4. Sale offers

This is the "first cousin" to a discount offer. A sale is really like a discount for a specified period of time. There are umpteen different names used for sales but most of them fall into the category of a seasonal sale or a reason-why sale.

As Paul Bringe, a well-known direct mail consultant, pointed out in *Direct Marketing* magazine, "A sale of known value goods can stand on its own feet. It needs no justification to be believable. But a sale on merchandise of unknown quality must have a 'reason why' if it is to be accepted. It must be an Inventory Reduction, Post-Holiday, Odds & Ends, Going-Out-of-Business or similar sale. All these explanatory terms have one purpose, to make the sale believable to the prospect."

5. Sample offers

A sample offer is designed to do just one thing: get your product into the prospect's hands. This is because a good sample of a good product will sell itself better than all the fancy words and pictures we can use to describe it.

When a sample offer is mentioned, many advertisers automatically think of a *free* sample. Yet I've seen test results that show it's better to make a nominal charge for the sample. Apparently people are somewhat suspicious of free offers and don't really expect to get something valuable for nothing. A nominal charge also helps screen out some of the curiousity seekers.

Another approach to the sample offer is to tie it to a tentative commitment. A number of magazines use this technique. The offer usually reads something like this: "Yes, please send me a free sample issue of (magazine) and enter my name as a trial subscriber for one year." The subscriber is told that if he or she is not satisfied with the sample copy, to just write "cancel" on the bill and send it back. Once again, it's hoped that the sample product will sell itself.

6. Time limit offers

If you want somebody to take a specific action, it often helps to give him or her a time limit to do so. And if your offer is really a special one, this approach makes it seem even more so. It implies the offer is so generous that you cannot afford to continue it indefinitely.

Limited-time offers work because consumers know they must make up their minds if they want to get in on the deal you're offering. This tends to force a quick decision and avoids procrastination. It's usually best to mention a specific date rather than a time period. For example: "This free gift offer expires June 27," rather than "This offer expires in 10 days."

A number of time limit offers have become favorites for specific types of products or services:

- An enrollment period, widely used in selling mail order insurance.
- Prepublication offer, used by publishers to offer a savings before the official publication date of a new book.
- Charter offer, ideal for introducing new clubs, publications, and other subscription services.
- Limited edition offer, proved effective for selling coins, art prints, and other collectible items.

7. Guarantee offers

Earlier we reviewed the basic money-back guarantee which helps overcome the customer's reluctance to order an unknown product by mail. You can often use an extended guarantee, and, if the product is sound, have little or no increase in returned goods. For example:

- If you have a spring promotion on a fishing lure, you can offer a six-month guarantee and tell the customer to use it for the entire summer fishing season.
- If you are selling an annual investment service, tell the customer that he or she can get a full refund any time within twelve months.
- If you are selling a magazine subscription, offer to refund the unexpired portion of the subscription any time before it runs out.

8. Build-up-the-sale offers

Most direct marketers are interested in increasing the size of their average order. A number of special offers are designed to accomplish just that. They're structured so the customer can easily order more than one item or add something to the basic purchase.

A good example is the deluxe offer. A book publisher might offer a certain volume for $9.95 in a standard binding. On the order form the publisher gives the customer the alternative of ordering the same volume in a deluxe leather-bound edition for only $2.00 extra. It's not unusual for 10 percent or more of those ordering to select the deluxe option.

Also in this category is the multiproduct offer—two or more products featured in the same ad or mailing. This and other similar offers should be tested carefully. Giving the customer a choice can sometimes depress results because indecision sets in and he or she doesn't order at all. But, used wisely, such offers can be effective in building up the sale. The best proof of this is the success of catalogs, which are really multiproduct offers featuring as many as a hundred or more different products.

9. Sweepstakes offers

Today's sweepstakes must be a "guaranteed winner" type of contest in which all prizes are awarded and the prospect can enter whether or not an order is placed. To afford an attractive prize structure, you usually need a fairly large mailing universe, which is why you see sweepstakes used mainly for general interest magazines, popular merchandise offers, and catalogs.

Sweepstakes types include preselected numbers, drawings, everybody wins, and involvement sweepstakes. It's not unusual to see a sweepstakes improve results by 50 percent or more.

One reason sweepstakes offers work is that the dramatic excitement of big prizes attracts attention. This in turn focuses interest on the product or service being offered. But the psychology of how consumers react to sweepstakes is also interesting. Although it isn't so, a great many customers *think* they have a better chance to win if they place an order. So, if the prizes are really attractive to them, many will place an order who would not have done so otherwise.

10. Club and continuity offers

These offers are favorites with the record clubs, book clubs, and other publishers. Some of them have also been successfully used for other special-interest clubs. While there are many variations, as shown in the 99 Offers checklist, let's look at just the three most popular ones as they might be viewed by a consumer:

Positive option. You join a club and are notified monthly of new selections. To order a particular selection, you must take some positive action, e.g., send back an order card, before the club will ship.

Negative option. As with the positive option, you join a club and are notified monthly of new selections. However, unless the rejection card is returned by a specific date, the publisher has the right to ship. Under the terms of membership to which you agreed when joining, non-action on your part is considered a "yes" vote for that month's selection.

Automatic shipments. This variation eliminates the advance notice of each new selection. When you sign up for the book club offer, you give the publisher permission to ship each new selection automatically, usually every month or two, until you notify the publisher to stop. It's commonly called a "till forbid" offer.

All the club and continuity offers get somewhat complicated and must be spelled out clearly. It's best to make sure the consumer understands how the offer works and what he or she is agreeing to in advance.

These offers and their variations might seem similar but their results can be substantially different. A positive-option book club, for example, might only get 5 to 10 percent of its members to accept each monthly selection. On the other hand, a negative-option club can get 20 to 30 percent of the members to accept a monthly selection. So the negative option results can be five or six times better!

11. Specialized offers

This group frankly includes all the leftovers that don't fit neatly into one of the other categories. Many of them are rather specialized and only fit a certain type of direct marketing operation.

A good example is what I call the "philanthropic privilege." This is the basis of almost all fund-raising offers. When you give a contribution, you get nothing tangible in return. But your contribution, coupled with thousands of others, brought in by an extensive direct marketing program, helps make the world a better place in which to live.

Another example that dramatizes what was said earlier about being able to combine two or more offers is the self-qualification. With this offer, you provide a choice of options to get the consumer to indicate his or her degree of interest in your product or service, such as different check boxes on your order form for a free booklet and a free demonstration. Those who request the latter qualify themselves as more-serious prospects and should get more-immediate attention.

Presenting your offer most effectively

Once you've zeroed in on the offer or offers you are going to use, give some thought to the best way to present your proposition. What part of the offer should be emphasized? How should it be worded?

A good example of how you can take the same basic offer and present it in different ways comes from one of the leading book clubs. The club tested the following three offers. To help you compare them, I've added alongside of each what the customer gets and what the customer pays.

	Customer gets	Customer pays
1. *Two books free* (if you agree to join and buy four more books at $2.00 each)	6 books	$8.00
2. *Two books free if you buy one now* (and agree to buy three more at $2.00 each)	6 books	$8.00
3. *Three books for only* $2.00 (if you agree to buy three more at $2.00 each)	6 books	$8.00

Note that in each case the customer winds up with the same number of books and pays exactly the same amount. Yet, at first glance, the offers seem quite different. And when they were tested, offer number 3 produced a much better response than the other two!

The last word on offers

If you have a limited mailing list universe, it might make sense to vary your offer from one mailing to the next. Different things appeal to different people. Some consumers will never respond to one type of offer, even if they receive it a dozen times or more. By using a change of pace, you can pull in some people with one offer and then come back next time with another offer that pulls in others.

Make sure the offer is featured prominently in your ad or mailing package. If you have a free gift offer, it's usually more effective to enclose a separate gift slip rather than put the gift offer in the circular. If you have a guarantee, put an official-looking certificate border around it. If you have a free trial offer, make sure it's played up strongly in a heading or subhead and not buried in the body copy.

Checklist of 99 proven direct response offers

Basic offers
1. Right price
2. Free trial
3. Money-back guarantee
4. Cash with order
5. Bill me later
6. Installment terms
7. Charge card privileges
8. C.O.D.

Free gift offers
9. Free gift for an inquiry
10. Free gift for a trial order
11. Free gift for buying
12. Multiple free gifts with a single order
13. Your choice of free gifts
14. Free gifts based on size of order
15. Two-step gift offer
16. Continuing incentive gifts

17. Mystery gift offer

Other free offers
18. Free information
19. Free catalog
20. Free booklet
21. Free fact kit
22. Send me a salesman
23. Free demonstration
24. Free "survey of your needs"
25. Free cost estimate
26. Free dinner
27. Free film offer
28. Free house organ subscription
29. Free talent test
30. Gift shipment service

Discount offers
31. Cash discount
32. Short-term introductory offer
33. Refund certificate
34. Introductory order discount
35. Trade discount
36. Early-bird discount
37. Quantity discount
38. Sliding-scale discount
39. Selected discounts

Sale offers
40. Seasonal sales
41. Reason-why sales
42. Price increase notice
43. Auction-by-mail

Sample offers
44. Free sample
45. Nominal charge samples
46. Sample offer with tentative commitment
47. Quantity sample offer
48. Free sample lesson

Time limit offers
49. Limited-time offers
50. Enrollment periods
51. Pre-publication offer
52. Charter membership (or subscription) offer
53. Limited edition offer

Guarantee offers
54. Extended guarantee
55. Double-your-money-back guarantee
56. Guaranteed buy-back agreement
57. Guaranteed acceptance offer

Build-up-the-sale offers
58. Multi-product offers
59. Piggyback offers
60. The deluxe offer
61. Good-better-best offer
62. Add-on offer
63. Write-your-own-ticket offer
64. Bounce-back offer
65. Increase and extension offers

Sweepstakes offers
66. Drawing-type sweepstakes
67. Lucky number sweepstakes
68. "Everybody wins" sweepstakes
69. Involvement sweepstakes
70. Talent contests

Club and continuity offers
71. Positive option
72. Negative option
73. Automatic shipments
74. Continuity load-up offer
75. Front-end load-ups
76. Open-ended commitment
77. "No strings attached" commitment
78. Lifetime membership fee
79. Annual membership fee

Specialized offers
80. The philanthropic privilege
81. Blank check offer
82. Executive preview charge
83. Yes/no offers
84. Self-qualification offer
85. Exclusive rights for your trading area
86. The super-dramatic offer
87. Trade-in offer
88. Third-party referral offer
89. Member-get-a-member offer
90. Name-getter offers
91. Purchase-with-purchase
92. Delayed billing offer
93. Reduced down payment
94. Stripped-down products
95. Secret bonus gift
96. Rush shipping service
97. The competitive offer
98. The nominal reimbursement offer
99. Establish-the-value offer

Direct Marketing's Testing Laboratory

General advertisers spend about $75 million a year for research and copy testing to find out which ad or TV commercial *might* move the most merchandise. But they are forced to rely largely on assumptions such as: The ad that gets the highest readership score will sell the most goods. Or people who *say* they'll buy a product will actually do so. Assumptions like these can best be classified as wishful thinking.

Perhaps the one unique thing about direct marketing is its ability to scientifically test different ideas and approaches to find out what works best. Not by measuring opinions. Or readership. Or promises. But by counting the actual orders received.

Even direct marketing professionals with years of experience have difficulty predicting exactly what will strike the consumer's fancy. This point was really driven home to me a few years ago when I put together a panel session on testing for a Direct Mail/Marketing Association conference. My fellow panelists and I presented eight testing case histories, using slides to show the mailing packages or ads that were split-tested. Each member of the audience had a scoresheet so he or she could pick his or her favorite before the results were revealed.

When we finished not a single one of the 400 direct marketing pros in the audience had picked more than six of the eight test winners! But somebody had correctly picked all eight winners, namely, the consumers who had voted by sending in their respective reply cards and coupons.

That, of course, is why advertisers invest money in testing. Nobody can consistently predict how the consumer will react to specific products, selling methods, and creative approaches. Some tests turn out as you hope and expect they will. Others may be disappointing, but you still learn something. Before looking at the major areas to test, let's consider the basics for a solid testing program.

Eight testing ground rules

1. *Test a single element* or *a completely different approach.* These are the two main ways to get meaningful test results. First, you can test a single element or variable in your ad or mailing package. One letter against another, for example. Or one ad headline against another. If all the other elements of your ad or mailing remain the same, you know any difference in results can be attributed to the one element you changed, such as the letter or the ad headline.

On the other hand, you can test two completely different ads or mailing packages against each other. In this case, you won't know exactly which element accounted for the difference in results. But you do know which ad or mailing package did best. By testing two completely different approaches, you stand a greater chance for a substantial difference in results.

So, when you're launching a new program or looking for breakthroughs, it's usually best to concentrate your testing on completely different approaches. Once you have a winning ad or mailing package, it often pays to test its individual components. In so doing, you isolate what's making the difference and find ways to further improve results or reduce costs.

2. *Be prepared to record test results.* By assigning each ad or mailing package a separate key number, you have the mechanism to record responses and measure test results. In direct mail, the key number can appear anywhere on your reply card or order form. For space advertising, the number is often buried in a corner of the coupon. You can also work it into your return address, such as assigning a different department number for each effort.

A key number can be strictly numerical, such as Dept. 204. Or it can be a functional abbreviation, such as WSJ8279 to stand for the *Wall Street Journal* insertion of August 2, 1979. How you do it isn't important. But keeping a master record is.

3. *Work on the "beat the champ" principle.* In sports activities, a new champion is never crowned until the old one is counted out. Smart direct marketers operate the same way. Their most successful current mailing package or ad is considered the champ. This is the "control" mailing or ad against which all new approaches are tested. They continue to use the control, without making any significant changes, so long as it keeps working.

In general advertising, an ad or campaign is often changed when the agency or client gets tired of it. In direct response advertising, a successful control is often continued for years, until it wears out or you find a new approach that beats it.

4. *Make sure your tests are statistically valid.* Each portion of the test should be large enough to be meaningful. You can use probability tables to quite accurately determine the mailing quantity or ad circulation required. In addition, the list for each part of the test must be selected on the same random basis. Thanks to the fact that virtually all large lists are maintained on computers today, this is relatively simple. Moreover, all test mailing pieces should be mailed at the same time. And all test ads appear in the same issue. Otherwise, you introduce timing as another variable that can affect test results.

5. *Analyze your results carefully.* If you sell by mail, it's important to measure results based on the "net" dollar return. With a mailing, for example, you should take into account such cost factors and variables as the quantity mailed, production cost of each mailing package, products and premiums, fulfillment expense, and collections. Likewise, if you use lead-getting advertising, look beyond the number of inquiries produced. Your analysis should include the conversions or actual sales that result from each lead-getting effort. Experience has shown that it's a good idea to track all future transactions with a customer by the original key number or source code. This way you can measure the long-range value of a customer and see if one approach attracts better repeat buyers than another. It's also valuable to do a written report after each test to summarize the objective, test plan, results, and action

taken (Exhibit 10). As time goes by, these can become extremely valuable reference tools.

6. *Test for yourself.* It's nice to learn what you can from the testing experience of others. But don't assume someone else's results will turn out the same way for your market, your product, and your offer. It's better to test for yourself—and find out.

7. *Don't think test results are forever.* Just because something worked best for you five years ago or even two years ago doesn't mean it's best today. Your market changes from year to year even if your product or service doesn't. Important elements of your ads or mailings should be retested regularly. Especially those that are being used in volume and can represent substantial result improvements or cost reductions.

8. *Finally, avoid the disease of overtesting.* Some direct response advertisers get carried away with what's known as "trivia testing." They test one envelope color versus another. Or whether underscoring certain words in a headline improves response. What's wrong with testing these things? They generally make a very minor difference in results. So, unless you mail millions of pieces or run space with very large circulation, the minor difference won't amount to much. There are so many bigger or more important factors that can be tested instead.

Exhibit 10. Written test report.

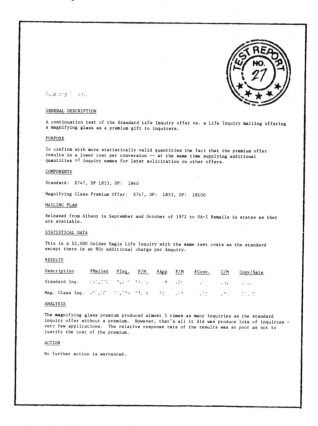

Major areas to test

If you want to learn some meaningful things by testing, you have to concentrate on testing meaningful points. Things like pricing and payment options, offers and premiums, formats and copy. Let's consider each of these areas individually and look at a few actual testing examples to show how significant they can be in affecting results.

Pricing and payment option tests

When you are launching any new product or service, it's important to test a variety of prices. It's not uncommon to find one of the higher prices pays out best.

Example: A 293-page business manual was launched with a three-way price test—$29.95, $39.95, and $49.95. The $29.95 price pulled the most responses. However, the second highest price—$39.95—was the most profitable in terms of the net dollar payout.

Pricing is also important on sample offers, and the results can be completely different depending on the product and market involved.

Example: On a product sample offer to fund-raising groups, a 25¢ offer pulled 58 percent better than asking $1.00 for the sample. On a product sample offer to business firms, however, a $1.00 offer helped establish the value of the product and actually produced more responses than a free offer.

Also important are the payment options under which a product or service is offered—cash, bill me, or charge card privileges. For instance, you would naturally expect a bill-me offer to produce more responses than a cash offer. But exactly how much better do you think it might do?

Example: A bill-me offer will usually do about twice as well as the same item offered only on a cash basis. Even on an inexpensive $9.95 item, I've seen a bill-me offer do 77 percent better than a cash offer. (After taking bad debts and collection costs into account, it was still much more profitable.)

Offers and premium tests

The product and pricing you establish are often considered to be your basic offer. But there's a lot you can do to sweeten that offer by the use of premiums, sweepstakes, or other incentives. Premiums alone provide plenty of testing opportunities. And a good premium need not be expensive.

Example: A 25¢ package of flower seeds, offered as a bonus with the first volume in a set of gardening books, boosted response by 42 percent. On a $50.00 item being offered to business firms, a premium costing less than $1.00 caused a 20 percent improvement in results.

While a premium offer will almost always do better than no premium, it's important to realize that a good premium will work a lot better than a poor one. This is an area that's often overlooked in testing but one that certainly bears exploration.

Example: On a mailing to PTA groups, three different premiums were split-tested. All had been carefully chosen to tie in with the known interests of the audience. Yet results showed that the most attractive premium offer did 51 percent better than the least attractive item. And the winning premium in this case happened to be the least expensive one!

Formats

Next to the offer, the phsyical format of your ad or mailing is one of the most important areas for testing. Do you use a No. 10 envelope, a 6 × 9, or a 9 × 12 size? Should you use two-color printing or four-color? Do you run a full-page ad with coupon or use a bind-in reply card? For example, take a personalized computer letter. The same basic copy approach with the addition of computer personalization can often boost your response by 25 percent or more. Likewise for a full-page ad with a bind in card. Even though your costs can be two to three times higher, your results can be more than four times greater.

Copy testing

We've talked about testing pricing, offers, and formats. What about *copy,* which many think of as the heart of an ad or mailing package? Copy, too, is certainly worth testing, especially headlines and letter copy. One of my favorite examples concerns two letters that were tested in selling an electric home organ by mail. The first letter presented the product story and features in a good, professional way. It was well written and covered all the bases. The second letter differed in only one respect. About a third of the copy was devoted to explaining how much each member of the family would benefit from having this organ in the home—the father, mother, and children. The writer felt it would be easier to sell this expensive product if the prospect could visualize the whole family enjoying it. As you may have guessed, the second letter did better—34 percent better, in fact.

There's an important message hidden here about copy testing. The second letter wasn't written any better than the first one. But there was a "big idea" behind the copy that made it more successful. So, when you get involved in copy testing, be sure to test copy that's based on completely different ideas or approaches.

If your budget permits you to test a number of copy approaches, it's not a bad idea to include one that might be considered "way out." An unusual or offbeat copy approach sometimes produces a real breakthrough.

Putting it all together

If you believe you're ready to go into business and open up your own testing laboratory, wait a moment! One other important principle to maximize your testing success is needed. The best way to realize how important it can be is to look back at the examples we've just covered. We've seen price and payment options that have improved results by 77 percent, premium offers that boosted results by 51 percent, format and copy tests that boosted results by 34 percent. The important thing is to do some testing in as many of these areas as you can, and then put the pieces together to really parlay your success.

Example: A test mailing program for an association soliciting membership called for a·variety of testing. An invitation format did 26 percent better than a standard 6 × 9 mailing package. An inexpensive premium boosted response by 49 percent over a nonpremium offer. And the best letter copy accounted for a 32 percent increase. When the best format, offer, and copy were combined, the new mailing package substantially boosted response! The result was a very profitable mailing.

How to test a new venture

In making the first test of a new venture, some direct marketers make the mistake of trying to test as inexpensively as possible. More often than not, the result is a small test that produces poor results. Little if anything is learned from such a test. For you don't know if the same product or service might have been a winner with the right test approach. So your first goal in testing a new venture is to have a soundly constructed test program that will get you some definite answers on whether your proposition has potential drawing power.

If you launch a new venture with a direct mail test, your testing should be concentrated on the two factors that have the most significant impact on results—lists and offers. With a sound test plan, I've found you can usually get the answers you want with a 50,000-piece mailing program.

Let's suppose you're a manufacturer of microscopes. You have a microscope starter kit for the educational market. And you want to see if you can use direct marketing to sell grammar schools. You know that microscopes are not widely used in grammar schools. You believe, however, that the key buying influences are principals and fourth and sixth grade teachers.

The basic offers you believe to be most important are the sale of a single kit at $39.95, a classroom kit with enough microscopes and lesson material for an average size class, a free gift offer, and a 10 percent educational discount.

The test matrix

The test matrix you develop (see Exhibit 11) allows you to test all these variables with a single mailing of 50,000 pieces. If you study the matrix, you will see it includes four list segments and four offers with 10 test cells, each assigned a separate key number. While every offer is not mailed to every list segment, you have concentrated the test quantities in the areas you think are most likely to work. And you can extrapolate the results for the other areas.

Let's say, for example, that fourth grade teachers prove to be the best list segment and the free gift is the strongest offer. You didn't test the free gift to fourth grade teachers. But when mailed to the fifth grade teachers, the free gift offer did 18 percent better than the nongift offer; to principals, it did 23 percent better. You can safely assume that the free gift will work about 20 percent better when mailed to fourth grade teachers.

Naturally, it would be great if every test cell produced results at breakeven or better and it was simply a question of which area was most profitable. But it's much more likely for a test matrix like this to produce some profitable cells and some unprofitable ones. And that's why you want the test to be big enough to uncover the areas that can prove profitable.

Exhibit 11. Microscope test matrix.

LIST	Offer A	Offer B	Offer C	Offer D	TOTAL
4th Grade Teachers	5,000 Key 101A				5,000
5th Grade Teachers	5,000 Key 102A	5,000 Key 102B	5,000 Key 102C	5,000 Key 102D	20,000
6th Grade Teachers	5,000 Key 103A				5,000
Principals	5,000 Key 104A	5,000 Key 104B	5,000 Key 104C	5,000 Key 104D	20,000
TOTALS	20,000	10,000	10,000	10,000	50,000

Offer A - Single Kit
Offer B - Classroom Kit
Offer C - Free Gift
Offer D - 10% Discount

What to test on a proven venture

Once you have proved some success with a new venture, you naturally expand the test to a bigger universe. As a rule of thumb, most marketers believe you shouldn't expand a test more than five to ten times the quantity you originally tested. So, if your total universe is bigger than that, you use it up in chunks or stages. At this point your testing program logically should include an expansion of the successful things you originally tested, as well as refinement testing that can improve results or reduce your costs.

As an example, let's go back to the manufacturer of microscope kits. Assuming the initial test proves successful, refinement testing could include:

- Testing private school lists versus public schools
- Testing secondary lists, like curriculum coordinators or PTA groups who might buy the kits for their school
- Testing other free gift offers
- Testing new copy approaches
- Testing a more elaborate mailing package with the inclusion of a sample lesson

- Testing a lower cost or "stripped down" package with a smaller outer envelope, less expensive circular, and so on
- Testing a four-color circular versus a two-color circular
- Back-end tests to stimulate reorders after the initial shipment

How to test lists

Naturally, your objective is to come up with as many profitable lists as you can, to reach the maximum universe that can be successfully mailed for your product or service. It's usually best to test a variety of logical list types or categories. And, when you find a successful list, test as many similar ones as you can find.

Many direct marketers have their own pet theories for list testing. But let's look at the guidelines used by a leading list user and a leading list broker. The list user is Old American Insurance Company. The firm's written guidelines for list testing and continuation were developed by Steve McDaniel and Jerry Burke. The guidelines include:

1. Always test the "presumed" best segment of the list first, such as hot line buyers or buyers rather than inquiries.
2. Use selectivity factors that have proven successful on other mailings for this same policy, such as sex and state selection.
3. If the initial test of 10,000 pieces projects acceptable results, reorder 50,000 pieces. If still acceptable, order the entire list.
4. Reorder additional names on a successful list as they become available, and try to remail a successful list every six months.
5. Test other segments of a successful list. If appealing to buyers works, try the inquiries. If soliciting one-year-old buyers works, try two-year-old names.
6. Test a successful list for other suitable policies.

The broker is Dependable Lists, Inc. In a booklet, "How to Test a Mailing List," the firm suggests that you always mail one or more proven lists at the same time you do list testing to get comparative results.

Knowing what to do about a list that's a real winner or a real loser is no problem. But when your results are marginal, at or near breakeven, list evaluation can be a problem. Dependable Lists wisely points out that a marginal list probably includes some profitable and some unprofitable segments. Before discarding the list, you should see if there is some way to increase response by changing the selectivity you used. You may end up with a smaller list but one that is well worth mailing.

How to test space and broadcast

While the media are different, you can apply some of the same principles used for testing lists. Start with areas most likely to work and then expand the areas that are successful.

Magazines. Pick the magazine categories that are most likely to work for your product or service, such as sports, women's service, or shelter magazines. Certain magazines seem to have a special mail order or direct response character. So it usually makes sense to start off with the strongest direct response publication in each category, the one that carries the most direct response advertising. In some cases, you can run an A/B split test in the same publication. Or, in the case of publications with regional editions, you can often use telescopic testing to test six to eight ads in different regional editions of the same issue with each of the ads split-tested against the same control ad.

Newspapers. Select at least three to five markets for a good test and use the leading paper in each market. A/B split tests are rarely available except in the case of newspaper inserts. If you want to test two or more inserts that are the same size and format, you can have the printer "shuffle" them so they will arrive at the paper premixed. Experience has shown that this is much more reliable than sending the paper two different inserts and leaving it to them to give you an accurate split test.

Radio and television. Here, too, it's usually best to select three to five proven markets for a good test. One of the leading agencies specializing in direct response television uses markets like Sacramento, Portland, New Orleans, Albany, Tampa, Orlando, Miami, Indianapolis, and Chicago for the majority of its testing. Care should be used to select the right stations and time buys for your direct response offer. It is virtually impossible to test different spots in the same market and get meaningful results, which is one of the limitations of broadcast testing you have to live with.

Dry testing and the FTC

On a new venture, direct marketing firms must choose between "wet testing," in which the product is produced and fulfilled, and "dry testing," where a product is advertised before going into production, and in fact, is only produced if the test results warrant it.

Naturally, dry testing can offer attractive financial savings. Through the years this technique has been widely used in the publishing field. Instead of making a heavy investment in editorial and book production, the publisher would simply spend the necessary amount to run an ad or mailing. The order form was designed to seek actual orders, not opinions of whether somebody might buy. To avoid "biasing the test" the publisher neglected to mention that the books weren't yet available or might never be produced.

Recently, at the request of a publisher, the Federal Trade Commission issued an advisory opinion on dry testing. The FTC does not object to this method of testing, provided that:

- No representations are made to mislead the public that the books have been or definitely will be published.

- Adequate notice of the conditional nature of publication is made.

- If the books aren't published, notice should be given to those who subscribed within four months.

- There is no substitute of other books for those ordered.

The testing of seasonal propositions

If your results vary from month to month throughout the year, as they do for most direct marketers, it's naturally best to concentrate your testing in your strongest season. This is when you can expect the best test results. And, because you are probably promoting heavily at that time of the year, you can easily measure new mailing packages or lists against your control package and your proven lists.

However, you can also test safely at other times of the year. *Provided* you know what differences in results to expect. For example, let's say January is your best month, as it is for most direct marketing offers. For various reasons you want to make some tests in June.

You do your mailing and it pulls an even 2 percent, but your breakeven is 2.5 percent. Using your historic figures, you know that if January results are rated at 100 percent, your June results are usually 67 percent. So January is usually half again better. You can confidently expect to mail in January and do about 50 percent better, which would mean a profitable response of 3 percent.

Probabilities and realistic test sizes

One of the age-old questions in direct response advertising is, "How large should a test be?" If you test too large a quantity, you spend more than is necessary to obtain reliable test results. And too small a quantity wastes money because you can't have much confidence in the results.

Probability tables can provide a scientific approach to minimizing your testing risk. One of the best explanations I've seen on the subject appears in a booklet called "Computing Probabilities," published by Alan Drey Company, a leading list broker. The booklet likens direct marketing probabilities to tossing a coin. Just as there are only two ways a coin can land—heads or tails—only two things can happen to your order card. It either comes back or it doesn't.

Probability tables are based on statistical formulas that take into account the relationship of *confidence* (how sure you can be that your test results are valid), *the limit of error* (how close your next results should be to the test results), *the sample size* (number of coins tossed or mailing pieces observed), and *the expected response* (the number of orders).

Most direct marketers work with a probability table that has a 95 percent confidence level. In other words, 95 percent of the time, the results from a follow-up mailing or ad should fall within a prescribed range of the test results, e.g., plus or minus two-tenths of a percent.

But experienced direct marketers also know there are times when the quantities called for by probability tables simply aren't realistic. You may find that the tables call for mailing hundreds of thousands of pieces on each side of a test. With most budgets, that just isn't realistic.

While it isn't always practical to follow probability tables for all your testing, I strongly recommend you become familiar with them. Then work out test sizes you can live with. As an example, here are the guidelines one large publisher uses for testing: mailing package tests—10,000 to 25,000 pieces; price tests—50,000 to 100,000 pieces; and list tests—5,000 pieces.

Finally, in list testing, you should be aware of a common fallacy. When you work with probabilities, the size of the total list or universe has no bearing whatsoever on the test size. Therefore, it's perfectly valid to test the same number of pieces on a small list as you would on a giant one.

Improving your testing program

I've always believed that most direct marketing firms don't do as much testing as they should. And they don't spend enough time studying and analyzing test results. Let's see how these two areas can be improved.

First of all, testing can be expensive, and this no doubt discourages many advertisers from doing more testing. As was mentioned earlier, a direct marketing firm should regard testing the same way a manufacturing firm views research and development. You invest money in testing or R & D to learn something for the future.

A manufacturing firm I worked with spends almost 10 percent of their sales dollars on R & D. They have achieved sales leadership in their field by introducing innovative products with unique features and benefits.

One way for direct marketing firms to put more emphasis on testing is to allocate a definite percentage of their budget for this purpose. Stan Rapp of Rapp & Collins calls this a self-renewing testing budget. He knows that a sound testing program will usually improve results, and that the increased profits can offset what was spend on the test. So the testing budget continues to renew itself.

When in comes to analyzing test results, it's easy to look at the bottom line and make a quick judgment on what worked best. You can get a lot more out of your testing budget, however, if you creatively analyze the results. For example, one large client I know has an eight-member creative group that meets monthly to review all current test results. The actual mailing samples or ads are reviewed, along with the figures. Each test is individually discussed. From those discussions come many ideas for new creative approaches, marketing strategies, and additional testing.

Obviously, you can't expect all your tests to wind up as big winners. If you test wisely, however, you build up a tremendous amount of knowledge that's bound to increase your sales and profits.

The last word on testing

Tests can become quite complicated. And, because they often entail minor changes in ads or mailing packages, there is a lot of opportunity for errors in test execution.

It's a good idea to write up your test strategy showing the objective of each test and explaining how it will be executed. Then make sure every one concerned gets a copy of your test plan. As an example, let's return again to the microscope kit mailing covered earlier in this chapter. The following chart shows how that 4-way test might be written up (see Exhibit 12).

Exhibit 12. Test strategy statement.

KOBS & BRADY ADVERTISING, INC.
625 N. Michigan Avenue. Chicago. Illinois 60611
(312) 944-3500

Test Strategy Statement

client: ABC COMPANY

project: Microscope Mailing

TEST	OBJECTIVES	METHOD
Single Kit	To test the potential of the grammar school market, and provide a benchmark against which other offers can be measured.	Develop basic mailing package ... including 6 x 9 outer envelope, 2-page letter, brochure, and order card.
Classroom Kit	To increase the average order and profitability by offering a larger kit with enough microscopes and lesson material for an average size class.	Change main brochure illustration to show classroom kit. Describe kit fully in letter, and change order card to include price and details of classroom kit.
Free Gift Offer	To improve response by offering a free gift. Gift will be an attractive poster showing magnified illustrations as if seen through a microscope.	Add 5 1/2 x 8 1/2 gift slip to the package. Mention free gift in P.S. on the letter, and add to order card description of the offer.
10% Educational Discount	To determine whether a discount will be more effective than the single kit at full price or the free gift offer.	Play up discount in the price area of brochure and letter. Also emphasize the discount on the order card.

6

Developing a Multi-media Plan

People, people, people.

A media plan is the people end of marketing. This is one way we bring our selling message to the people who have the ability and desire to buy—our prospects and customers.

A constant need exists to learn more about these prospects and customers. What common denominators do they have? How do we reach them most effectively? What medium, or multi-media combination, delivers them at the lowest cost per order?

Most direct marketers today use a variety of media. Let's review the major media that have proved to be most effective for direct response, pointing out some of the things that have been learned about using each of them efficiently. Then see what's involved in developing your own multi-media program.

Direct mail: Still number one

In total advertising expenditures direct mail comes in third, behind newspapers and television. But for most direct response advertisers, direct mail has been the top medium and gets the largest share of their media budget.

About 350,000 businesses have bulk mail permits, which allow them to mail at the lower third class postage rate. They send out more than 32 billion pieces of mail a year, including third class and catalogs.

Five big advantages

While one can list a lot of possible advantages for direct mail, many such advantages are not unique to the medium. They might apply equally to magazines or television, for example. But I think these five advantages are quite special and account for direct mail's widespread use.

1. *Selectivity and personalization.* You can select a mailing list that zeroes in on a certain type of person or a specific geographic area. You can pick only people with known interests or a specific buying history, with little or no wasted circulation. Also, you can make your message a personal one that capitalizes on that selectivity.

Such as a computer letter that addresses each individual by name. Or a printed letter that includes copy directed to the specific lists selected.

2. *More flexibility.* Your mailing package can be as simple or elaborate as you wish. You can include a four-color circular that opens up as big as a tablecloth, or, in some cases, include a sample in the mailing. You control the distribution, so the quantity of a mailing can be as small as you like or as large as the available universe. And you can mail whenever you prefer.

3. *Most suitable for testing.* While other media permit some types of testing, none offers the widespread test capability provided by direct mail. Thanks to the computer's ability to select a perfect Nth name sample, your mailings can include as many split tests as necessary to provide a wide variety of answers from a single mailing. It's not unusual for large mailings to include 50 or more test cells.

4. *Maximizes profit from your customer list.* As was pointed out earlier, the classic formula for direct marketing success is to build a list of satisfied customers and then go back to them for repeat sales. Direct mail is the only medium that allows you to concentrate your promotion efforts on just your previous customers.

5. *Highest response rate.* Compared with other media, direct mail will usually produce the highest percentage of response. So, if direct mail pays out for you, you can build your sales, profit, and customer list more rapidly.

The disadvantage of cost

The major disadvantage of direct mail is that it is very expensive. It's hard to make even a simple mailing today for less than $150 per thousand, especially a prospect mailing that includes list rental charges. By comparison, you can buy most other media at a cost per thousand that ranges from $3.00 to $35.00. So direct mail must produce a much higher response than other media to give you a comparable cost per order. The fact that it's used so widely is proof that direct mail can overcome the high cost and still pay out.

Mailing lists

It's almost impossible to over emphasize the importance of mailing lists to your direct mail success. If your mailing doesn't get to the right prospects, it doesn't have a chance. The more expertise you develop in this area, the better your chances for success.

Lists may be classified in three basic categories: (a) house lists—your own customers or inquiries. They normally produce a much higher response than any other list you can rent. (Lists are normally rented for one-time usage, not purchased.) (b) Response lists—prospects who have responded to the offer of another advertiser. You can select an endless variety from merchandise buyers to magazine subscribers. Whether they are buyers or inquirers, it's their propensity to respond by mail that makes them valuable. And the offer to which they responded previously can tell you a lot about their interests. (c) Compiled lists—names gathered from a variety of sources, such as auto registrations, telephone directories, or appliance warranty cards. In the business field, individual's names are compiled from various business directories. Moreover, the name of virtually every business firm in the country has been compiled into a master business list, broken down by Standard Industrial Classification, or SIC.

Most major lists offer some selectivity (at a slightly higher rental fee) to help you target specific market segments. You can select only males, for examples. Or eliminate certain states. Or choose between a firm's buyers and inquirers. Buyers names will generally produce better results than inquiry names or compiled lists. The more recent a group of customers has bought, the more likely they'll do so again. If you get into large-volume mailings based on similar lists, it usually pays to use a merge-purge computer program to eliminate duplicates.

The best advice for selecting lists is deceptively simple: Find out as much as you can about who your customers are—age, sex, geographic concentration, and so on. Then rent lists with similar characteristics or selectivity. If you don't have demographic information on your customers, you can select lists to suit the product being offered. The late Bob Dale, a well-known consultant, used to sum up his list advice this way: "Find lists of recent mail purchasers of similar or allied products in the same price range as the product or service you're selling." Naturally, the lists that best fit this description will probably belong to your competitors. So you have to search out lists that are suitable, but noncompetitive.

The best source of more detailed list information is a mailing list broker. A broker can supply you with data cards for virtually every list that's available for rental. Or, if you prefer to do your own research, you can consult the Direct Mail List directory published by SRDS which has information on more than 25,000 lists.

Most popular formats

There are literally hundreds of different variations available. But the most popular physical formats for direct mail fall into these categories.

- Self-mailer—any piece mailed by itself, without an outside mailing envelope.

- Number 10 Package—usually a letter, circular, and order form mailed in a number 10 envelope, the size used for standard business correspondence.

- 6 × 9 Package—like a number 10, except mailed in an envelope that measures 6 by 9 inches.

- 9 × 12 Package—like the above, except mailed in an oversized envelope that measures 9 by 12 inches.

- Catalog—a multipage format designed to present a variety of merchandise. Can be mailed in an envelope or as a self-mailer.

As noted, the number 10 package and the 6 × 9 and 9 × 12 usually have similar components. Each component—the envelope, letter, circular, order form, and often a gift slip—works together to do a complete selling job. Results usually decrease when you try to eliminate one of the components or try to combine two of them into a single piece. Popular variations on this standard mailing package include illustrated letters, simulated telegrams, invitations, computer letters, involvement devices, and catalog overwraps.

The importance of catalogs

Perhaps the oldest form of mail order promotion is the catalog. It's over a hundred years since Aaron Montgomery Ward started his business. Today, despite having hundreds of retail stores from coast to coast, Wards still does about 25 percent of all sales through its catalog division. But a Wards general merchandise catalog is a far cry from the typical direct marketing catalog. Most are specialized catalogs that carry a specific product line or type of product, such as gift foods, gardening and nursery stock, or office supplies.

Interestingly enough, most people don't think of catalogs as advertising mail. A catalog is considered something different, and catalog shopping is a favorite pastime for many consumers. This also occurs in the business market where catalogs are often used as buying guides.

Direct mail trends

Some trends that have already developed a strong pattern in the last few years are:

- More specialized list selection to increase response
- More use of lower-cost mailing formats, like self-mailers, to offset rising postage and mailing costs
- More use of mail in the business and industrial market to reduce selling costs
- Continuing growth in the number and variety of specialized catalogs.

If direct mail costs continue to rise, I anticipate more use of other media to get new customers. One of the advantages mentioned earlier is direct mail's ability to target promotion efforts to previous customers, and that's not likely to change. So direct mail will continue to play an important role in most direct marketing programs.

Magazines: mass or class

Next to direct mail, magazines are probably more widely used by direct marketers than any other major medium. The large-circulation magazines allow you to reach a mass audience; others deliver your message to a specific class or type of reader.

The main advantage offered by magazines include good color reproduction, which is important for many types of products; a long ad life; and a low cost per thousand. The latter is true primarily for consumer magazines. Business or trade publications usually have a much higher cost per thousand.

Another important advantage is that often you can test a variety of creative approaches or offers in space less expensively than you can in the mail. This is usually done with regional editions of large circulation publications. You pay a premium for regional editions in terms of a higher cost per thousand. But most advertisers are willing to pay this premium for a test knowing that they can run the winning ad in the national edition of the same publication at a much lower cost per thousand.

Disadvantages of magazine advertising include long closing dates (some magazines require your ad material three months before they come out), slower response because of the longer ad life and readership, and less space to tell your story. Even if you use a double-spread ad, you have much less room for copy and illustrations than in a typical direct mail package.

Standard ad sizes and formats include one-third page, half page, two-thirds page, full page, and double spread, with a coupon in a bottom corner of the ad where it's easy to clip out. Smaller ad sizes like two-inch ads or classified ads normally run without a coupon. Bind-in insert cards are expensive but can pull four to eight times as well as an on-page coupon. Full-page inserts or multi-page card-stock inserts are also available in some publications. Those in *TV Guide*, for example, have been very effective for direct response advertisers.

Making magazines work

Magazines with a direct response atmosphere generally produce better results than those without. These include publications that have mail order shopping sections, usually found at the back of the book containing a variety of small ads, and those that regularly run a lot of larger direct response ads. Other advertisers would not continue to use these publications if they weren't producing good results.

As in other media, the timing of insertions must be taken into account when you are scheduling magazines. Timing can affect your results by as much as 40 percent (see Exhibit 13). Assume, for example, that your cost per response is about $2.00 in January or February. That cost could climb to $2.80 in a June issue.

Exhibit 13. Magazine response by date of issue.

Issue	Cost-per response	Issue	Cost-per response
January	$2.05	July	$2.60
February	$2.00	August	$2.40
March	$2.20	September	$2.60
April	$2.50	October	$2.20
May	$2.60	November	$2.20
June	$2.80	December	$2.40

The position of your ad is also important. Experience shows that the first right-hand page and the back cover are usually best for direct response ads. These are followed by other cover positions and the front of the book. Unless you run your ad in a mail order section, positions at the back of the book usually produce a much lower response. One advantage of insert cards is that they tend to make the magazine fall open to your ad page. So even a poorer position will usually pull relatively better with a card.

Television: glamorous, new darling of direct response

Many advertisers think of television as a new medium. The fact is that television was used heavily for direct response back in the old days when wrestling matches were more popular than pro football and Milton Berle was a bigger attraction than Archie Bunker. Today, direct marketers use television in a much more sophisticated way.

Television's main advantages include immediate response, a wide range of stations and spot buys to choose from (most direct response advertisers buy local spots rather than network time), and the ability to visually show or demonstrate your product in action. Television is also surprisingly inexpensive for testing.

It's amazing to see how many advertisers believe they can't afford television although they think nothing of spending thousands of dollars to test a new space ad or mailing package. If you don't go overboard in planning the spot and if you use the right production sources, a television test program can cost less than $10,000—including creating the spot, producing it, talent, and buying time.

The medium, however, also has some disadvantages. First, the amount of copy time is severely limited. Even a two-minute spot includes only about 250 words, much less than a typical full-page ad or just the letter in a direct mail package. Each commercial has a momentary ad life and no permanent response device like order cards or coupons that can be saved for later ordering. So it's best to buy a flight of commercials on the same station with response usually building up over a two- or three-week period as the spot gets repeated exposures.

Finally, television can be more difficult to test than other response mediums. You can't get pure A/B split tests. So trying to test two or more different spots on the same station or on different stations in the same market is risky at best. That doesn't mean you can't do television testing. It does mean you have to approach TV testing somewhat differently to establish sound testing procedures and controls.

Specialized TV marketing programs

A relatively new approach that has proved successful for many direct marketers is TV support. The advertiser basically is using television to say, "Watch your newspaper or mailbox for this special offer." TV support only makes sense if you pretty well saturate a market with mass mailings or Sunday newspaper inserts. With the latter, for example, you would buy a support schedule with spots running from Friday through Sunday. While the cost of TV support might add from 8 to 10 percent to your costs, you can normally expect it to improve results by 25 to 30 percent.

Two of the largest users of TV support are *Reader's Digest* and Publishers Clearing House. According to *Advertising Age*, PCH recently spent $1,500,000 on TV support for a mailing of 20,000,000 pieces.

Another specialized use of television has become known as key outlet marketing. Rather than seek a direct response by mail or phone, advertisers use television spots to build traffic for a chain of retail stores in each market. The retailers accept the product on a consignment basis with a lower than normal margin, because they know it will get heavy TV exposure and produce rapid turnover.

Perhaps the best-known product to recently get this treatment is the Pocket Fisherman. The manufacturer, Popeil Brothers, reportedly sold a million and a half units the first two years. With a $19.95 selling price, that represents almost $30 million in retail sales!

Making television work

Direct response advertisers have found that television often requires a different strategy and offer, one slanted to the medium and the amount of time available to tell your story. The record spots you see, for example, don't normally promote a record club, they promote a special one-shot record package. Instead of selling a complete set of kitchen knives for $29.95, you may have to feature one or two of the most popular knives for $9.95.

While 30-second spots dominate the medium for general advertisers, direct marketers generally use longer spots. Sixty-second spots are commonly used for getting inquiries; 120-second spots for direct selling. Only for TV support is a 30-second spot normally adequate to do the job.

You also have to buy the right kind of spot at the right cost. In general, old movies, reruns, and various late-night or weekend shows produce much better results than prime time shows or sporting events. People are more likely to get up from their easy chair to get a pencil or place a phone order if it's a show they've seen before or to which they are not paying close attention. Because television time is a perishable commodity, television buys can often be negotiated at lower-than-card rates to give you a better chance to make your offer pay out.

Newspapers: built-in variety

Unlike most other media, newspapers offer a wide variety of sections, advertising formats, and reproduction methods. They're so varied they almost have to be considered as media within a medium. Besides this built-in advantage, newspapers offer short closing dates, immediate response, and broad coverage of a large and diverse audience. The closing date for regular ROP (run-of-paper) ads is usually only a couple of days before publication. And, because newspapers have a short life, they tend to produce orders quickly as with television advertising.

This broad coverage is made possible by almost 1,800 daily U.S. newspapers with an average circulation of over 61,000,000 on weekdays. At the same time, only 665 Sunday papers average almost 53,000,000 circulation. A number of leading direct response advertisers devote a major share of their ad budgets to newspapers.

Disadvantages of newspapers include poor ad reproduction and limited availability of color except in certain sections; results tend to be affected by adverse local news somewhat more so than in other media, probably because newspapers have such a short life; and there is no real standardization of page formats or advertising rates, especially for newspaper inserts.

What sections work best for direct response ads

While small ROP ads work consistently well for some advertisers, most direct marketers get better results from Sunday supplements, comic sections, mail order shopping sections, and newspaper inserts.

Some newspapers publish their own Sunday supplement, but most papers carry a syndicated supplement like *Parade* or *Family Weekly*. These supplements are usually printed by the rotogravure process and provide much better reproduction and color than the rest of the newspaper. They tend to carry a lot of mail order ads, especially for low price, impulse merchandise, and therefore have a good direct response atmosphere. The syndicated supplements, however, can be quite expensive to test. Unless you can get a leftover page or remnant space in specific markets, the minimum buy is normally a full geographic region.

Comic sections have also produced good results but seem to work only for certain specialized offers. In the past few years the comics have been used to promote mail order film processing, insurance, pantyhose, and books. Color reproduction is not as good as in the Sunday supplements. But most papers have the capability to affix a detachable card or mailing envelope to the page, which usually enhances response.

The most expensive newspaper space: inserts

On the other hand, newspaper inserts have become extremely popular for direct response in the last 10 years, despite the fact they're very expensive in comparison with other print media. Inserts are sometimes called preprints or free-standing stuffers. But all the terms refer to the same thing: a loose insert, usually printed in four-colors on coated or card stock that appears in the Sunday newspaper. Most advertisers use a single sheet or a four-page folder, but some prefer an eight-page booklet format or an insert enclosed in a 6 × 9 envelope.

Inserts are normally supplied by the advertiser, not printed by the newspaper. The printing cost of a typical insert can run about $20.00 to $30.00 per thousand. The charges by individual papers vary, of course, depending on the size and number of pages the insert contains. But, even for the same insert, newspapers often quote rates that range from a low of $17.00 per thousand to a high of $60.00 per thousand. (In general, the rates are more favorable in larger markets.) With proper media selection, you can currently expect the total cost of your newspaper insert (printing and media) to run between $37.00 and $64.00 per thousand.

Why have inserts proven so effective, despite this higher cost? First, the insert is a dramatic format that stands out and gets individual attention much as a mailing package does. Second, the advertiser has enough space to do a complete selling job, even for a complicated proposition like that of a record club. Third, inserts usually have a built in reply card or an order envelope to facilitate response. And, finally, while the cost is high compared to other media, it's still only about half what postage alone runs for direct mail.

Direct response advertisers have found that inserts have a better chance to pay out if distribution costs are carefully controlled. That usually means eliminating from the schedule any papers whose cost per thousand is too high. Most newspapers also ask the advertisers to supply a fairly large quantity of additional inserts to cover spoilage in inserting; advertisers have found they can often reduce or eliminate this excess without seriously affecting results.

Also, testing by size of market is important with newspaper inserts as well as with other newspaper formats. For example, a recent test on a low-priced women's product showed that response in markets with 500,000 circulation or less was 40 to 50 percent better than in larger markets.

Some newspapers also have poor quality control on their inserting equipment. One series of spot checks I conducted showed that only 80 percent of all sample papers were properly inserted with one insert per paper, while 10 percent had multiple copies of the same insert and 10 percent were missing the insert entirely. If newspapers can solve this problem, results should improve accordingly.

Supplementary media: unglamorous, but productive

While direct mail, magazines, television, and newspapers are the major media for direct marketing, a number of other more-specialized media shouldn't be overlooked. Chief among these are co-op mailings, postcard co-ops, package inserts, and telephone selling.

The first three share an important common denominator: they're all relatively low-cost because, by the very nature of a co-op or package insert, you are sharing the advertising vehicle and distribution costs with other advertisers.

Take co-op mailings. You can choose a mass consumer mailing, such as Donnelley's Carol Wright co-op, a 6 × 9 envelope with as many as two dozen inserts ranging from cents-off coupons to direct response offers. Or take a co-op designed to reach a specialized audience segment like one directed at teen-agers. Still others have been started by advertisers for mailing to their house lists. By getting other advertisers to share the costs, they can distribute their own messages at little or no cost. Some co-ops are also available as newspaper inserts.

Package inserts are similar to co-op mailings, except that your message is distributed with another advertiser's product shipments.

Postcard co-ops or postcard publications have been developed primarily in the business and professional market. Most were started by the publishers of trade journals as another low-cost way for advertisers to reach the same audience. Some take the form of bound booklets with each advertiser having its own detachable reply card. Others are a series of loose reply cards mailed in an envelope.

About 250 postcard co-ops are currently available. Results for most advertisers have been quite good. Message space on the cards is limited, so they're used primarily for getting inquiries or sales leads. But, if you can get your story across in a small amount of space, these co-ops can also be effective in producing direct orders.

Telephone selling is a much more expensive medium. While many advertisers provide their customers a means to place an order by phone (such as a toll-free 800 number), when you think of the telephone as an advertising medium, you have to think in terms of its use for outgoing calls.

In my experience, it's hard to overcome the high cost per call and make the phone pay out when you're using it to reach cold prospects. But it can be effective in more specialized applications such as calling previous customers. Or following up inquiries from an ad or mailing. Or calling people who have not responded to the early renewal notices from a magazine or insurance company.

The rather recent development of using taped messages for telephone calls is very effective. With this technique, you tape record a sales message lasting a few minutes, normally using a well-known personality or top company official to add appeal. A telephone communicator then places the call, gets the prospect on the line, and requests permission to play the message. After the tape message has been played, the communicator comes back on the line to answer any questions or take the order.

One medium widely used by general advertisers is radio. But, with few exceptions, I have not seen it widely used for direct response. It has the same disadvantages as television but lacks the visual impact and demonstrability that make television an effective selling tool.

Still other specialized media include matchbook advertising, inserts in paperback books, and literature racks in supermarkets. All have produced good results for certain direct marketing applications. While their volume is usually not large enough to sustain a program by themselves, they can be a good supplemental source of orders or inquiries.

Combination media programs

While each medium naturally has to be considered individually in terms of its ability to perform profitably for your product or service, most advertisers no longer limit their marketing program to a single medium. There are exciting opportunities for combining two or more media in an effective program such as the use of TV support for a large-scale mailing program or newspaper insert campaign. Other natural combination media programs are using space advertising to produce inquiries combined with a mailing or series of mailings used to follow-up and convert the inquiries into sales; and using preprint mailings, in which you mail an advance copy of an ad to a publication's subscriber list. When media are used in logical combinations like these, the results are usually synergistic: your bottom line comes out better than if you had used each medium individually.

Developing your media plan

In chapter 5 we reviewed some guidelines for how to test major media. Another logical question that remains is how do you decide which medium to use first?

To start with, you may want to review the multi-media cost/potential chart (see Exhibit 14). It provides some examples of the average cost per thousand and the potential universe for various media. Naturally you want to use media that will be cost efficient. And the larger the universe of a medium that works for you, the greater your sales potential.

There are also other things to think about. First is the ability to reach your target audience with different media. Direct mail is ideal for some products or services because you can zero in on the right prospects with specific mailing lists. But, in other cases, no list is available that efficiently delivers the audience you're after.

Take, for example, a direct marketing firm selling clothing for big and tall men. It would be nice if the firm could just mail their catalog to such a list. But to my knowledge, no such list is available. So such a firm would have to use a medium like space advertising to ferret out prospects, to get somebody to tell the company he's big or tall by requesting their catalog.

Second, the amount of space needed to adequately tell your story is another consideration. A simpler offer can be promoted with space or television. A more complicated product such as a highly specialized pocket calculator with sophisticated engineering functions probably requires direct mail to do the major selling job, although, as already noted, other media could be used to produce inquiries for such a product.

Third, does the product really need demonstrability? If so, television is the logical answer. Take a product like a paint sprayer that can be adjusted to spray so finely that you can write your name with it. You might use a picture or a series

Exhibit 14. Multi-media cost/potential comparisons.

		Average Cost Per Thousand	*Potential Universe*	
1.	**Direct mail**	$150 – $250	60,000,000	Homes
			4,000,000	Businesses
2.	**Magazines**			
	TV Guide black-and-white page	$ 2.80	18,300,000	Circulation
	Family Circle four-color page	$ 5.96	8,350,000	Circulation
	Family Circle 4/C page & card			
	(includes $3.75/M for printing)	$13.30	8,350,000	Circulation
	Administrative Management			
	B/W page	$32.63	52,562	Circulation
3.	**Spot TV (non-prime time)**			
	Two-minute sell commercial	$10.28	73,240,000	TV homes
	Thirty-second support commercial	$ 2.57	73,240,000	TV homes
4.	**Newspapers**			
	Six-page newspaper insert (includes			
	media and printing)	$37 – $64	52,805,000	Circulation
	Four-color comics page	$ 8.19	40,108,000	Circulation
	Parade supplement, inside B/W pg.	$ 5.12	20,575,000	Circulation
	ROP ad, B/W, 1,000 lines, daily	$ 7.80	61,714,000	Circulation
5.	**Supplementary**			
	Co-op mailings: Mass audience	$7 – $20	250,000 to	35,000,000
	Target audience (both plus printing)	$15 – $30	25,000 to	2,000,000
	Package inserts (plus printing)	$25 – $40	5,000 to	12,000,000
	Postcard publications	$6 – $50	4,000 to	400,000

Note: Above figures are based on Fall 1978 rate card costs. Special reduced rates are available in some publications and newspapers for certain advertisers, such as mail order, schools and book publishing companies. Also remnant and standby space (when available) is significantly lower in cost.

of pictures to show that feature in a mailing package. But it's much more effective to see somebody on television actually doing it.

The fourth consideration is your profit margin, which must be related to the media cost. With a low-cost product—selling, say, for less than $10—it's almost impossible today to get a sufficiently high direct mail response to make your mailing profitable. But it certainly is possible to make space advertising pay out for a product in that price range.

The last word on media

Finally, there are some refinements to consider in choosing media. Many of them revolve around the advantages and disadvantages of the individual media we've discussed. If, for example, you have a product where four-color is necessary to show it off to best advantage, you're limited to media that provide good color reproduction.

To help you review the possibilities for your multi-media program, you'll find the chart summarizing the advantages and disadvantages of each medium a handy reference (see Exhibit 15 on the following page).

Exhibit 15. A comparison of major media for direct response

Medium	Advantages	Disadvantages
Direct mail	Selectivity and personalization More flexibility Most suitable for testing Maximizes customer list profit Highest response rate	Most expensive cost-per- thousand
Magazines	Reach mass or class Good color reproduction Long ad life Low cost-per-thousand Often test inexpensively	Long closing dates Slower response Less space to tell your story
Television	Immediate response Wide choice of time buys Visual product demonstration Relatively inexpensive to test	Limited copy time No permanent response device Difficult to split test
Newspapers	Wide variety of choices Short closing dates Immediate response Broad coverage	Poor ad reproduction Limited color availability More affected by local news No standardiza- tion of for- mats/rates

7

Industrial Direct Marketing

Today, business and industry are more and more recognizing the potential of direct marketing as an effective bottom-line marketing tool. In fact, it is becoming a profit center of major proportions for thousands of companies. It's only logical. Industrial advertisers have always relied heavily on direct mail to pinpoint their specialized and selective markets. DMMA estimates that 30 percent of all direct mail advertising is directed to business firms. And the past few years have seen a growing use of other media by industrial direct marketers.

Maybe industrial direct marketing isn't so different

Some believe that industrial buyers can't be sold the same way as consumers. They reason that the industrial buyer is only interested in nuts-and-bolts facts. He or she can't be persuaded with flashy four-color circulars. The buyer doesn't have time to play with involvement devices. Yet some of the case history chapters in Part Three will prove otherwise.

Here's what Herb Ahrend, president of Ahrend Associates, says on the subject: "The industrial buyer is a human being. He has the same desires, hopes, hang-ups, and fears as the consumer. Indeed, he *is* the consumer outside of business hours! Yet many people still believe that a dull recital of facts and figures is enough to sell industrial goods by mail." Ahrend concludes: "Remember that the industrial buyer is different from the consumer in only one significant respect—he is spending company money, not his own."

Differences beyond the basics

Many of the basics of direct marketing covered in other chapters—things like offers and testing—apply equally well to the business or industrial field. But there are some differences that should be recognized. First, the audience is usually smaller. It's simply a more limited universe. For example, there are only about four-million business firms you can reach by mail, compared to about 60 million homes on consumer mailing lists.

But this can be an advantage, as Dick Hodgson points out in his *Direct Mail and*

Mail Order Handbook (Dartnell, 1974): "The creative industrial direct mail advertiser can work within well-defined boundaries—something which the consumer advertiser frequently lacks. A pinpointed audience enables the direct mail advertiser to use the medium to its fullest potential by being able to personalize many of his mailings."

Second, less testing is generally done in industrial direct marketing. To some extent, this is a function of the more limited universe. Let's say you have only 25,000 prospects and four mailing packages you want to split test. If you test them with 5,000 pieces each, that only leaves 5,000 names to come back to with the winning package.

While you have to approach testing somewhat differently, it doesn't mean you should ignore it altogether. Roy Ljungren, advertising manager of National Cash Register Company, has extensive experience in industrial direct marketing. As he pointed out in a recent article in *Industrial Marketing* magazine, "We can learn something from every mailing we make. Many direct mailings made today by industrial advertising managers should have some testing aspect as a by-product of the regular mailings they make. If you make enough meaningful tests, you will build up a fund of knowledge that will give you the edge when betting on the success of future mailings."

Third, still another difference is that most industrial sales entail a bigger ticket or unit of sale. Just as in personal selling, it often takes more than one call to close a sale. In fact, a much-quoted study by the National Sales Executives Club showed that 80 percent of all sales are made *after* the fifth call. When you combine the bigger unit of sale with the limited universe available, it becomes obvious that most industrial direct marketing involves repeated efforts aimed at the same market segments.

Finally, many industrial firms sell through dealers, distributors and wholesalers. Sometimes the firm's entire distribution is done this way. Other times the firm might have its own offices and salespersons in some geographic areas with dealers in others. This is not necessarily a limitation, but it does have to be taken into account in planning an industrial direct marketing progam. In lead-getting mailing programs, for example, you often have to "sell" dealers on participating in the program.

Three main application areas

As in the consumer field, many specialized ways exist to use industrial direct marketing. But the "big three" are to get leads, to make direct sales, and to reinforce the sales effort. Let's take an overview look at each area before going into more detail.

1. *To get sales leads.* While there may be a great many potential prospects for your product or service, there's usually a smaller and more select number who represent the prime prospects. These are the ones who are disenchanted with a present supplier; the ones who are most receptive to new methods and new ideas.

Direct marketing can help you identify and separate these prime prospects by generating sales leads for your salespersons or for the salespersons of your dealers or distributors. Regardless of whom he or she works for, a good salesperson should be able to close a higher percentage of calls when working leads than when making cold calls. In fact, it's not unusual for the closing percentage to be twice as high—and that can mean a dramatic reduction in your sales costs.

2. *To make direct sales.* A lot of people don't realize that industrial products can be sold by mail. But many of them are, including ad specialties, calculators, corrugated file boxes, printed products, office supplies, and maintenance items. Many are also expendable products that are suited to repeat business.

Actually, industrial mail order is quite flexible. You can sell a single product, aftermarket supplies and accessories, or have a full-line catalog. Some firms sell entirely by mail. Others use direct marketing to cover certain territories where they don't have a sales force. Still others employ a sales force to distribute certain products and use direct marketing for others. The latter often includes lower priced products that don't have sufficient margin to justify normal selling costs and commissions.

3. *To reinforce the sales effort.* Sometimes you know your salespersons are covering their markets and calling on most of the right people. They know who their prime prospects are and really don't need sales leads. You can, however, still use industrial direct marketing to reinforce their sales effort, to deliver background information on the company and its products, and to make sure the message gets through to everyone who influences the buying decision.

Reinforcement efforts can take the form of pre-approach mailings. Or a sales call can trigger an automatic follow-up mailing series. Or you can develop a special high-impact series of mailings for only a small group of top prospects. Even such devices as institutional mailings or house organs fall in this category of supporting the sales effort.

Other more-specialized applications of industrial direct marketing include bringing prospects to you (such as building attendance at a trade show exhibit), signing up new dealers, or getting needed information through research mailings. But let's concentrate the balance of this chapter on some things you should know about getting leads, making direct sales, and reinforcing the sales effort.

Lead development programs

As was pointed out in chapter 4, inquiries themselves are easy to get. But you have to decide what kind of leads you want and then structure your offer accordingly. To get a lead, you usually have to offer something in your ad or mailing.

That something might be a free booklet, a free gift, or just more information. Or it might be along the lines of a free survey, free estimate, or free demonstration.

The late Ed Mayer, a great student and teacher of direct mail, once wrote a booklet for National Business Lists call the "Q Concept." Here's how he explained the title: "The Q Concept is just a phrase, of course. But it is one that puts all the power you can muster right where it belongs: on Quality and Quantity. By developing direct mail support for the man in the field with the Q Concept as a guiding principle, you'll be directing your energies toward the essential need: the right quality of sales leads, in the right quantity."

What's the right quality or quantity mix for your firm? That's something only you can decide. It might depend on your competitive position, the size of your sales force, or even its level of sophistication. For a relatively young and inexperienced sales force, many sales managers believe in providing them with a good quantity of leads. This gives plenty of face-to-face selling experience. On the other hand, if you have a staff of higher-paid and more-experienced sales representatives, you probably don't want to waste their time chasing down loose leads.

Remember, what it boils down to is this: The more you promise to send or give away, the more leads you will get—but the lower the quality of leads. Conversely, you can get a smaller number of better-qualified inquiries by just making your offer less generous.

Don't be fooled by cost-per-lead

You naturally have to keep in mind that getting leads or inquiries is only the first step in the selling process. Making the sale is the real payoff. And how you vary the quantity/quality mix has a real bearing on your cost per sale.

As an example, let's say you test two different direct mail offers. The first is a free gift offer and pulls a 2 percent response. The second merely offers free information and the response rate is 1 percent. To simplify matters, let's assume that both mailings cost the same $160 per thousand and that the cost of the gift itself is nominal. The first chart (see Exhibit 16) shows the cost per lead from the two mailings. The free gift mailing is the clear winner with an $8.00 cost per lead compared to $16.00 for the free information offer.

Exhibit 16. Cost per lead.

	Quantity Mailed	Percent Response	Number of Leads	Cost of Mailing	Cost Per Lead
Mailing A					
Free gift offer.......	1,000	2	20	$160	$ 8.00
Mailing B					
Free information offer	1,000	1	10	$160	$16.00

But let's go a step further. Let's now assume that the sales force closes 15 percent of the free gift leads, while, with the better quality free information leads, they close 20 percent. The second chart (Exhibit 17) takes these closure rates into account, as well as the cost of the sales calls and mailings. While the second mailing results in one less sale, the cost per sale is only $564.00 versus a comparable cost of $699.00 on the more generous offer.

These response rates and closure figures are purely hypothetical. But they illustrate the dynamics of the quantity/quality equation as well as the effect the closure rate and the cost of sales calls have on the end result.

How to improve lead quality

In launching a new lead-development program, I've found it's usually best to start off aiming for quantity. That way you establish that you can get leads and you gain some experience with closing ratios.

Exhibit 17. Cost per sale.

	Number of Leads	Cost of Sales Calls*	Total Selling Costs†	Percent Closure	Number of Sales	Cost per Sale
Mailing A						
Free gift offer....	20	$1,936	$2,096	15	3	$699
Mailing B						
Free information						
offer..........	10	$ 968	$1,128	20	2	$564

*Based on $96.79 as average cost per industrial sales call.
†Includes cost of mailing and sales calls.

It's then relatively easy to tighten up the leads and improve the quality. You can do this by making the offer itself less generous, such as switching from a free gift to free information. Or you can make it harder to respond. In space advertising, for example, you can ask the prospect to write you for more information instead of supplying a coupon in the ad.

You can also use a self-qualification offer in which you give the prospect a choice of options. Your reply card, for instance, might provide a choice of "send me more information" or "have a salesperson phone me for an appointment." Those who select the latter are obviously better-quality leads and should be worthy of a sales call, while the free booklet requests might simply be fulfilled by mail.

The systems approach

A sound lead-getting system has many essential characteristics that have to be monitored and coordinated for optimum results. The accompanying chart (Exhibit 18) shows how the elements of the system interact and provide feedback to fine-tune the program. It was developed by Russ Lapso, now an account supervisor at Rapp & Collins. Here are some of the key points he makes:

- Determine how many leads your sales force should be able to handle within certain time parameters.

- The marketing team needs to be aware of the entire selling process. Have your advertising people spend a few days in the field and get first-hand selling experience.

- Communicate with the sales force to sell them on the value of the leads they receive. Point out the science of testing and explain that while they might occasionally get a few unqualified leads, those are a necessary evil of the testing process that will lead to more sales.

- To ensure tight control, leads should always come back to a central location, like the home office, to be recorded and distributed.

- Following up a direct response lead may require special sales techniques. In many cases, a prospect may not really expect a sales call, and the salesperson needs to have a full repertoire of door openers.
- A list of unsold inquiries should be set up for future promotions and used regularly.

Exhibit 18. Components of the lead generator system fall into three areas. The shaded boxes on the left reflect elements of the System Input. All the white boxes are part of the Leads-to-Sales Process. And the shaded box on the right represents System Output. The diagram shows how the interrelated elements provide feedback to fine-tune the program.

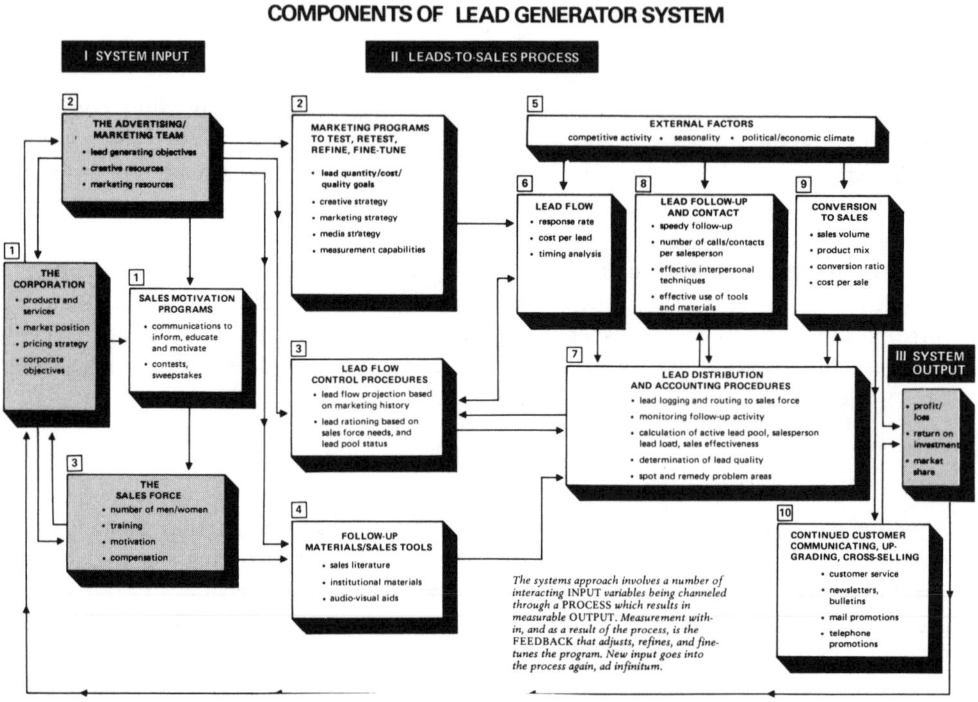

COMPONENTS OF LEAD GENERATOR SYSTEM

Checking up on the system

Finally, any system like this must be monitored to control both lead flow and lead accounting. The ideal procedure is to control flow so salespeople are neither drowning in leads or starving for them.

Too many leads boost the cost per sale because the sales force begins to treat them too casually or lets them get cold before they follow up. Too few leads can result in salesperson downtime and is harmful to morale. You must continually review the size of your active lead pool to determine whether mail and media promotions need to be stepped up or held back.

The other monitoring device is lead accounting. The objective is to keep tabs on all leads received and follow them through the selling process. This enables you to get a feeling for lead quality and salesperson efficiency. You can calculate the cost per sale by individual salepersons or by source of lead.

While a lead-generation system requires some effort to establish and monitor, it can also provide handsome dividends. One industrial client I've worked with carefully analyzed all the expenses and results of their program and found that every dollar they invested in lead-getting promotions had generated $24.00 in additional sales.

Guidelines for inquiry handling

With all that has been written through the years on the value of inquiries and how to handle them properly, it's amazing that so many firms still do such a poor job. Writing in a recent issue of *Direct Marketing* magazine, Robert Ingalls reported on a study he made. He responded to 50 industrial ads that offered more information, not with a coupon or bingo card, but by writing a letter.

Here are some of the findings: sixteen percent of the firms did not even bother to respond at all. Of those who did respond, only 30 percent included a letter with the material they sent, and only 42 percent enclosed a return form or indicated where to get additional information. The over-all impression was that most firms just slapped some literature together and mailed it without much planning.

While inquiry handling procedures vary widely from company to company, here are the basic steps that I've found are important:

1. *Have a system.* Keep it as simple as possible. Try to process the inquiry and record and capture the data you need without getting too complicated. Some firms use a snap-out carbon form to make multiple copies of the inquiries. One company I know uses a simple 8½ × 11 form, staples an inquiry reply card to it, and makes photocopies for distribution and follow-up (see Exhibit 19).

2. *Answer inquiries promptly from the home office.* You can't control how quickly a salesperson will follow up an inquiry in person, but you can at least acknowledge the inquiry from the home office. A well-done letter should be used, indicating the name and phone number of the local salesperson or dealer. If the prospect is really hot, he or she can contact them directly. If your promotion has offered a free gift or booklet, most salespersons prefer to deliver it in person and use it as a door opener. But your letter can still acknowledge the request and promise that the gift or booklet is on the way.

3. *Remind the prospect of his or her request.* If you send out literature by mail, make sure the envelope is marked with copy like, "Here's the information you requested." This reminds the reader of his or her interest. And, if a secretary sorts out important mail from advertising, it will usually get into the priority stack.

4. *Keep accurate records.* Inquiries should be recorded by individual promotion

key numbers. And the same key number should be recorded on any lead control forms so the sales closures can be tracked back to the inquiry source. A follow-up system should be used for the sales force. This can be a simple card or form that's returned to report the results of each lead they receive. Or you can use a weekly or monthly lead accounting form, one that asks salespeople to report the status of all leads still active.

Exhibit 19. Simple inquiry follow-up form.

PAYROLL LEAD PROGRAM

Lead No. ______

Sales Rep. ______

Date Lead Received ______

______

No. of Employees ______

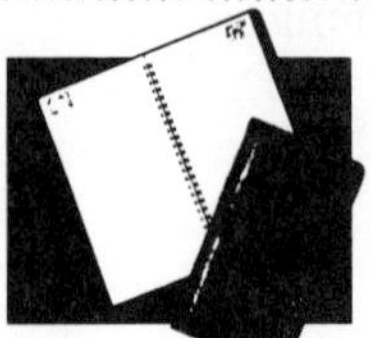

Free! Pocket Executive Planner for 1976!

Handiest way to manage your time. Removable phone index, lie-flat pages, many other deluxe features. You'll receive this get-acquainted gift along with your free copy of the booklet on *Payroll Management*.

Please return this certificate for your complimentary copy of

PAYROLL MANAGEMENT: Asset or Liability?

Gentlemen: I would like to receive a copy of *Payroll Management: Asset or Liability*. I am interested in learning how my company can turn its payroll system into a flexible, information-generating tool for management, while lowering the overall cost of payroll preparation. Of course I will be under no obligation whatsoever.

Signature ______

(If the following information is not shown on the label at right or is incorrect, please indicate below.)

Print name ______

Title ______

Phone ______

I am also interested in receiving information on the following Stat Tab program(s):

☐ Accounts Payable ☐ Accounts Receivable ☐ Inventory Control ☐ General Ledger C1

	TYPE OF CONTACT			RESULT		
Date of Contact	Meeting Held	Meeting Scheduled*	Other	Sale Closed	Sale Effort Continuing	Sale Effort Discontinued

Industrial mail order

By comparison with the number of firms who use lead-getting programs, industrial mail order activity is not nearly as widespread. However, I think there's a lot more of it around than most people realize, since many efforts are directed at specialized market segments without wide exposure.

Some industrial mail order promotion is done through space advertising. Most, however, is done with direct mail and governed by essentially the same factors that affect consumer mail order efforts.

There are a few differences, however, in industrial mail order methods that are worth noting. First, the envelope is probably less important. Because the majority of executives have their mail opened or screened by a secretary, many do not even have a chance to see envelopes or teaser copy. Plain, businesslike envelopes appear to have a better chance of getting by the secretary than more elaborate ones.

The most common formats used are number 10 envelopes and 9 × 12 envelopes. Both usually employ standard 8½ × 11 components that are comparable to normal business correspondence. Report formats are often effective, using a booklet-style piece that simulates a regular business report (see Exhibit 20). Self-mailers also tend to work better in the business market than they do for consumers. Most industrial or business seminars, for example, are promoted with some type of self-mailer format.

Exhibit 20. Report format mailing in the style of a medical journal, used by Michigan Bell Telephone for mailing to medical assistants.

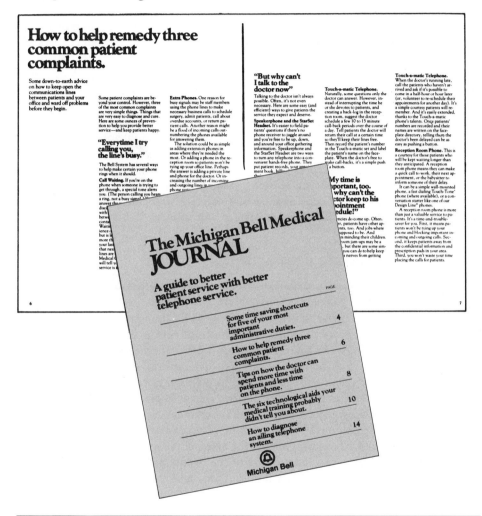

There also is less four-color printing in the business market. Not because it isn't effective, but because the smaller market segments mean that the cost of photography and separations add a larger percentage to the in-the-mail cost. On the other hand, sampling seems to be more widely used in the industrial market, especially for ad specialties and printed products. Many firms selling these items enclose samples in their mailings. Some offer a sample for a nominal charge. Baldwin-Cooke, for instance, sells desk diaries to businesspeople for Christmas gifts and offers a sample for $2.00.

Catalogs for industrial selling

Many industrial firms have found the catalog an ideal way to sell the industrial market. Catalogs can carry a firm's full line of products or be used for aftermarket supplies and accessories. Many general advertisers who provide catalogs for their sales force make the mistake of thinking they will be acceptable for direct marketing. They usually are not.

One reason is that a salesperson's catalog ordinarily doesn't carry enough copy to do a complete selling job. It may, for example, just provide the product specs and rely on the salesperson to explain how the product works, describe the benefits it provides, and answer questions. Many such catalogs don't even include prices because the salesperson always carries a separate price list. A good mail order catalog, by contrast, usually has attractive product illustrations, tells a complete selling story on each item, and has the price right near it.

Many industrial mail order catalogs have started with a single product line, have met with success, and have expanded into other product areas. Fidelity Products in Minneapolis is a good example. The firm was started as a direct marketing subsidiary of a corrugated box firm to sell storage files for business correspondence. Today, the firm has a 120-page catalog that offers a wide variety of products for both office and plant use (see Exhibit 21).

Reinforcement selling programs

As was noted earlier, reinforcement efforts can take the form of pre-approach or sales call follow-ups. These are usually direct mail efforts that are left up to the individual salesperson rather than being controlled by the home office.

Many salespeople, however, don't do as much of this as they should, primarily because they would rather be out on the street making sales calls than sitting in the office writing letters. Recognizing this, some firms supply salespeople with a manual of stock letters that can just be turned over to a secretary for typing and mailing.

National Cash Register goes a step further. It has created more than 125 stock direct mail campaigns aimed at specific market segments and product applications. Salespeople get a semiannual index to these campaigns plus a supply of request cards. To initiate one of the campaigns, the salespeople merely jot down the prospect's name and address and the number of the campaign they want him or her to receive. The card is sent to NCR's home office, and the whole thing is handled automatically.

The place for showmanship mailings

Another type of reinforcement selling program is a series of showmanship mailings. They're sometimes called impact mailings, dimensionals, or spectaculars. They're usually done as a series of efforts aimed at a small group of top prospects. And each mailing has a gift or dimensional enclosure of some type.

An example is a series of mailings done a few years ago by Market Development Corporation, a leading compiler of college student mailing lists. The company

Exhibit 21. Fidelity Products catalog.

wanted to reach a select number of top prospects and communicate some sales points about the college market in a dramatic, memorable way.

As a result, the firm created a hypothetical college student to serve as spokesperson for the mailing series. A series of five handwritten mailings were sent out at one-week intervals, starting with the student's arrival at college early in September. Each mailing included an interesting college-oriented gift, a pendant, drinking mug, fraternity paddle, and so on (see Exhibit 22). While each piece subtly got across

Exhibit 22. Market Development showmanship mailing.

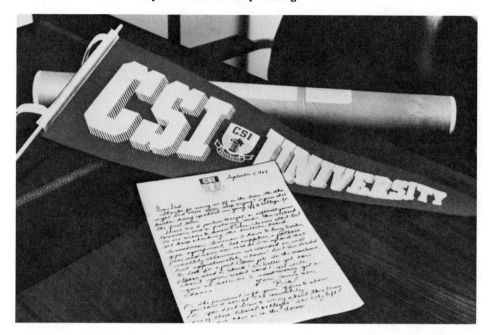

some sales points about the size and spending power of the college market, prospects were kept in suspense until the final mailing, before Market Development's name was revealed.

The entire campaign was directed at just 200 top prospects, and the cost came to $25.00 per prospect. After the campaign, all executives were called on. A month later, the firm had already written more than enough business to pay for the campaign with many leads still active. And the campaign was so well received that it even generated fan mail from top executives.

Mailing campaigns like this certainly cost more than normal direct mail efforts. But when you compare the expense with the $96.00 or higher cost of a single sales call and take into account the potential sales a group of prospects can represent, the cost can be viewed as quite reasonable.

Industrial lists and media considerations

The importance of mailing lists was stressed in chapter 6. However, there are special considerations that apply to industrial list selection and testing.

First, the availability of business lists by the government's Standard Industrial Classification (SIC) numbers is a terrific aid in defining and pinpointing your market. This four-digit numbering system classifies companies by the activity in which they engage. All major activities are assigned a two-digit code number. As the activity becomes more specialized, a third and fourth digit are added to identify subgroups. For example, here are the SIC numbers and descriptions for furniture manufacturers:

25	Manufacturers of Furniture and Fixtures
251	Manufacturers of Household Furniture
2511	Manufacturers of Wood Household Furniture, except Upholstered
2512	Manufacturers of Wood Furniture, Upholstered

The accompanying chart (Exhibit 23) shows some of the major SIC groups used for direct mail along with the number of U.S. names available from a leading business list compiler.

Exhibit 23. Major market segments available by SIC number.

SIC number	Description	Quantity
1500-1799	Contractors	423,937
2000-3999	Manufacturers	318,642
4000-4999	Transportation, communication & public utilities	142,428
5000-5199	Wholesalers	377,129
5200-5999	Retailers	1,702,650
6000-6599	Financial institutions & services	447,336
7010	Hotels & motels	66,681
7200-7300, 7500-7699	Personal & business services	694,730
8111, 8911, 8931-8999	Legal, architectural, engineering & accounting services	210,901
8011, 8021	Doctors & dentists	285,674
8200	Schools & libraries	173,648
8660	Churches	151,777

Buying influences and list titles

A long-standing debate persists in industrial direct mail circles on whether it's better to mail to executives by name or title. Some claim that mailing by name gets a little better readership and response. Others believe that the turnover of job changes and promotions is so high you have a better chance of getting your mail to the individual you really want with title addressing. Lists with individual names are more expensive to rent and maintain and are not always up-to-date. I've seen test results where title addressing has pulled better than individual names and vice versa. So this is an area I suggest you test for yourself.

Related to this is the importance of finding the right position title or titles to mail. Sometimes several persons within a firm can influence the buying decision, and it's often necessary to mail more than one title. Response can also vary widely by title. In one recent test for a client selling financial services, two seemingly logical titles were tested and keyed accordingly, and one pulled 69 percent better than the other.

Three ways to get your mail to Mr. Right Guy

It's nice to have a situation where the product or service you're selling is always purchased by somebody with a specific title like office manager or treasurer. But sometimes the buying decision for certain products or services is made by a person with one job title in firm A, another title in firm B, and still another in firm C. This is especially true in small- to medium-size firms.

One way to solve this problem is to address by functional title, such as "to the executive who buys Christmas gifts," or "to the person in charge of office supplies," or "chief financial officer." These are not titles that appear on business cards, but they generally get your mail delivered to the right person, regardless of his or her actual title.

Another approach that catalog mailers have found effective is to print a buck slip or "Route to" box near the address area. They normally preprint three different titles and leave a couple of blank spaces so the recipient can fill in additional names and titles.

Still another way to solve this problem is to write a polite "we need help" letter to company presidents. Tell them you have important information available on a specific subject, like planning meetings, but you don't know who in the firm makes decisions about such meetings. Ask for the name and title of the individual who's responsible and provide a postpaid card for the reply. It's not unusual for a well-done letter like this to get a response as high as 50 percent, and you'll often get the name of more than one individual to contact at the firm.

Helpful services for business list users

Thanks to today's computer technology and the sophistication of the SIC numbering system, major list compilers or service bureaus can provide important services to help you in targeting your industrial direct marketing program. As an example, all of the following are available from National Business Lists in Chicago:

- Customer profile analysis showing the number of customers you have in each SIC area and the percent of penetration.

- Availability reports, indicating the number of firms available in the specific SIC's and geographic areas you want.

- Dealer marketing programs that provide counts, prospect listings, and mailing labels broken down by each dealer's territory.

- Prospect record cards that provide salespersons with a complete file of all prospects in their area for specific SIC categories.

- Phone numbers to be added to your customer list by feeding in the names and addresses you have and computer-matching with NBL's master list of business firms.

Trade journals and bingo cards

Some business or trade journals have paid subscribers while others are made available on a no-cost or controlled-circulation basis. Publishers claim the latter get just as high readership as paid circulation books, and maybe they do. But when you're looking for a direct response, such as an order, my experience is that paid circulation books usually pull somewhat better.

Also, many business publications offer "bingo" cards as a reader service. Instead of filling out coupons or writing letters to get advertised information, the reader simply fills out a single card, circles the numbers that correspond with the ads he or she wants to reply to, and mails it back to the publication. The publication, in turn, forwards the inquiries to the advertisers specified.

One recent study by the Center for Marketing Communications estimated that bingo cards generate more than 50 million requests annually for information. But a study the Center made of business publication readers showed that 43 percent of the respondents receive material too late to be useful.

Perhaps the length of time it takes publications to process and forward these inquiries helps explain why their quality is usually not as high as coupons returned from ads. A few years ago, a large industrial direct marketer tested the pulling power and conversion of bingo-card inquiries versus coupons. The marketer used an attractive full-page ad with a coupon. Below the ad the publications inserted the bingo card number to be used to get the same information. The conversion rate on coupons was 5.5 percent compared to less than 1 percent for the bingo card inquiries. So, if you want better-quality leads from your space advertising, use a coupon in your ads instead of a bingo card number.

Postcard co-ops

These publications were referred to in chapter 6 but bear repeating because they're being so widely used for industrial direct marketing. Examples of some of the roughly 250 postcard publications available include *The Accountant's Marketplace,* *Coal Age* postcard mailings, *Hospital Pharmacy* response cards, *The Office Mailer,* and *Travel Weekly's Supplyline.*

I've seen them used effectively for both generating sales leads and for producing orders. However, since space is limited, they have to be designed and planned carefully to provide a complete selling story. Examples of both inquiry and selling cards are shown in Exhibit 24.

The last word on industrial direct marketing

Industrial direct marketing is one of the fastest-growing segments of the direct marketing field. Whether you use it for getting sales leads, generating orders, or reinforcing your sales efforts depends on your particular marketing situation.

While the size of your market might impose some restrictions on what you can do, try to do as much testing as practical. You'll gain information by which you can continually refine and fine-tune your promotion efforts. And don't be afraid to apply some of the offers and selling techniques you see being used for consumer direct marketing. You may be surprised to find they work equally well for industrial direct marketing.

Exhibit 24. Montage of postcard co-op cards (some for selling, some for inquiries).

8

Creativity and Idea Generation

Until now, we've been concentrating on direct marketing fundamentals and how they are applied in launching a *new* direct marketing program. It's time to shift gears and talk about *existing* direct marketing programs for products or services that have already been developed and tested. They might be winners, but you're looking for new approaches to make them even better. They may just be marginal, and one good idea could put them over the top. Or they might be losers that need a complete overhaul.

An excellent way to improve results on an existing program is to come up with a strong, new creative approach. That's why this chapter is devoted to creativity and idea generation. I'm sure you all know what creativity is, so I won't try to provide a formal definition. But here's my favorite fun definition: Creativity is a husband who can come home late every Friday night from the same poker game and keep coming up with a new excuse.

Many copywriters are in the same boat as that husband: They've written so many ads or mailings for a certain product that it gets pretty hard to come up with new ideas. I won't try to cover the basics of copywriting, but I will try to suggest some ways to get new ideas and develop breakthroughs.

Test new appeals or positionings

Much more has been written on the subject of developing a new ad or mailing than improving an old one. There are, however, some good suggestions for improving a mailing package in *Successful Direct Marketing Methods* (Crain Books, Chicago):

> One of the best ways I know is to come up with an entirely different appeal for your letter. For instance, suppose you're selling an income tax guide and your present letter is built around saving money. That's probably a tough appeal to beat. But to develop a new approach, you could write a letter around a negative appeal—something people want to avoid.
>
> Experience with many propositions has proved that a negative appeal is often stronger than a positive one; yet it's frequently overlooked by copywriters. An appropriate negative copy appeal for our example might be something like, "How to avoid costly mistakes that can get you in trouble with the Internal Revenue Service."

Or, "Are you taking advantage of these six commonly overlooked tax deductions?" Another good technique is to change the type of lead on your letter. If you're using a news lead, try one built around the narrative approach. Or develop a provocative question as the lead. Usually a new lead will require you to rewrite the first few paragraphs of copy to fit the lead, but then you can often pick up the balance of the letter from your control.

During the past few years, a lot of views have been voiced in general advertising circles about "copy positioning," i.e., how you position your product or service in the reader's mind. The classic example is 7-Up's Uncola campaign which positioned the product as a related alternative to the popular cola category.

The same positioning technique can be used in direct marketing. *Highlights for Children* has long used a successful space ad to sell gift subscriptions. But instead of positioning their product just as another magazine, the publisher positions it against the toys and clothes usually chosen as kids gifts:

> Would you pay $7.95 for a child's gift that won't be outgrown, broken, worn out, lost or forgotten six months after Christmas?
>
> In a day and age when fads in toys and trinkets appear and vanish almost before you turn around, *Highlights for Children* could be one of the most exciting Christmas presents you will ever give.

The hypothesis approach

Several years ago I heard Tom Collins of Rapp & Collins explain a method he sometimes used in developing new space ads. Here's how the technique works: Before starting to write an ad, you develop a series of hypotheses. You then build a separate ad around each hypothesis, which can be tested to prove or disprove it. Collins went on to explain that hypotheses are usually made about the prospect, the price or offer, the product, or the ultimate benefit of using the product.

Collins then proceeded to show how U.S. School of Music came up with a new control ad. This mail order music school had been running an ad with a large picture of a woman playing the piano and a headline, "The secret of teaching yourself music." Collins hypothesized that, today, a teenager interested in the guitar was a better prospect than the woman playing the piano. So he made a few changes in the ad such as substituting an appropriate photo, and it was a big winner.

Even though I respected Tom Collins as one of the great direct response writers, I frankly thought this two-step creative process was unnecessarily complex. That is, until I had occasion to use it. And then I became a true convert.

I've found the hypothesis approach has some inherent advantages, especially when you're trying to come up with a whole series of ads or mailing ideas. For one thing, you don't wind up with as many look-alike or similar ads. Normally, when you ask a creative person to develop a half-dozen ad approaches, you tend to get one idea and five or six variations of it. If you were to test these minor variations, you would naturally expect only minor differences in results. And most marketers are looking for breakthroughs, not minor differences. So it's desirable to test ads that are more distinctly different.

In other words, the hypothesis technique stretches your thinking and forces you to go beyond the obvious. That, of course, is where potential breakthroughs often come from. Still another advantage is that, once the hypothesis is developed, you have a strong platform for building the ad. The technique provides direction in creating a headline, developing graphics, and writing body copy.

For an example of how the technique works in practice, you may want to review the *Skeptic* ads in chapter 19 which were developed by using this approach. But, if you're still somewhat unsure about the technique (as I was), try it out for yourself on your next creative assignment. Granted, it's easier to hypothesize about some products than others, but I think you'll find it's a very adaptable technique. It works equally well for large and small ads and direct mail as well as space.

Proven copy appeals

Most copy appeals are timeless because they stem from basic human needs and wants that don't change much from year to year. As proof, I offer the accompanying chart (Exhibit 25) which was a favorite of Victor Schwab, one of the founders of Schwab and Beatty Advertising. It's at least twenty years old, and yet still quite timely.

Exhibit 25. Timeless copy appeals.

People want to gain:

Health
Popularity
Praise from others
Pride of accomplishment
Self-confidence
Time
Improved appearance
Comfort
Advancement: social–business
Money
Security in old age
Leisure
Increased enjoyment
Personal prestige

They want to do:

Express their personalities
Satisfy their curiosity
Appreciate beauty
Win others' affection
Resist domination by others
Emulate the admirable
Acquire or collect things
Improve themselves generally

They want to save:

Time
Discomfort
Risks
Money
Worry
Embarrassment
Work
Doubts

They want to be:

Good parents
Creative
Efficient
Recognized authorities
Up-to-date
Gregarious
"First" in things
Sociable, hospitable
Proud of their possessions
Influential over others

Source: Victor Schwab, *Mail Order Strategy* (Hoke Communications, 1956).

You might find the exhibit to be a handy checklist next time you're looking for a new copy appeal or approach. Just select two or three different appeals that fit your product or service and see how strong a creative strategy or headline you can come up with for each one.

An organized approach for beating the control

Top creative people are not always able to verbalize their approach to creativity. An exception is Sol Blumenfeld of Sol Blumenfeld & Associates. I like his organized method for idea generation, which he calls a five-track approach to beating the control:

1. *The subtractive approach.* This seeks to improve the effectiveness of a given mailing by reducing costs, thereby reducing the cost per inquiry or sale. One way to do this is by using a "stripped down" version of a winning package such as going from a 6 × 9 size to a number 10 size, using a smaller circular, eliminating one element from the package, and so on. Another way to accomplish the same thing is to develop a new mailing that's more economical such as a self-mailer. These approaches usually won't outpull the control in percent response, but they can often produce a lower cost per order.

2. *The additive technique.* This means adding something to a control package that may increase its efficiency in excess ratio to any increased costs. Usually it involves inserts. A classic example is the so-called publisher's letter, which was originated by Paul Michaels when he was with Greystone Press. At other times the mere addition of a token, stamp, or other involvement device can provide a substantial boost in results.

3. *The extractive approach.* This technique entails drawing on the contents of an established ad or mailing and extracting a thought or idea that can be built up as the main appeal. Blumenfeld cites an example for a publication's subscription campaign in which he picked up a very human appeal that was buried in the body copy of their control ad. He developed it into a· new headline, which substantially beat the control.

4. *The segmentive technique.* As you might guess, this one entails segmenting your market and developing one or more special promotions aimed at those different segments. Blumenfeld points out that correspondence schools often use a special women's package, because they have found that their normal packages simply don't work as well with the female market. Likewise, record clubs often use separate packages for country music, teen, and classical market segments. Understandably, this technique requires that the copywriter be familiar with the list universe to which he or she is writing and its customer profile.

5. *The innovative approach.* This category is characterized by Blumenfeld as being highly original, even wild. He believes that every test series should contain at least one or two ideas that fall into this category, because they can often produce more dramatic improvements in results than the other approaches.

Breakthrough thinking techniques

The human brain is similar, in some ways, to a computer. Researchers at a leading university have tried to estimate the brain's storage capacity in computer terms:

How many "bits" of information can the brain store? The answer they came up with is 10^{28}, or 10 to the 28th power. That may not sound like much—until you see it spelled out (see Exhibit 26).

Exhibit 26. Human brain's computer-like storage capacity.

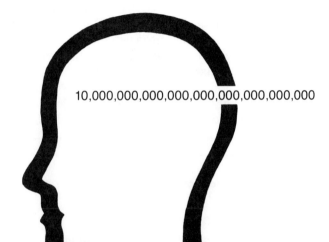

How does the brain function and use all that information? The way you are probably most familiar with has been called the "judgmental thinking mode." This is the everyday process we use to think things through in a logical step-by-step way. The mind moves sequentially from point A to point B and so on.

For creative idea generation, however, there's another way to "think about thinking" that can be extremely useful. It's become known as the "lateral thinking mode." It's simply a state of mind where the restrictions of critical judgment can be suspended for a time. This allows the mind to wander freely into unchartered areas in search of new ideas.

Techniques for lateral thinking

A number of techniques have been developed to arrive at a lateral state of mind and improve the idea flow. Some merely provide the proper setting for idea generation, such as group meetings where critical judgment is suspended. Others offer a method in which the brain randomly is exposed to outside stimuli which can spark new ideas. These lateral thinking techniques let you mentally step back and look at your problem from a fresh perspective.

Here are some of the lateral thinking techniques I've found to be quite helpful.

Brainstorm meetings. Some marketers believe that brainstorm meetings should be pretty much unstructured; just "let the ideas flow." I prefer what I call "directed brainstorming." Everyone at the meeting gets background information in advance. The meeting then follows an agenda or list of questions to focus idea generation on a specific area or problem. Chapter 12 describes how one idea developed at such a brainstorm meeting literally increased Sunset House sales by more than $6 million!

The exciting part of a brainstorm meeting is how ideas are built up by the group. One participant tosses out an idea. It has potential but needs further development. Somebody adds to it. One person suggests a variation. And another. The idea that's finally built up may not bear much resemblance to the original. But that original rough idea was the stimulus that started the process.

An important rule for brainstorming sessions is to avoid negative comments on ideas that are expressed. You don't want to inhibit participants from throwing out any idea, no matter how wild it is. The accompanying chart (Exhibit 27) provides other rules used by a leading ad agency for its brainstorming sessions.

Exhibit 27. Ad agency rules for brainstorming.

Select a Leader

Let the leader take all responsibility for contact with reality; everyone else in the brainstorming meeting is to "think wild." The duties of the leader are:
- Take notes on all the ideas expressed.
- Set a time limit on the meeting, such as 60 minutes.
- Set a quota on ideas to be generated, such as 60 ideas in 60 minutes.
- Admonish any critical thinkers in the group—no negative thinking allowed.
- Say "stop" when an idea has been built up enough.
- Help start new ideas if things lag.

Rules During Brainstorming

- Suspend all critical judgment on any ideas expressed.
- Let the leader handle all contact with reality. The rest of the group should "let go" at all times and just react to ideas.
- As each new idea comes, let the leader express the simple meaning.
- As each new idea is expressed, the participants should begin to build up the idea expressed.
- Keep building each idea till the leader of the group says, "Stop."
- Remember, humor and "play" atmosphere are desirable and important to the process. Don't be afraid to have fun!

Three-Phase Process

Brainstorming is part of a three-phase process. Make all preparations before brainstorming starts. Do all critical analysis after brainstorming stops.
- Before you start, carefully define problem(s) in writing. Set quotas for ideas. Set a time limit. Review the above rules with the brainstorming group.
- Establish the "formal setting," then *brainstorm*.
- After the session is over, use your normal, everyday judgment to logically develop ideas, selecting the best ideas from all of the alternatives available.

Random word association. This involves selecting a few words at random from a dictionary and "bumping them up against" the problem you're trying to solve. You start by looking at the various definitions of the random words. Then see how these definitions stimulate new thinking about the problem. Here's an oversimplified example. Let's say you're selling a woman's purse by mail. A competitor suddenly comes along who "knocks off" your product and starts running ads in the same magazines you've been using. Your results have been hurt and you need a new ad to boost response.

You open the dictionary. The first word you spot is "secure." One of the definitions is, "to free from risk of loss." Is there a way to strengthen or dramatize your guarantee to emphasize the high-quality features of your product and offer the consumer better protection?

The next word you spot is "victory." You notice that one of its definitions is "winning in a competition, performing better than others." Can you, perhaps, do a competitive rundown that shows how your purse compares with Brand "X"?

As in brainstorming, your objective is to generate as many different approaches as possible. You don't stop when you come up with a promising idea. You continue until you have a full list of alternatives. Then you switch to a judgmental thinking mode to sort them out and select the best option.

Transfer analysis. With this technique you consciously try to transfer a successful idea from another area to the problem you're working on. I've seen it used to isolate the key elements of successful products and then transfer them to a completely different product category.

Here's an example often used by Howard Gibson, president of New Product Insights, a firm that specializes in this technique. Let's say you're trying to develop ideas for new insurance promotions. One of the successful products you study is Crest toothpaste. This product's most important feature is that it contains flouride. What consumer benefit does it offer? Professional treatment, which formerly had to be applied by a dentist, can now be applied by the individual. The core idea is *something that allows you to do your own analysis or treatment in lieu of a professional.* Okay, transfer it to insurance. Maybe you should develop a personal assessment form so the indiviudal can select the policy that best fits his or her needs without a salesperson breathing down his or her neck. Perhaps a direct marketing insurance firm can mail out an immediate-issue policy that the consumer can activate to put in force and provide instant protection.

The secret of lateral thinking is exposing yourself to outside stimuli. And it helps to build up experience that your brain can store until you need it. By attending direct marketing luncheons, seminars, conferences, and courses. By reading industry publications, like *Direct Marketing* magazine. And by monitoring what competitors are doing in the marketing arena.

How to stimulate ideas

Getting good ideas is obviously easier said than done. But there are things you can do besides staring at a blank layout pad or a blank sheet of paper in your typewriter. One good approach is to explore various alternatives for changing the creative strategy you've been using.

An excellent booklet on the subject, called *How to Get that Great Advertising*

Idea, has been published by The Mind Institute in Canada. Here are some of the stimulating questions the booklet poses, plus a few related ones I added.

Can I alter timing? Is there a way to set a period of time that alters normal sales patterns and creates a benefit? Can a push normally done in the winter months be done in the summer? What offers could be used to preseason buyers? Can a Florida land company time its ad or mailing to break right after a big snowstorm up north?

Can I make an opposite? If a negative headline is working, can you use a positive one? What strengths are there in your product that can be emphasized by their opposites? Is there a way to make your message more believable by simply changing a common word or two? U.S. News & World Report book division accomplished the latter with its great headline, "Get rich slowly." (See Exhibit 28.)

Exhibit 28. U.S. News & World Report ad.

Can I use sensory appeal? Can you link the natural human senses to product attributes to create benefits? Is there a texture, odor, beauty, sound, taste or combination of these than can be incorporated? Should some special paper stock be used for the mailing? How about scented inks? A plastic record? Or can you just create sensory appeal with a mouth-watering food picture?

Can I demonstrate? Is there a key way to show product appeal through graphic demonstration? Can the product be pictured under excessively hard use to demonstrate strength? Would a chart aid in demonstrating? Can you use a series of action photos to provide the equivalent of a TV demonstration?

Can I make an association? What may be associated with the product to create a different appeal? Can the product be linked with a physical thing? A circumstance? An event? Can associations be made with current social trends? Or with nostalgic things of the past?

Can I do the unexpected? Is there a combination of art and copy that would create a startling improvement in readership? Are there humorous connotations in the product appeal or applications? Is there a sacred cow in the industry that your product proves wrong? Is there a way to make the mailing package so valuable that people will not only read it but want to save it?

Can I combine? What can be combined, physically or conceptually, with the product appeal? Can a related product be combined as a premium offer? Can newness be combined with tradition? Can a product benefit be combined with a specific industry or prospect need?

The consumer perspective for idea generation

Still another approach for developing new ideas is to completely change your perspective. Stop looking at the product or service as something you want to *sell*. Instead, look at it as something others might want to *buy*. Try exposing yourself to how consumers think about your offer.

One way to do it is with focus group research. A small group of consumers that fit your market profile have an informal discussion, led by a trained interviewer. They might be shown product samples and asked about how and why they use the product. They might be asked to review and comment on advertising claims. Sessions are taped so you can play back and study the comments.

You can get the same kind of straight-from-the-shoulder consumer feedback by making a few random phone calls. Pick some names from your customer list or a prospect list you're using. Look up the numbers and call them. Warning: Keep in mind that you're only talking to a small number of people that may or may not be typical of your marketing universe. The results won't be statistically valid. But what consumers say and how they say things can often stimulate ideas.

Dick Hodgson, one of the great creative pros in the direct marketing field, recommends another technique to get that consumer perspective. He suggests you review a random sample of the "white mail" you get from customers. This is a common term for various consumer correspondence—complaints, inquiries, and compliments. Dick finds that it allows you to get a handle on what main benefits appeal to people, what problems they have understanding your offer or copy claims, and what language the consumers use in talking about the product or service.

I think Chris Stagg, a top free-lance writer, sums it up well with this quote from a recent newsletter published by The Kleid Company: "No professional in the direct response business can create a winning package when he doesn't know *everything* there is to know about the human being he's writing to. When a writer creates in a marketing vacuum, he creates a loser."

Idea-starter questions

Finally, here are a few parting shots that I've found can often lead to new ideas and result in improvements:

- Can you make it easier for the prospect to take action?
- Can you make your mailing package look or seem more personal, as if it's coming from a real person rather than a giant company?
- Can you dramatically prove your copy claims?
- Can you make a more elaborate or expensive package pay out better than the one you're using?
- What would you like to build into your mailing package if cost were no object? Is there a way to do it less expensively?
- Does your space ad zero in on your most logical prospects instead of trying to appeal to everyone?
- Can you emulate the creative approach of an ad or mailing package you really admire?
- Is there a way to flatter the reader without overdoing it?

9

Management and Marketing Improvement Areas

Years ago the mail order field was populated primarily by entrepreneurs, and their management style was best described as "seat-of-the-pants." Today, whether you call it mail order or direct marketing, it's a different situation.

Management usually has to be concerned with all the things faced by any other business, such as buying or manufacturing, inventories, personnel, and financing. But managers also have some special problems and concerns unique to direct marketing. And, in most cases, top executives have a heavier-than-normal involvement in the marketing functions of the company.

In this chapter, we'll cover some of the advanced areas of management and marketing that can have a big impact on improving and building an existing direct marketing program.

Establish the value of a customer

It's amazing how many direct marketing firms think they know what they can afford to spend to get a new customer, but really don't. Why? Because they don't know what kind of repeat business they can expect from a customer. So they look at their revenue and costs for the initial sale. And they assume that if they at least breakeven on this sale, they'll make some money on repeat business.

What's wrong with this approach? Nothing. Except that it's a very shortsighted view, as with some people who say, "I don't believe in credit; I pay cash for everything." Businesspeople who use this breakeven approach should have a profitable operation. But, on the other hand, by neglecting to take into account the value of repeat business, such businesspeople are also limiting their growth. Simply because they are only willing to proceed with ads or mailings where they can at least breakeven. In so doing, they are automatically excluding other publications, other lists, or other media that don't quite reach the breakeven point on the first sale but can be profitable in the long run.

One of the best discussions of the subject I've seen is in Julian Simon's book, *How to Start and Operate a Mail Order Business*. Simon says: "It is amazing and sad to see how much profit mail order firms forego by not correctly estimating and using the value of a customer." Here's the approach he recommends for calculating the value of a customer:

1. Take a fair random sample of the names of customers—active and inactive—who first bought from you about three years ago. (Simon recommends 300 customer names but I suggest you use at least 1,000.)

2. Add up the total dollar amount they have purchased in the three years since the date of their first purchase.

3. Divide by the number of customer records in your sample.

4. Multiply by the percentage that represents your average profit margin.

Sounds simple enough, doesn't it? Let's try it out. Suppose you have a catalog operation selling inexpensive gifts and novelty items. You randomly select 1,000 three-year old customers and get a computer printout or manual summary of their buying history. They have placed 775 orders during this period with a total value of $9,300. Dividing that figure by 1,000 gives you a $9.30 average per customer. Naturally, some customers have bought a lot more; some a lot less. But what you want is the average.

You have a 20 percent profit margin, which means the value of each new customer is $1.86. That's what the average customer you acquired three years ago was worth to you in terms of future profits. And if you really want to grow and expand, you should be willing to invest up to $1.86 to get a new customer instead of just trying to acquire customers on a breakeven basis.

To help dramatize the value of repeat business, let's suppose you somehow manage to double it. For our purposes, it doesn't really matter whether customers place more orders, larger orders, or a combination of the two. The 1,000 customers now account for $18,600 in total sales. If you go through the rest of the calculations, you'll find you can now afford to spend twice as much for a new customer, $3.72 instead of $1.86.

As Simon wisely points out, you should take into account the cost of your capital since you will be effectively investing your money for up to a three-year period. And if your list rental income is substantial, that revenue should also be considered in calculating the value of a customer.

The impact of a growing customer list

Knowing the value of a customer is half the battle. The other half is to understand the importance of a growing customer list on your bottom line. It comes down to very simple economics. The cost of mailing to a group of customers and a same-sized group of prospects is almost identical (the customers are actually cheaper to mail because you don't incur list rental expense); yet your response from customers is much greater.

Let's look at an example I think is pretty realistic. We'll take a firm that goes into direct marketing to sell collectibles. The first offering is a series of five china plates. We do a P&L calculation, taking into account all direct costs. It shows that, allowing for attrition, the series would produce net sales of $173.81 per order. The gross profit, before promotion costs, would be $93.46 per order. Here are some more assumptions:

• The mailing packages costs $300 per thousand.

- The expected response rate from prospect lists is 0.5 percent, which would generate 500 customer names from every 100,000 pieces mailed.
- The P&L statement shows that this response rate would give us a profit of $167.30 for every thousand pieces mailed.
- There are 500,000 prospect names available for such an offer.
- We have product resources sufficient for development of twelve similar collectible offers a year. To simplify our example, we'll assume that all future offers would have a response rate and P&L identical to those of the plate series.

The first chart shows a five-year plan for prospect mailings (see Exhibit 29). As you can see, the plan calls for 12 mailings a year to the full prospect universe. Our profit percentage is a consistent 19 percent. And our promotions will bring in a total of 30,000 new customers a year.

Exhibit 29. Prospect mailings.

Year	Mailings per Year	Quantity per Year	Total Sales	Total Profit	Percent Profit
1.......	12	500,000	$5,214,300	$1,003,800	19
2.......	12	500,000	5,214,300	1,003,800	19
3.......	12	500,000	5,214,300	1,003,800	19
4.......	12	500,000	5,214,300	1,003,800	19
5.......	12	500,000	5,214,300	1,003,800	19

Note: At a response rate of .005, each mailing produces 2,500 new customers. Therefore 12 mailings produce 30,000 customers per year.

The second chart (Exhibit 30) shows a five-year plan for customer mailings. The 12 mailings a year would be the same as those used for prospects. But there are two important differences. First, the size of the customer list is growing year-by-year as we generate new names from the prospect mailing program. Second, we assume a response rate of 3 percent instead of 0.5 percent, which reflects the higher response expected from a firm's own customers. As a result of the higher response rate, the customer list can be expected to produce a consistent profit of 46 percent.

Exhibit 30. Customer mailings.

Year	Mailings per Year	Customers Mailed	Total Sales	Total Profit	Percent Profit
1.......	12	15,000*	$ 938,574	$ 433,890	46
2.......	12	45,000	2,815,722	1,301,670	46
3.......	12	75,000	4,692,870	2,169,450	46
4.......	12	105,000	6,570,018	3,037,230	46
5.......	12	135,000	8,447,166	3,905,010	46

*Based on 30,000 customers acquired by the end of the year. The number 15,000 is used to represent an average for the year.

The third chart (Exhibit 31) simply combines the totals of the first two, to reflect both the prospect and customer mailings. The dollar amount of sales and profits grow steadily year by year. Even more significant is the growing profit percentage. This, of course, is a reflection again of the increasing customer list with its higher and more profitable response rate. As the years go by, a higher percentage of the total mailing volume is concentrated on the customer list and, therefore, the profit percentage grows accordingly.

Exhibit 31. Prospect and customer mailings combined.

Year	Total Sales	Total Profit	Percent Profit
1	$ 6,152,874	$1,437,690	23
2	8,030,022	2,305,470	29
3	9,907,170	3,173,250	32
4	11,784,318	4,041,030	34
5	13,661,466	4,908,810	36

Importance of new product development

New products are the lifeblood of any business. It's a rare company indeed whose product mix will be the same five years from now as it is today. So, new product development is essential not only to sustain your present sales volume but also to meet the growth goals established by most businesses. Just one solid new product can have a big impact on the sales and profit picture.

Most firms are always on the lookout for new product ideas. Some firms use a new product committee that meets regularly to review the possibilities open to them. Others charge one person with the responsibility for generating new direct marketing product ideas. For most, however, this is a function that marketing management has to oversee on a part-time basis, along with all other management responsibilities and current activities.

The key factors are that management makes a formal commitment to new product development, establishes a budget for development and testing, and sets up some mechanism or reporting system to ensure that this area gets attention on a regular basis.

A structured new product program

One of the most exciting new product development programs I've participated in was for the mail order division of Encyclopaedia Britannica. This was a joint effort on the part of the client and its ad agency. And the year-long effort was a highly structured program to initiate, evaluate, and develop suitable ideas. Here are the ten steps that were followed:

1. *Brainstorming.* Encylopaedia Britannica's present product line, reputation, and editorial strengths were reviewed. Then through a series of brainstorm meetings and individual assignments, the agency began developing new product ideas. The

result: 58 product ideas were presented to the client with a brief one-paragraph description of each concept.

2. *Idea evaluation and refinement.* A committee of six people—three from the agency and three from Britannica—then reviewed and voted on each product idea. From this review, 16 ideas were judged as suitable for further exploration.

3. *Concept marketing plans.* For each new product idea, a mini-marketing plan was written which briefly explained the concept, the rationale behind it, the market segment it was aimed at, the competition faced in the marketplace, if any, the proposed offer and operation (e.g., one-shot sale, monthly shipment plan), the suggested pricing, any problem areas anticipated, and an indication of the investment required to launch the product.

4. *Idea evaluation and refinement.* The concept marketing plans were then reviewed by the agency-client team. Four ideas were eliminated for one reason or another, and then there were 12.

5. *Focus group research.* Visual presentations of the 12 remaining new product ideas were prepared along with a brief description. A total of five focus-group research sessions were then conducted using the visual presentations. Some groups consisted of only women and some of only men with all participants carefully selected to represent the potential market segments. Each product idea was exposed to at least two of the focus group sessions.

6. *Idea evaluation and refinement.* Based on this qualitative research, five more product ideas were either completely eliminated or sent "back to the drawing board" for major revision. While most of the remaining ideas had been enthusiastically received in the research sessions, some suggested refinements were made in a couple of them to strengthen the product concepts.

7. *Profit projections.* The agency then developed cost estimates for testing the seven remaining products, which included layout and finished art, production of engravings or separations, and direct mail or space media cost. These were used to develop profit and loss statements covering the test as well as a five-year expansion program for each product idea.

8. *Idea evaluation and refinement.* As a result of the profit projections, three of the ideas were approved for immediate testing, three were "tabled" for various financial considerations, and one was recommended as a possible joint venture with another company.

9. *Development of creative materials.* Direct mail and space advertising were then created for the three ideas initially approved and a joint venture was set up for the fourth. Important tests were planned. Media was scheduled. Ads and direct mail materials were produced.

10. *Marketplace measurement.* The final evaluation of the new product ideas came from consumers who cast the critical votes by sending in the respective ad coupons and reply cards. At this point it appears that one of the products is a big bomb. Another showed some life but not enough to be profitable. And the other two are winners.

In any type of new product development, whether in general advertising or direct marketing, the success ratio is usually pretty low. Most firms believe they're doing quite well if they get one winner out of every five products actually tested. This structured program for new product development has already produced two winners for Encyclopaedia Britannica, including the Fix-It-Fast card reference file (see Exhibit 32). So the batting average on this program is excellent.

Exhibit 32. Fix-It-Fast ad.

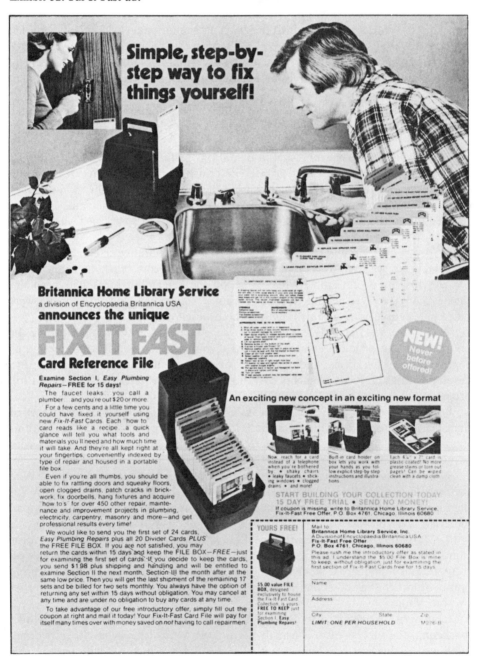

A revolving review of existing products

While it's exciting to be involved in the birth of a successful new product, management should not overlook the opportunity for revamping or improving existing products. Very often, once a product has become established, it gets promoted regularly along with the rest of the product line.

But seldom does management make a full-scale review of existing products. One client I've worked with has recognized this shortcoming and has done something about it. The company has established a product audit committee. It meets every other month for an in-depth review of one product. The review includes product features, pricing, recent promotion efforts, results, and how the product is paying out. The committee members then brainstorm new ideas ranging from product improvements to new promotion ideas. Decisions are made. Actions are taken. As a result, many existing products have been substantially improved and product life lengthened.

Finally, in thinking about product improvements or new products, don't limit your scope. How you define your business often has an important bearing on the range of product ideas that will be considered. A good example is the Franklin Mint, which started with commemorative coins. If the firm had limited its business definition to commemorative coins, Franklin would not have enjoyed the substantial growth it has. Instead executives regarded themselves as being in the collectibles business and have branched out from coins and ingots to a wide variety of other collectible products.

The untapped potential in list selectivity

Much has been said and written, especially in recent years, on the value of list selectivity. As mailings become more and more expensive, the proper selectivity allows you to cut back on your mailing quantity and zero in on the people most likely to respond. Very often selectivity can even make the difference in whether or not a list pays out for you.

Yet I think this potential resource is largely untapped by the majority of direct marketers. Not by the giants like Fingerhut and Publishers Clearing House. They've worked on this problem for years and their list selectivity has become highly sophisticated.

But, apparently, most medium-size and smaller firms have not devoted enough time and energy to this important area. This was largely borne out by a recent study made by Doubleday. The company analyzed all the list rental orders for their book buyer lists over a six-month period. The results are shocking:

- Less than 25 percent of all the orders requested any selectivity other than an Nth name sample for testing.
- Less than 15 percent used any ZIP code selectivity.
- Less than 5 percent did any selectivity by demographics.

This led Doubleday to publish a helpful booklet titled *How to Use Mailing List Selections*. The booklet concludes that, "Most mailers are not as familiar as they like to think they are with selections. Too many mailers are underestimating what selections can do for them, or maybe they're afraid that selections are too complicated for them.''

In any case, the booklet spells out the basic types of selectivity available on Doubleday's lists and most other lists. They include active or expire names, title or sex selections, amount paid, credit qualification, recency or hot-line buyers, type of product purchased, and geographic area.

Identifying prime prospects

Naturally, the way to find out which selectivity factors are most important for you is through testing. Beyond these individual criteria, however, other methods are available to identify and zero in on your prime prospects. Some direct marketers will make a large mailing and analyze their responses to find which ZIP codes performed best and worst. Others do the same thing by taking their entire customer file and comparing the number of customers in each ZIP area to the total population of that area. Those areas with the highest penetration are the ones used in renting prospect lists, while those with the lower penetrations are eliminated. Industrial direct marketers often use a similar technique to analyze penetration by SIC codes.

A more advanced technique is regression analysis, which is sometimes called multiple correlation. Most people make it sound terribly complicated. Rose Harper, president of The Kleid Company, a leading list brokerage firm, describes it rather simply: "What it comes down to is doing a test mailing and then analyzing your returns to find out exactly how the people who did order differ from the people who didn't order." If you need an incentive to pursue things like this, Harper points out that these studies will usually allow you to double your response rate.

The value of research

Until recently, most direct marketers have tended to think that formal research was unnecessary. "Why do that type of research," they might say, "when we're constantly researching everything we do by testing? Our tests show us exactly how people respond to a given offer or copy approach, not how they tell us they would respond."

There is a lot of truth in that remark. Testing is a built-in research mechanism that is extremely valuable. But it also has its limitations. When we test package A versus package B, sure, we find out which works better. But we don't find out why. And we really don't learn much about the nonresponders to help us sell them the next time around.

I'm happy to report that the old attitudes about research are changing. Most of today's sophisticated direct marketers use research regularly. In its simplest terms, research is a tool for fact finding and decision making. Here are three broad research applications for direct marketing, as outlined by Allen Sorkin of Sorkin-Enenstein Research Service at a recent DMMA seminar.

Product evaluation. What do consumers really think of your product? It is possible through product and concept research to determine the features of a product that are liked and disliked and how they relate to consumer buying intentions. The opinions and needs of consumers are evaluated to determine the viability of a particular product or products. This can not only indicate a product's likelihood for success, but suggest modifications that could improve its position in the marketplace.

One direct marketing firm I know had been enjoying a consistent 15 percent sales increase for about 10 straight years. Then some stiff competition came on the scene and sales dropped 30 percent the following year. Product research was undertaken to compare the firm's product with the competitor's. The study showed clearly that the competitor had three unique features which were highly favored by consumers. These features were adopted plus two others that consumers had rated high. As a result, sales shot up 40 percent the following year.

Market segmentation research. Who is your market and how do you appeal to them? This type of research gathers demographic information about your customers and prospects—age, income level, and so on. You can also do research to compare responder and nonresponder groups from the same mailing list or publication to see how they differ.

I've often been amazed to see how few direct marketing firms have customer profile information on their own list. They think they know who their customers are, but have no hard data to back up their beliefs. Yet this is one of the most inexpensive types of research because it can usually be done with a mailed survey to a small, random sample of the customer file.

Promotional materials research. Is your message getting through? What copy or design elements of envelopes, brochures, or ads do consumers respond to most favorably? Least favorably? How do they rate your pieces compared to competitors? A well-done research study will not only help you sharpen and fine tune your promotional materials, it will usually suggest new ideas for future creative efforts.

Many types of research studies can be employed to accomplish these three objectives. They include focus groups, in-depth personal interviews, phone surveys, and mail panels. Some are quantitative: They involve enough people or interviews so the results are statistically valid. Others are qualitative: The results are not statistically valid, but they still give you some valuable indications of consumer attitudes and motivations. It's best to work with a professional research organization, people who can give you good guidance on the types of studies that best serve your objectives.

Does research really pay? Here's what David Soskin, Book-of-the-Month Club's former advertising director, said on the subject in a recent issue of *Direct Marketing* magazine: "At Book-of-the-Month Club, we have found that extensive research before testing has helped us to find the best product or product combination to sell, the best offers to test, the creative strategy to use, and the most effective media to get our message across. Oftentimes we find that headlines and offers which we think are clear are not to those persons being interviewed. This helps to eliminate problems that might come up later."

Start your own competition

How do you substantially increase sales when you think you might already be saturating the market with your present product line? Or, you have so many competitors it's difficult to win a bigger share of the market?

One possibility is by competing with yourself, establishing a second company name to sell the same type of products. This idea might seem far-fetched, but it's really what the big soap companies, cosmetic firms, cigarette companies, and auto manufacturers have been doing for years to increase their share of market. And I know of at least two direct marketing firms that have successfully started their own competition.

In the first case, the objective was to meet competition head-on. The client concerned had a successful premium-priced product for the business market. Suddenly they were "knocked off" by another firm selling a similar but much less expensive version of the same product. So they started their own lower-price version which they marketed under a different name.

In another case, a firm selling the school market had a dual buying influence. Some purchases were made by principals and faculty, others by students. This firm had the bulk of the total market, but executives believed they weren't getting as much of the student business as they should. Maybe their catalog was too conservative, they reasoned. So they started another catalog under a different name. The product line was almost identical but they gave the catalog a more youthful feel with mod art and copy.

The results? In both cases, the second companies have brought in "plus" sales without hurting the original product line. In the second example, the new catalog operation has been growing much more rapidly than the original one. And there are some obvious economies. By utilizing the same office and personnel, you can increase your volume with an effective decrease in overhead because you're actually spreading your overhead across two operations instead of one.

Foreign markets

Another way to expand sales and profits when you think you've saturated your market is by expanding beyond U.S. borders. Some large direct marketers already have substantial foreign operations. International sales accounted for 48 percent of the total revenues of Time-Life Books in 1978 and 42 percent for Franklin Mint.

It's generally conceded that response rates on direct mail in foreign countries are higher than in the United States. Not just slightly higher, but often as much as 50 percent or more higher. This is probably because most foreign countries receive less mail per capita than in this country. They are still largely virgin territory for direct marketing. List availability is a problem in some countries but is largely offset by list exchanges and heavier use of space advertising to get new customers.

If you're just beginning to consider foreign operations, the logical starting points are Canada and Europe. To help you compare their potential to the U.S., the accompanying chart (Exhibit 33) provides a handy summary of population, households, and other key statistics.

Thirteen overlooked paths to sales and profits

Having been involved in developing marketing recommendations for numerous clients and having analyzed the present operations of others, I've noticed a lot of commonality. Following are some techniques that seem to apply equally well to a wide variety of companies in different types of businesses. You might call them activities most direct marketers don't do enough of:

Exhibit 33. Comparison of United States and foreign markets.

Country	Population (000)	Households	Average Size of Family	Gross National Product (millions)
United States	213,540	72,867,000	2.9	$1,688,800
Canada	22,831	6,041,305	3.8	189,900
Belgium	9,801	3,161,000	3.1	66,900
Denmark	5,060	1,872,000	2.7	38,100
France	52,743	17,537,000	3.0	348,300
West Germany ...	61,829	22,453,000	2.8	451,200
Great Britain	56,042	18,920,000	3.0	216,500
Ireland	3,127	NA	NA	7,900
Italy	55,812	17,989,000	3.1	164,300
The Netherlands .	13,654	4,178,000	3.3	87,200

Source: *O.E.C.D. Observer,* May 1977; U.S. Dept. of Commerce, Canadian Government, and European Community Information Services.

Mail your customer list heavily. Some firms hit their customers only a few times a year. But, unless you have a seasonal operation and assuming the availability of product, customers can generally be profitably mailed at least six times, often twelve times, and sometimes even more frequently.

Use telephone selling. Especially good for large ticket items or renewal efforts to previous buyers. One firm selling to the business market started experimenting with telephone selling two years ago and now has nine people working on phone sales.

Develop special offers to get new customers. It's obviously easier to send the same mailing or catalog to customers and prospects alike. But it's not always the smartest approach. Sometimes prospects require a more complete or elaborate selling story. Customers, on the other hand, often respond best when your copy acknowledges a previous purchase.

Use enough leverage where it counts. In an inquiry-producing situation or a two-stage selling method, the heaviest effort is devoted to getting the initial inquiry or response. Often the conversion or follow-up effort doesn't get enough attention. Because the quantity of names in this second stage is small, a few added dollars well spent can mean a big improvement in the final profit picture.

Sell unrelated merchandise to customers. Because somebody starts out as a "widget" buyer, it's all too easy to think of him or her as just that. However, your customer list will usually respond to a great variety of products and services, many quite different from the basic or original offer that brought them in.

Have enough follow-ups in a series. For example, someone arbitrarily decides there should be three mailings in a series. The firm tries it and all three pay out. The odds are that the series could and should be expanded to four, five, or more mailings—so long as each mailing continues to pay its own way.

Segregate large customers. We often find that 20 percent of a firm's customers account for 80 percent of the sales volume. These large customers should get special sales attention, whether by mail or phone, to keep them buying. And the more you learn about them, the better the chance of finding more just like them.

Develop customized products for specialized markets. I have found that some markets can best be tapped by a product that seems to be tailor-made for their needs. This might be as simple as changing the product name or a few minor features or it might require a whole new product approach. A number of specialized markets are large enough to be worth cultivating in this way. The method can be more effective than trying to sell the same thing to everyone.

Try for multiple-unit sales. The idea is to sell more units on each order by mailing to individuals, firms, or groups who represent a multiple market for the product. Those who receive the mailing can act like middlemen or agents to multiply product distribution and sales. This works well in the school market, for example, where the teacher gets students to sign up for various programs. In other situations, you can use "twofer" prices and volume-order discounts.

Use MGM programs. The initials stand for *member get a member,* which is a fancy way of saying, go after customer referrals. Satisfied customers can be your best salespeople. You can merely ask for referral names or provide a small gift as an incentive. Best proof of how well this works is the record clubs who constantly feature MGM programs.

Promote list rental. Most firms with a list on the market leave the promotion up to a list broker. But it's such a profitable area that it should get more attention, either from a list manager or yourself. And the universe of potential list users is so small that a nominal budget can have a big impact.

Develop a catalog. While many direct marketers rely entirely on catalog selling, many other marketing situations exist in which a catalog could provide supplementary sales even if it's used only for the customer list or aftermarket sales. Catalogs provide an opportunity to offer a wide variety of products and consistently get better readership and retention than solo mailings.

Look beyond the next twelve months. If an organization expects to be in business for more than a year or two, it should have marketing objectives for the next five years. A five-year plan should include future products, services, and markets to be explored. And some of them should be under active consideration right now.

10

Fulfillment and Back-end Marketing

Mail order pioneer Max Sackheim liked to admonish clients to "make customers, not sales." And the distinction is more than a subtle play on words. It is recognizing that you don't build a business on one-time sales. You build it on repeat business—on customers who like your products, who are pleased with your service, and who are therefore likely to buy from you again and again.

One of the most knowledgeable people I know in this area is Walter Marshall of Rapp and Collins. "Most of us spend the large part of our day working hard to find new copy themes, new offers, new products, or new media," he says. "All of this effort is geared to bolstering the front-end position and improving the bottom line. But how many of us look to the back-end as a way of improving profitability? Is it possible that the fulfillment department can be just as important a profit center as the marketing department? The answer, I believe, is yes."

The importance of the back-end

Another real expert on the subject is Stan Fenvessy, president of Fenvessy Associates, a direct marketing consulting firm. In a recent talk, he described fulfillment as "the full circle of handling an order from its initiation by mail or telephone until the customer is fully satisfied."

Fenvessy went on to outline the eight elements or steps that are part of fulfillment:

1. Ordering tools and techniques including the product numbering system, order form design, and ordering instructions
2. Receiving mail and telephone orders
3. Processing orders
4. Checking credit
5. Maintaining inventory
6. Sending merchandise or subscriptions
7. Billing
8. Handling complaints

Fulfillment is important for two big reasons. First, to make the original order stick. The majority of direct marketing purchases are made on impulse, and virtually all carry a free trial or moneyback guarantee. If fulfillment isn't handled promptly and efficiently, your returned goods rate can and will increase.

Second, good fulfillment builds customer satisfaction. As Fenvessy says, "Only a satisfied customer will order again. She must receive everything she ordered, promptly, properly packed, the invoice must be clear and accurate, and she must have the assurance that any problems will be resolved fairly, quickly, and courteously."

How long are customers willing to wait?

The FTC recently established a 30-day rule for most mail order sales. In effect, it says that, unless you tell the customer shipping will take longer in your front-end ad or mailing, you must either ship the order in 30 days or give the customer an opportunity to cancel his or her order.

How do consumers feel about the subject? I haven't seen any surveys dealing with the 30-day rule itself. But some years ago, *Better Homes & Gardens* did an interesting subscriber survey on mail order shopping. One of the many questions asked was, "How long are you willing to wait for an item ordered through the mail to be delivered?" Here are the results in percentages:

Less than a week	1
One week	6
Two weeks	37
Three weeks	28
Four weeks	13
Five or six weeks and up	4
Did not answer	11

Note that almost half the audience preferred to wait no more than two weeks. Nearly three-fourths expected their order in no more than three weeks. And this question was asked only of respondents who said they ordered through the mail. How many other consumers never bother with mail order shopping because they have the feeling, perhaps based on past experience, that it "takes forever?"

Slow fulfillment can cost you money

Compared to the tremendous volume of testing done on front-end marketing to make the initial sale, there has been relatively little done on the back-end. Enough testing has been done, however, under controlled conditions, to establish quite clearly that good fulfillment is more than just a nice gesture. Here are a number of examples cited by Walter Marshall in a recent article in *Direct Marketing* magazine:

Speed shipping. A record club was taking about five weeks to get its first shipment to new members. In testing the effect of getting the first shipment out sooner, 5,000 orders from a single magazine insert were split into two groups. Half got standard fulfillment; the other half were handled under a "speed ship" plan that got the first shipment to new members in about two and one-half weeks.

Six months later a computer analysis was done on both groups to measure two key factors. First, the payment of the invoice that came with the initial shipment. The "speed ship" group had a 17 percent higher payment rate than the control group who got standard fulfillment. Second, what's known as the "take per member" was measured, i.e., the number of club selections purchased during the six-month period. The "speed ship" group won again with a "take" that was over 20 percent higher than the control group. The test was later verified in even larger quantities and, as a result, the club's entire fulfillment operation was streamlined.

Acknowledging orders. Knowing that customers had to wait a few weeks to get their first shipment, a major book club wanted to test the addition of an acknowledgment mailing to let new members know their order had been received and was being processed. The mailing used contained a personalized thank you letter and an eight-page booklet that described the club's operations.

The test group received this acknowledgment mailing, which was sent first class. The control group merely received its introductory shipment. And both groups got their introductory shipment at the same time. The results showed that the test group, who received the acknowledgment, came out ahead on all three scores being measured: Their conversion rate was 10.4 percent higher, the bad debt rate was 18.7 percent lower, and the returned goods rate was 44 percent lower.

Handling inquiries. Still another test Marshall cites was for a direct marketing firm who advertised to generate inquiries for their catalog. Management wondered if they could save money by sending out their catalog via third class instead of first class, knowing the former method would add about a week to the delivery time. They tested and found their percent of catalog sales was 19 percent lower for the third class group.

Good service helps, not hurts

In addition to speedier fulfillment, other tests have shown that good customer service also pays out. Years ago executives of mail order companies were scared to death to put anything in their shipping cartons about how to send back merchandise because they felt it would increase their returns. Some even kidded about trying to develop self-destruct cartons so that, once opened, the carton couldn't be used to send the merchandise back. Finally, one of the giant catalog firms made a test. On the back of the packing slip, instructions were given on how to return merchandise the customer was unhappy with. There was no increase in returns and the normal returns were easier to process because customers followed the instructions given them.

Still another tack was taken by a firm selling movie camera outfits on a free trial basis. The firm was experiencing an abnormally high returned goods rate. Research disclosed that many returns were being made for very minor reasons. If the customer couldn't figure out how to work the camera or if the bulb didn't work on the projector, the customer would just pack up the whole outfit, ship it back, and forget the whole thing.

To solve the problem, a card was inserted in all shipments telling customers to call the factory toll-free if they had any questions or problems. The return goods rate was cut by about 25 percent, and the phone expense turned out to be a mere fraction of the sales and profits that were saved.

Order conversion and renewals: key leverage points

Many direct marketing situations call for a series of mailings to get conversions or renewals. Most insurance companies, for instance, have to convert policyholders who inquire or accept an introductory offer to pay their first regular premium. Magazines have to renew subscriptions, usually annually. These are key leverage points, and just an increase of a few percentage points can make a big improvement in your bottom line.

In my experience, it's important that a conversion series be given enough efforts. Most firms I know use a five- to seven-piece series, though some use as many as a dozen efforts. The series should have a lot of variety in format and copy approach so each effort has a good chance to get opened and produce action. This area is certainly worthy of testing. A magazine recently did extensive testing on their renewal series using the creative efforts of three top copywriters and boosted their renewal rate 50 percent.

One relatively new technique that I've seen work well in the conversion and renewal area is called the surprise gift or goodwill gift. The technique was first tested by a magazine. The publisher sent subscribers an art poster about a month before the normal renewal series started. It was an attractive gift, apparently sent for no reason at all. And there was no invoice or renewal order card in the mailing, just a friendly cover letter. The poster added about 15 percent to the cost of the magazine's regular renewal efforts. But those subscribers who received the free poster renewed at a 26 percent higher rate than the control group who just received the normal renewal series.

I've seen the surprise gift work equally well for others, including a direct marketing insurance company. The company sends a Norman Rockwell print in advance of its regular conversion series (see Exhibit 34).

Getting that second order

Another key leverage point for most direct marketing firms is the second order. Yet, companies often treat all customers alike. They make no special effort to get an individual to order a second time, ignoring the fact that a two-time buyer is much more likely to become a good long-term customer.

Let's consider some figures to prove the point. One firm sells a gift item with an annual repeat factor. Out of 100 new customers, 49 will buy again the following year. But, of those who place a second order, 68 percent will buy again the third year, and 76 percent of these will also buy the fourth year. Once a buying pattern is established, customer loyalty and repeat purchases remain high.

The same principle applies in fund raising. Officials of one charity found that they lost 53 out of 100 new contributors the following year. But, of the 47 who donated a second time, 85 percent were still contributing four years later!

The message is clear: Getting that second order is important. Therefore, special renewal or promotion efforts directed to first-time buyers can pay big dividends.

On a continuity shipment plan, where customers receive new selections on a monthly or bimonthly basis, you have a built-in opportunity to presell—not only the second shipment, but every future shipment. Many publishers use what is sometimes

Exhibit 34. Rockwell print surprise gift mailing.

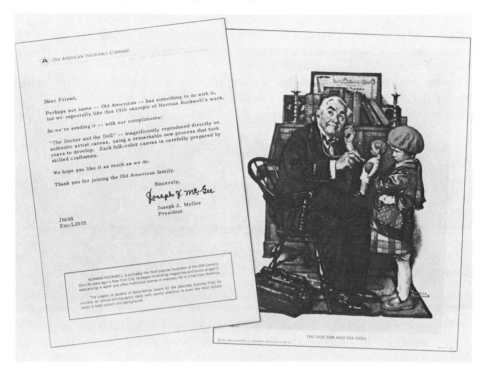

called a "running resell." They enclose a letter or flyer with each shipment that previews what's coming next month. It not only can increase the acceptance rate or "take" of the next selection, it can cut down the expense of processing returns from customers who decide in advance that they don't want the selection.

Are you maximizing customer value?

Virtually all direct marketers will acknowledge that their customer list is their greatest asset. But varying degrees of sophistication are shown on how well they utilize that asset. Most have learned the basics, of course. They keep their list segmented by year of last purchase because they know the most recent buyers perform better than the older ones. And, through testing and experimentation, they've gained some idea of how many times a year they can profitably mail each group.

But those really are the elementary methods. The more advanced direct marketing practitioners go well beyond this. They know that some two-year old customers are better than others, maybe because their last order was a large one or because they had purchased frequently for some time and temporarily had become inactive. They adjust their promotion efforts accordingly to concentrate as much mail as possible on the customers whose past history proves they are most likely to buy again.

They do it by using a recency/frequency/monetary formula, commonly known as RFM. The technique was pioneered back in the thirties by the giant mail order catalog houses. In that depression era, these leading marketers found they could no longer afford to give their expensive catalog to everyone who bought from them in the past. They ended up virtually cutting their catalog circulations in half with only a slight decline in sales and a sharp increase in profits.

The original systems have become even more sophisticated today thanks to the fact that RFM formulas can be established and controlled by computer. In his *Advertising Age* column, Bob Stone recently discussed how an RFM system is set up:

"In its simplest form, a point system is established with purchases broken out by quarters. A typical formula might be as follows:

Recency points:	24 points—purchased in current quarter
	12 points—purchased 4 to 6 months ago
	6 points—purchased 7 to 9 months ago
	3 points—purchased 10 to 12 months ago
Frequency points:	Number of purchases times 4 points
Monetary points:	10 percent of each dollar purchase with a ceiling of 9 points (ceiling avoids distortion from an unusually large purchase)

"The points allotted vary among those using RFM formulas but the principles are the same. Once the system is established and point values are confirmed, the opportunities for maximizing profits are phenomenal."

Applying the RFM formula

Using Stone's typical formula as an example, let's see how it might be applied by a catalog marketer. We'll assume that the firm puts out eight catalogs a year and has 100,000 names in its customer file. The firm assigns RFM points as indicated above and finds that its customer file breaks out as follows:

Points	Number of Names
75 or more	13,000
50 to 74	22,000
25 to 54	46,000
0 to 24	19,000

At this point, judgment and testing come into play. But a typical mailing plan might call for an annual catalog frequency like this:

Points	Number of Names	Catalogs
75 or more	13,000	12
50 to 74	22,000	8
25 to 54	46,000	6
0 to 24	19,000	3

As you can see, the top two categories would get all eight catalogs. The top group, in fact, would get a remail of the four strongest books, ideally with a different cover. The bottom two groups, however, would get less than eight catalogs. The lowest group might get a book only in the best months—perhaps January, August, and October—when they have the best chance of paying out.

The above plan calls for a total mailing of 665,000 catalogs. If, on the other hand, the firm were to mail all eight catalogs to its entire 100,000 list, it would be mailing 800,000 books. In our example, we would end up mailing 135,000 less catalogs and probably do as well or better in the sales department.

This is, of course, an over-simplified example. Many RFM formulas become quite complicated. Time-Life Books has its house list broken into 105 identifiable segments. The example, however, shows that the same system can be applied on a smaller scale by any direct marketer with a substantial list. And it's not unusual for the better segments of a list to perform six to ten times as well as the poorer segments.

One firm's building-a-name program

You can't maximize customer value unless you really work at it. The most sophisticated back-end marketing system I've seen is that used by Old American Insurance Company under the direction of Martin Baier. The firm has about 500,000 policyholders and an elaborate system called Building-A-Name.

The system is dedicated to the premise that when the firm gets the name of a new policyholder, a structured program should be used to build up his or her value to the company. The program includes a variety of efforts to convert introductory offer policyholders, renew them, upgrade them with increase offers and policy riders, sell other policies, and reactivate those who fail to convert or renew. Over 200 offers are mailed in the course of the year, and the system is constantly refined by evaluating and analyzing each effort.

Pretend you're a customer

Everyone likes to think his firm is doing a good job on fulfillment and customer service. But are your orders really shipped as fast as you think they are? Are all the correct forms and enclosures being used? Do complaints get handled efficiently? Are inquiries processed promptly?

I've always made it a practice to answer ads or mailings and check up on the fulfillment of the clients with whom I have worked. I've seen a number of surprises or "things nobody happened to think about." Many potential problems were quickly corrected. Try it yourself. Send in the coupons or order cards from your own ads or mailings. Under a decoy name, of course. Or have a friend do it. See how long it takes to get a shipment. Find out if the merchandise is received in good condition and can be easily repacked for returning it. Learn whether returns are acknowledged. Find out what it takes to get a problem straightened out and how many past due invoices you get in the meantime. Learn whether the form letters being used convey the proper customer service attitude. You may be surprised.

Consumerism—what to do about it now

In this chapter, I hope we've made the point that good fulfillment is good business. But the FTC, Better Business Bureaus, and newspaper "action line" columnists still receive an alarming number of mail order complaints every year. Direct marketers must work at reducing them or "Big Brother" will do it for us. Consumerism isn't about to go away and it's time we do something about it. Here are some "idea starters" to consider, if you aren't already using them:

Simplify your guarantee. A leading mail order nursery did this recently. The firm dropped the confusing legal terms. The refund and replacement policy was explained in simple, everyday language. The result was a sharp drop in customer complaints and correspondence.

Acknowledge orders. Many customers probably wouldn't mind waiting for merchandise delivery if they at least knew their order had been received and was getting your careful attention. A simple postcard is usually enough to do the trick. While sending a card will add somewhat to your ordering processing cost, it should greatly reduce customer inquiries, look-ups, and correspondence expense.

Ship merchandise more promptly. Stan Fenvessy says your goal should be to get your order into the customer's hands the calendar week after the one in which the order was placed. It may not always be possible. But the closer you can come, the better.

Don't bill before you ship. This must be near the top of a mail order buyer's "pet peeve" list. He or she sends an order, waits up to a month, then receives an invoice before the merchandise arrives. If there's even a slight chance that the invoice will arrive before your shipment, enclose a note explaining that the order has been shipped and should arrive shortly. And, by all means, point out that payment need not be sent until after the order has been received.

Acknowledge returns and cancellations. If the average customer sends back merchandise, he or she wants to know you received it. And, when the next statement arrives, he or she might be a little irritated that the returned goods haven't been credited yet. Or wonder why he or she gets another monthly club mailing after telling you to cancel. Easy solution: Send an acknowledgement card telling the customer you got the returned goods or cancellation request, explain that it may take a couple of weeks to process it, and don't be alarmed if you get another invoice or mailing in the interim.

Answer correspondence promptly. How many stories have you heard about people writing a book or record club two, three, or four times before they got a problem straightened out? What happens to all those first letters that never seem to get answered? Use a form letter with check-off boxes, if necessary, but give the customer the courtesy of a reply. And then follow through to get the problem straightened out so he or she doesn't have to write you again—with copies to the BBB, FTC, and anybody else he or she can think of.

Handle serious complaints by phone. The goodwill you'll generate by calling is nothing short of amazing. When you consider the high cost of a personal letter today, you may actually save money by using the telephone.

Appoint your own consumer affairs manager. You may prefer to call him or her a customer service manager. It needn't be a full-time responsibility. But make one person responsible for keeping customers happy, seeing that orders go out promptly, that complaints are handled properly, and so on. Then encourage customers to direct their inquiries to that person. Pyschologists tell us that customers would much rather write to a real person than to a computer.

Finally, stop and think about what it costs you to get those customers in the first place. It naturally makes good dollars-and-sense to keep them happy, and keep them coming back.

11

Hewlett-Packard:
How Industrial Direct Marketing
Solved a Distribution Problem

Pocket calculators have become so commonplace in the last few years, that it's hard to imagine how we ever got along without them. But until 1972 we did. Most calculators were big, bulky things that sat on a desk. A few portable electronic ones were on the market, but they were still quite large and performed limited functions. If you didn't have a calculator handy, you used a pencil and paper. Or if you were an engineer or scientist, you relied on your trusty slide rule. But Hewlett-Packard changed all that when the company introduced its HP-35 pocket calculator.

In the process, the company developed a program that one industry leader has described as the direct marketing success story of the decade! For it marked the first time direct marketing had been used to sell such an expensive and complicated product, to successfully penetrate highly specialized market segments, and to do so in tremendous volume.

Why HP's new product couldn't be sold the traditional way

Hewlett-Packard had built an enviable reputation among engineers and scientists for its extensive line of testing, measurement, and computation equipment. Products sold from $1,000 to $100,000. Like that of other companies in the electronics field, HP's distribution came primarily from its own sales force of field engineers.

Then in January 1972 the firm announced the HP-35, a pocket calculator that did much more than just add, subtract, multiply, and divide. It performed over a dozen log and trig functions that are commonly used by engineers and scientists. And it could be priced at $395, despite the fact that desk-top machines with the same capacity were then selling for over $1,000.

HP had a good product value, a ready market, and a sales force. But the firm still had a major problem. The sales organization was geared to big-ticket sales. And traditional selling costs were out of the question for individual sales of a $395 product.

The marketing strategy HP developed was to use the sales force only to go after quantity orders and try direct marketing to get individual orders. After talking to some experts in the field, the firm realized that direct marketing had the capability of providing sales at an efficient cost. But there were some problems to overcome here, too.

First, HP needed a direct marketing package that could explain the product's technical capability without the aid of a field engineer to answer questions. Second, the firm had to convince prospects to order a $395 product by mail, sight unseen. Third, marketers had to find or develop enough specialized mailing lists to make the volume interesting.

The HP-35 pocket calculator mailing

It was decided that direct mail would be used for the initial direct marketing test. The creative strategy that evolved was designed to overcome the first two problems noted above, namely, to capture the product's exciting capability on paper and to present the technically oriented audience with enough facts and figures to make a buying decision (see Exhibit 35).

The result was a rather elaborate mailing package with each component doing part of the selling job. A 9 × 12, two-color envelope established identity with engineers by showing a wide variety of handwritten log and trig problems. The copy was simple: "Now there's a better way to solve problems like these. Hewlett-Packard has the answer."

A one-page letter was headed with a 300-year old quote from a famous mathematician: "It is unworthy of excellent men to lose hours like slaves in the labor of calculation." The letter emphasized the time-saving advantages of the calculator, describing it as an electronic slide rule.

The four-color brochure was die-cut to dramatize how the HP-35 fit into a shirt pocket. It also showed the product in use, explained its features, and illustrated the complete accessory package.

Another insert was an eight-page Capability Report. It was done in the style of an engineering report complete with line drawings of the product. For convincing skeptical readers of product performances, it even included three typical problems with a comparison of the solution times using a slide rule versus the HP-35. (Naturally, the HP-35 came out well ahead.)

The order card was 8½ × 11 in size. To invite action, it had an actual-size illustration of the HP-35 that could be punched out and slipped in a shirt pocket. The copy invited the reader to test the real thing by detaching and mailing the card. It emphasized the 15-day free trial offer. Payment options included credit cards, cash, and bill the company.

In total, the mailing package contained over 4,500 words of copy—more than many short stories!

Test packages

Three variation packages were tested. The first included the components listed above plus a three-dimensional pop-up of the calculator to dramatize its pocket size. The other two packages were both tested because there was some concern that the basic package might be too "slick" or commercial for a technical audience. So one package was tested without the four-color brochure. And a smaller package was developed using a more ordinary-looking product data sheet in place of the four-color brochure and capability report.

Exhibit 35. First HP-35 mailing.

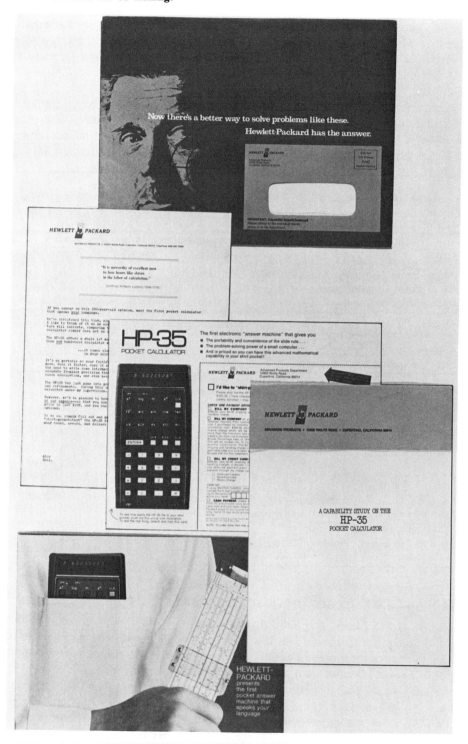

Selection of lists

Nine lists were chosen for the first mailing in May 1972. Two were Hewlett-Packard house lists. The other seven were prospect lists. They were chosen to represent a wide variety of categories including three different engineering disciplines, scientists, R&D specialists, chemistry book buyers, and engineering and technical magazine subscribers.

Each prospect list selected was relatively large so that if the test worked, a fairly substantial quantity of names would remain for a continuation mailing. The total universe of all nine lists was just over one million names. As the test matrix shows, one of the largest lists was used to split test the four packages (see Exhibit 36).

Exhibit 36. Hewlett-Packard HP-35 test mailing. Nine lists, with a total universe of over one-million names, were tested for the first HP-35 mailing. One of the largest lists was used to split-test the 4 packages.

List	Total quantity available	Quantity mailed	Mailing format*
HP prospects (house organ subscribers).	200,000	3,915	D
HP desktop calculator owners.........	7,245	7,245	D
McGraw-Hill subscribers:............	167,000	3,969	A
(engineering & technical		3,991	B
job categories from		1,600	C
manufacturing firms)		3,969	D
Electrical & electronic engineers.......	105,000	3,127	A
Civil engineers.....................	51,800	3,080	A
Mechanical engineers...............	41,000	2,991	A
Research & development executives....	185,000	2,943	A
Physical & biological scientists........	170,000	2,996	A
Van Nostrand Reinhold:............	97,500	2,989	A
(chemistry book buyers & prospects)			
Totals	1,024,545	42,815	

*A— 9 × 12 envelope, one-page letter, 4/C brochure, Capability Report, order form
B— Same as A but without 4/C brochure
C— Same as A but with Pop-up
D— #11 envelope, three-page letter, 2/C data sheet, order form

---

Less than 50,000 pieces provided the answers

A total of 42,815 pieces were mailed, and, because of the high unit of sale, the response needed to breakeven was less than two orders per thousand. The results added up to one of the most successful first tests I've ever seen. Eight of the nine lists topped breakeven! One list went over 1 percent in response, more than five times the breakeven. Over-all response wound up over 300 percent greater than the breakeven quota.

Two of the test packages—the control without the four-color brochure and the data sheet package—showed some promise. But neither did as well as the strong results on the control. And the pop-up also failed to improve results. A postmortem analysis speculated that the engineers got too involved in playing with the pop-up and how it worked and were distracted from the HP selling story.

The one-two punch of space and mail

Space advertising was slated to follow shortly on the heels of the initial test mailing. Because of the complicated selling story, the firm decided to use a simple but dramatic format—a full-page, four-color ad with a big picture and brief copy (see Exhibit 37). Initial insertions appeared in *Business Week* and a variety of engineering and technical publications, with a black-and-white version of the same ad placed in the *Wall Street Journal*.

The ad offered a free copy of the HP-35 Capability Report, the same one that had been developed for the mailing program. In addition to the report, the inquiry answer package included the other components of the control mailing with only minor copy changes in the envelope and letter to acknowledge that the package was being sent at the reader's request. No salesperson follow-up was planned so the mailing had to do a thorough selling job.

The ads plus publicity releases on the new product generated so many thousands of inquiries that the mailing package had to be quickly reprinted. Results were carefully tracked from each inquiry source, and more than 10 percent of all inquiries were converted into sales. This represented an incredible $39,500 in sales for every thousand inquiry packages mailed out! Needless to say, the combination of space and mail proved highly profitable.

How HP's program grew and evolved

From this initial success, Hewlett-Packard expanded its direct marketing program with a steady stream of follow-up mailings, ads, and new products. The second HP-35 mailing in October 1972 was expanded to over 850,000 pieces. A number of tests were made to fine-tune and refine the results. Most new packages did not do as well as the control, which went on to win the DMMA Silver Mail Box as the best mail order mailing of the year. However, one computer-personalized package showed good promise. It included a computer letter plus a computer-personalized order form that dramatized the free trial offer. It was also smaller and less expensive than the control and provided the first indication that HP could cut back to less elaborate mailings after the initial promotion had familiarized prime prospects with the product capabilities. This package was used extensively for subsequent mailings on various products (see Exhibit 38).

The HP-80 calculator for the business market

Because the HP-35 was so successful in the scientific and engineering fields, HP decided to market another pocket calculator for the business and financial fields—the HP-80. It had 40 different preprogrammed functions to solve time and money problems. And it carried the same $395 price tag.

The HP-80 was launched in January 1973. At that time, Hewlett-Packard was

Exhibit 37. HP-35 space ad.

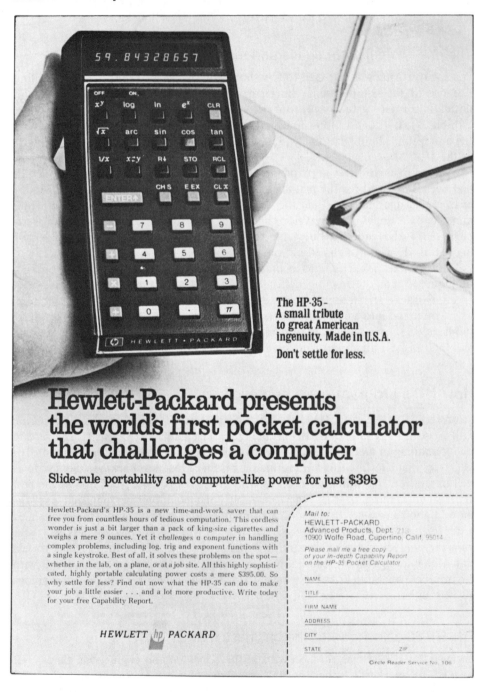

The HP-35 –
A small tribute
to great American
ingenuity. Made in U.S.A.

Don't settle for less.

Hewlett-Packard presents the world's first pocket calculator that challenges a computer

Slide-rule portability and computer-like power for just $395

Hewlett-Packard's HP-35 is a new time-and-work saver that can free you from countless hours of tedious computation. This cordless wonder is just a bit larger than a pack of king-size cigarettes and weighs a mere 9 ounces. Yet it *challenges a computer* in handling complex problems, including log, trig and exponent functions with a single keystroke. Best of all, it solves these problems on the spot— whether in the lab, on a plane, or at a job site. All this highly sophisticated, highly portable calculating power costs a mere $395.00. So why settle for less? Find out now what the HP-35 can do to make your job a little easier . . . and a lot more productive. Write today for your free Capability Report.

HEWLETT *hp* PACKARD

Exhibit 38. HP-35 evaluation request package.

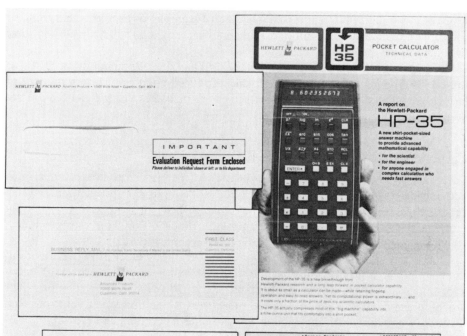

relatively unknown in the business market. The product capabilities were so new, that HP and its ad agency felt another elaborate mailing was required to tell the full product story. The package consisted of a 9 × 12 envelope, letter, order form, and four-color circular plus a report that included 10 examples of problems that could be solved with the HP-80. The entire mailing emphasized the product's ability to solve time and money problems (see Exhibit 39).

Over 350,000 pieces were slotted for the first mailing. While not as successful as the HP-35, the mailing was profitable and produced good results on a number of large lists. A couple of smaller and less expensive packages that were tested did not do as well as the more elaborate control.

Parlaying success with the HP-45

Later that same year, Hewlett-Packard unveiled the HP-45, a more sophisticated and advanced version of the original HP-35, at the same $395 price. With two successful direct marketing product launches under its belt, the firm decided to go right into a large-scale mailing without prior testing. Almost 600,000 pieces were mailed, which included a wide variety of scientific and technical mailing lists.

The 9 × 12 control mailing dramatized the product's superiority over the common slide rule. It pointed out that the slide rule had been invented over 100 years ago, and today there was a much better way to do technical calculations. The brochure provided full details on the more than 40 sophisticated functions and features (see Exhibit 40). The mailing was extremely successful and even more profitable than the earlier mailings on the HP-35 and HP-80.

The HP-65: selling a $795 pocket computer

Despite all Hewlett-Packard had learned about direct marketing, the next new product to come along posed a real marketing challenge. It was the first pocket-size programmable calculator—the HP-65. While the product resembled HP's other sophisticated pocket calculators in size and appearance, it was really like a miniature computer. It could be programmed to automatically solve long complicated problems in seconds using computer logic to make the right choices. With the aid of a mini-program card, the user could even record and store his or her own programs for future use.

Like a standard-sized computer, the HP-65 was introduced with support programs, or "software." In this case, the software represented packs of prerecorded cards for specific market segments and disciplines, plus a Users' Library for exchanging programs contributed by HP-65 owners. Here was a truly exciting new product. A personal computer selling for only $795! Yet, it was an extremely complicated product to explain and sell by mail.

Developing the marketing and creative strategy

Using research and past Hewlett-Packard history as a guide, the firm found it relatively easy to identify potential market segments. The market included such groups as electronics engineers, mathematicians, surveyors, statisticians, and

Exhibit 39. HP-80 time and money package.

Exhibit 40. First HP-45 mailing.

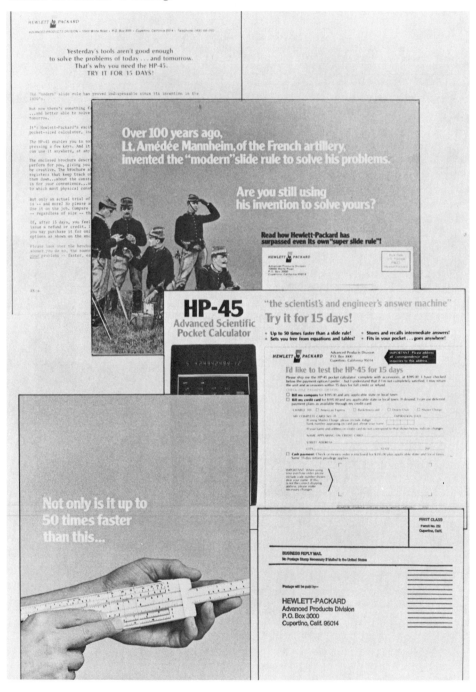

medical technicians. In developing the marketing and creative strategy, HP and its agency started wrestling with some difficult questions:

- How can we best sell a complicated $800 product by mail? Should we put major emphasis on the HP-65 machine itself (the hardware)? Or on the program packs (the software)? What about the dozens of built-in calculator functions and features?
- How do we tell each market segment about the 40 or so preprogrammed cards that would be of most interest for solving specialized problems?
- And finally, how do we capture the excitement and drama of this product on paper?

The creative strategy that evolved was to position the HP-65 as "the smallest computer ever made." Graphics were designed to dramatize the size and portability of the unit, by showing the product in use with a standard computer shown in the background.

Mailing package tells three-fold product story

The heart of the mailing package was a four-color, sixteen-page hardware circular. Copy was supported by numerous illustrations to "show and tell" all market segments how the HP-65 worked, using a "sectionalized" approach (see Exhibit 41).

The first section described the HP-65 as an answer machine that used preprogrammed cards for standard applications; the second, as a computer you could program yourself; and the third, as a sophisticated calculator with built-in functions operated at the touch of a key. To "back up" the hardware circular, a second main component was added to the package—the software circular. It showed the primary applications for each market segment, listing and describing over 200 prerecorded program cards available in optional accessory packs. To handle the Users' Library story, an insert sheet was developed stressing the benefits of a free one-year membership in this unique club.

Of course, the mailing included a letter, order card, and postpaid return envelope, all mailed in a 9 × 12 envelope (see Exhibit 42). The four-page letter was headed, "Now you can have your own personal computer!" The opening paragraph described a dream product:

> Imagine a computer that fits in your pocket. Imagine that it's no bigger than—and looks very much like—an ordinary pocket calculator but doesn't cost very much more. Now imagine this miniature marvel in *your* hands, as you try it out for 15 days and cut your problem-solving time down to seconds!

The order card was carefully designed to provide space to order the basic HP-65 outfit, as well as one of the optional accessory packs of prerecorded program cards.

Test package variations were also developed including an actual prerecorded card affixed to the letter to emphasize the programability of the HP-65. An inexpensive but unique lead-getting package was tested to reduce promotion cost on marginal lists, with the big 9 × 12 package used as a follow-up.

None of the test packages beat the control. But the over-all mailing results far exceeded HP's expectations. Almost everyone who ordered bought one of the optional

Exhibit 41. HP-65 hardware circular.

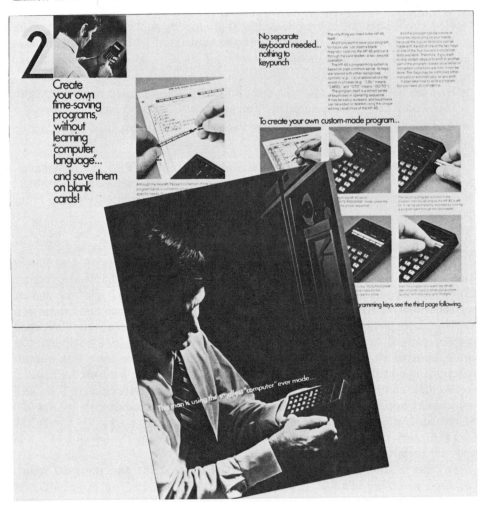

program packs bringing the average sale up to $838. The total response was so strong it helped create a five-month back-order situation for the HP-65! And the mailing was subsequently chosen as the winner of the coveted DMMA Gold Mail Box as the best mailing of the entire year.

An overview of HP's first two years of direct marketing

The mailings we have just reviewed represent the main thrust of Hewlett-Packard's entry into direct marketing. A lot more was involved than merely these introductory mailings. The HP direct marketing program included lot of follow-up mailings, space advertising, and specialized promotions—from accessory mailings to commuter train station booths that demonstrated calculators and took orders.

Exhibit 42. Complete HP-65 mailing.

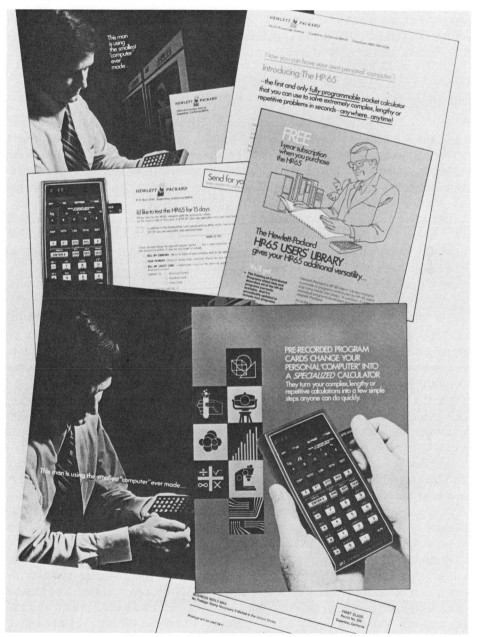

The Advanced Products group that had been formed to launch the marketing effort of the pocket calculators was soon established as a separate division. In the first two years after the announcement of the HP-35, the division reportedly had a sales volume in excess of $100 million, and profits on the direct marketing program were substantially above HP's targets.

Did direct marketing do it all?

No, not by a long shot. The field sales force, HP's international operations, and eventually the dealers accounted for the majority of traceable sales. But, besides producing a substantial portion of HP's pocket calculator sales and profits, direct marketing served as a catalyst. The large-scale introductory mailings announced new products, acquainted prospects with their features, and helped pave the way for sales through other distribution channels.

In addition the direct marketing program built a valuable asset in the form of HP's house lists. In just over two years, the firm developed 300,000 pocket calculator buyer and inquiry names. This list alone accounted for a large portion of the sales on each new product introduction mailing.

Some important things Hewlett-Packard learned about direct marketing

Looking back on HP's experience and test results, we can note that a number of strong patterns emerged. First, the best results came from launching each product with an elaborate package that did a complete selling job. Whenever a smaller or less elaborate package was tested at introduction time, it did not perform as well.

On the other hand, once a product had been launched and one or more large-scale mailings had been made, a less-elaborate package could be used effectively. Apparently the introductory mailings performed an educational function and built market awareness for the new product and its features.

Another important finding was that response dropped off sharply after product introduction. This may have been merely a function of the rapidly-changing pocket calculator industry where new product advancements, price reductions, and competition were growing steadily. But the first mailing on each new product was by far the most profitable. So, after the initial test on the HP-35, it made sense to build up the volume of subsequent introduction mailings.

A number of other things were learned. For example, it took a lot of list testing to build a large universe of technical and business names that could be mailed profitably; over 300 different mailing lists were tried. All three payment options proved viable with orders split roughly one-third each between credit cards, cash, and bill the company. Moreover, trying to make it easier to process the latter by requesting company credit information on the order card seriously depressed results.

Finally, several tests helped to dispel the myth that a technical audience needs only technical product information to make a buying decision. It was proved over and over that consumer-like techniques—such as four-color brochures, strong sales letters, and illustrated envelopes—produced much better results than more-traditional industrial mailings without the glamour and motivation.

How direct marketing opened retail distribution

Perhaps the most remarkable accomplishment of Hewlett-Packard's direct marketing program was that it opened another new distribution channel for the company. As an industrial products manufacturer, HP had never needed retail distribution. After the initial acceptance of the HP-35, however, the firm thought that engineering students might be good prospects. And, because most engineering students are located on a relatively small number of college campuses, college bookstores were visualized as important outlets.

Hewlett-Packard worked out an exclusive program with the National Association of College Stores (NACS) for their members to handle the HP-35. Then the entire program was launched with a special mailing to store owners and managers. The mailing included a covering letter on the NACS letterhead accompanied by an attractive presentation folder titled the "NACS/Hewlett-Packard College Bookstore Program." In the folder was an HP-35 product brochure, a special two-color brochure spelling out the details of the program, a flyer showing an ad designed for the school newspaper, and an order card (see Exhibit 43).

The package offered the store owner the opportunity to sell the HP-35 without having to invest in any inventory. HP would ship calculators to the store as the owner sent in orders. To join the plan, all the owner had to do was order one demonstration unit at a special discount price of $250, which was even refundable at the end of the school year.

According to *Business Week*, HP signed up over 350 college bookstores as dealers. And their results were sensational. One store owner reported that the HP-35 accounted for more than 40 percent of his total sales in one month. Another said: "It basically doesn't take any more effort to sell one than it does to sell a $3.95 bottle of cologne."

Naturally, with results like these, HP soon looked for other retail distribution outlets. Direct marketing had helped pave the way. All those mailings to engineers, scientists, and businesspeople had created a demand at retail where no previous demand had existed. Within a couple of years, Hewlett-Packard calculators had retail distribution nationwide through leading department stores.

An insider's viewpoint

The following comments about Hewlett-Packards's direct marketing program were provided by Duke Castle. (Castle supervised HP's direct marketing program for a number of years and is now Product Marketing Manager for the firm's Corvallis Division.)

> The Summer of '72 was one of the most exciting of my life. I had just joined Hewlett-Packard shortly after the HP-35 was introduced, and the atmosphere was electrifying.
>
> The HP-35 was to the scientific community what the first Polaroid camera was to the photographic world. People were awed at what it could do. They took it to Mount Everest, into outer space, drove cars over it, wrote poems to it; it seemed to do anything, survive anything.

Exhibit 43. College bookstore mailing.

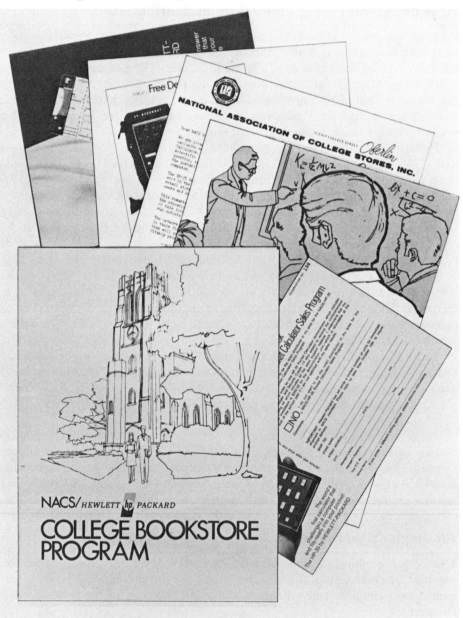

Our decision to use direct mail as a sales vehicle was both challenging and a little terrifying. As a conservative, scientific company we knew very little about the direct marketing business and were concerned about the possible "pots-and-pans" image that mail order might leave with customers.

Possibly the best decision we initially made was to retain the services of an experienced direct marketing consultant. With his help we selected an excellent direct response ad agency and the rest is history.

Looking back on the experience there are a few impressions that stand out.

One, direct marketing is one of the most scientific forms of selling I've ever experienced. We could test several different selling approaches simultaneously and accurately project the results within a matter of a few weeks.

Second, the most important ingredient to success is a good product, one that is not only well made but has a strong market appeal. Of all the testing we did, the greatest factor affecting success was the product. This may sound obvious, but it helped us keep our priorities straight.

A third thing that helped us with our retailers was that our warranty cards showed that for every order sent directly to the factory, five to ten customers would take the mailer down to their local dealer and buy from him. This "subsidized advertising" helped relieve the initial hue and cry that we were taking orders away from our retailers.

Today, sophisticated calculators are commonplace and a lot of the early excitement resides as a pleasant memory. However, our direct mail program is still active and remains a useful tool awaiting the development of the next revolutionary electronic product.

12

Sunset House:
How Sweepstakes Help Sell Millions
of Dollars Worth of Gifts and Gadgets

When you first look through a Sunset House catalog, you find an incredible array of specialty merchandise. Like a four-color flashlight, folding scissors, wireless light fixture, miniature tree, round playing cards, and toothpaste tube squeezer. Plus personalized items that range from address labels to pet identification tags.

Your first reaction might be to wonder who would buy these gadgets. Then you learn that Sunset House has a customer list of over six million buyers, puts out eight different catalogs a year with 500 to 600 items per catalog, and mails over 50 million catalogs annually. You probably begin to wonder instead how they do it.

Their success formula includes doing a lot of basic things right, such as finding many unusual items that either are not available or are difficult to find at retail plus the ability to efficiently process a large volume of small orders. The great majority of the firm's catalog items sell in the $1.00 to $5.00 price range and the average order is only around $10.00.

A tale of two sweepstakes

Another important part of the Sunset House success formula for more than a dozen years has been the use of sweepstakes. The company's first sweepstakes was done in January 1966. Virtually every catalog since then has featured a different sweepstakes contest. It's not unusual for a sweepstakes to improve results by 25 to 50 percent. An especially strong one can do even better.

Let's look at a couple of the most successful sweepstakes in Sunset's history. These have had a dramatic impact on the firm's growth and indicate some of the sophisticated techniques Sunset House has developed to effectively present a sweepstakes and maximize merchandise sales.

The Instant Winner Sweepstakes

The Instant Winner Sweepstakes was first used with Sunset's 1968 Christmas catalog. It is probably the most successful sweepstakes in direct marketing history! At the time, the firm had already been using sweepstakes for a couple of years. A lot of other firms were also using them—from direct marketers to the giant oil companies—and results had begun to decline somewhat. A fresh, new approach was clearly indicated. The typical sweepstakes of that period was a "lucky number" type. The advertiser offered a gigantic array of prizes that were worth hundreds of thousands of dollars. But the majority of prizes were not awarded because most people who received the preselected winning numbers didn't bother to enter. So their prizes went unclaimed.

The evolution of a big idea

Sunset House's ad agency had a meeting in December 1967 to brainstorm new sweepstakes ideas and approaches. Because I was fortunate enough to be at that meeting, I can recall quite well how the "big idea" evolved. As usual at brainstorm meetings, a great number of ideas were generated. Some good. Some not so good. But two were very interesting. One was to develop an instant winner type of contest where the customer or prospect could learn immediately whether his or her preselected number was a winner. The other was to do an "everybody wins" contest where every entrant would receive an attractive but inexpensive prize. We believed the two ideas had possibilities and might even be combined.

In discussing the practicality of the ideas, someone reminded the group that sweepstakes regulations require the advertiser to let people enter whether or not they place a merchandise order. This meant that the "everybody wins" prize would have to be fulfilled to a large quantity of negative entries, those persons who checked a box that said something like: "No, I don't want to order at this time, but let me know if I have won a prize."

After further discussion, it was felt that Sunset House could perhaps afford to give every entrant a low-end prize, costing about a dime, but it couldn't also afford the cost of processing all the winning entries and the postage to send out the prizes.

Then came the big idea: Why not require those who were entering the sweepstakes without placing an order to supply their own stamped, self-addressed return envelope? It not only would eliminate the postage expense, it would simplify the processing of winning entries.

The idea was presented to Sunset House management who also felt it had good potential. But it would have to be cleared by the U.S. Post Office, which regulates sweepstakes promotions through the mail to make sure they are legally acceptable. This took a few months. Because Sunset's Christmas catalog has always been their strongest book and the one mailed in largest volume, the first Instant Winner Sweepstakes was slated for the 1968 Christmas catalog.

How the sweepstakes was presented

A $250,000 prize structure was put together for the promotion with $10,000 in cash as the top prize. The other prizes included a new car, color TVs, sewing machines, movie outfits, and blenders. For the "everybody wins" prize, an attractive gold-finished pin was selected from a well-known manufacturer of costume jewelry. The pin made a perfect low-end prize. Sunset's customers are primarily women. Also, jewelry is a rather blind item. The average person can see a piece of costume jewelry and not know if it's worth $1.00 or $5.00. And the markup on jewelry is such that the item could be purchased for about a dime.

The cover of Sunset's Christmas catalog announced the $250,000 "Instant Winner" Sweepstakes with teaser copy that said, "See page 5. Discover instantly if you're a winner." (See Exhibit 44.) When the reader turned to page five, he or she

Exhibit 44. Cover of Instant Winner catalog.

WONDERFUL GIFT IDEAS BY MAIL FROM SUNSET HOUSE

$250,000 "INSTANT WINNER" SWEEPSTAKES
See page 5... discover instantly if you're a winner!

found a list of 152 winning numbers. Inserted between pages four and five was a two-color card that had a lucky number imprinted. Readers were instructed to check their number against the official winning numbers list (see Exhibit 45). And, of course, every reader was pleasantly surprised to find her number on the list, because *all* the lucky numbers were winners. So the reader quickly turned to the center of the catalog to see what she had won. All the prizes were attractively shown. The copy said: "If your number is a winner, then one of these fabulous prizes is yours." (See Exhibit 46.) At that point the reader knew she had won *something*. She didn't know what. But even the most inexpensive prize—the pin—looked attractive. A great many people decided it was worth entering this sweepstakes. Also, a large percentage of those decided to place an order at the same time.

Naturally, the entry instructions pointed out that, if you didn't wish to order, you must send a stamped, self-addressed return envelope along with your lucky number, to claim your prize. Some of the entrants did win the big prizes. But the great majority of them got that pin. (This might not seem like much of a prize, especially when compared to a color TV or $10,000 in cash. But since most people fall into the "I've never won anything in my life" category, it was still an acceptable prize.)

Exhibit 45. Page 5 of catalog and insert card.

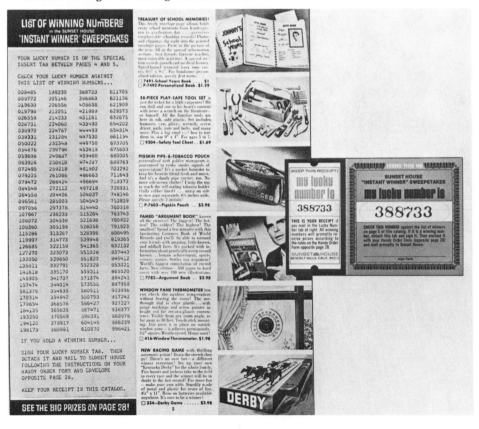

Exhibit 46. Page 28 of catalog with sweepstakes prizes.

Results? fantastic!

By whatever measurement you want to use, the Instant Winner Sweepstakes results were fantastic. Orders and entries started coming in so rapidly that merchandise had to be reordered from suppliers. And orders kept coming in right up until the December 15 contest deadline. A lot of merchandise was even brought in via air express to fulfill last-minute orders before Christmas.

When the final response was totaled, sales on the Christmas catalog were about 300 percent of normal! Whenever you're mailing in the millions on a proven proposition—and you triple results—it's pretty amazing. The ratio of orders to negative entries was even higher than normal—which means that in addition to a much higher response rate, a greater percentage of the responses were orders.

The instant winner treatment in space advertising

Knowing it had a big winner on its hands, Sunset House adapted the same idea to space advertising. The firm created another Instant Winner Sweepstakes with a similar prize structure that was used the following spring. The vehicle chosen was a Dutch door insert in *Parade* and *Family Weekly.* This is a format that Sunset had pioneered, using a multipage insert that was only half the depth of a full Sunday supplement page. It provided the effect of a minicatalog at a relatively inexpensive cost.

In this case, Sunset House used a 12 page, two-color Dutch door insert. The sweepstakes was handled almost identically to the catalog with a tip-on card used to provide the reader's lucky number. The cover strongly played up the Instant Winner idea (see Exhibit 47). While not as successful as the initial catalog promotion, the device still became the most successful Dutch door insert the firm had ever done.

Exhibit 47. Dutch door insert.

What made it work

The Instant Winner Sweepstakes was a fresh idea promoted at the right time. The promotion offered an attractive array of prizes along with the assurance that a person would get something for nothing simply by taking the time and effort to enter the contest. Within a few months, every one of Sunset's major competitors had copied the promotion and it was soon overexposed. But this single idea—the Instant Winner Sweepstakes—is credited with adding more than a million new Sunset House customers and more than $6 million in sales!

Sweepstakes like bingo

By 1973 the sweepstakes programs being used by Sunset House and other advertisers were quite different. New government regulations required a "guaranteed winner" contest where all prizes were awarded. (Also, it was no longer permissible to require negative entries to do something like supplying a stamped envelope, unless positive entries were required to do the same thing.) This meant winners were usually selected by a random drawing rather than a preselected lucky number. And, because all prizes had to be awarded, the prize structures had been reduced considerably. But the sweepstakes idea continued to produce good results. And Sunset House had developed a number of formats and promotion techniques that could be used effectively in conjunction with a sweepstakes. One of these was the use of a mini-computer letter affixed to the catalog. It took the form of an oversize label measuring about 3 × 4 inches which was affixed to the mailing area of the catalog cover. The label included the prospect's name and address as well as a brief computer-personalized message.

In itself, this mini-computer message is perhaps one of the most innovative catalog promotion ideas ever developed. And the main credit for it goes to Carl Carlson of Sunset House. First, it adds a personal touch to a catalog, just as a letter does to a solo mailing package. Second, it can be personalized like a regular computer letter with a different message for each recipient or audience group. Finally, unlike so many good ideas, it's remarkably inexpensive. This is because it really is just an oversize Cheshire label. It can be affixed for about the same cost as slapping a regular mailing label on a catalog.

Sunset House developed this mini-computer message and first used it in volume late in 1972. It was tried with two different catalog sweepstakes and both had produced good results. So the stage was set for an attempt at a new application of the same technology. The opportunity came with Sunset's January 1973 catalog. The sweepstakes slated for this catalog was a game like bingo. But, for legal reasons, the term "bingo" couldn't be used in some states. So the game was called "Match-a-Line Zingo."

How the sweepstakes was presented

The prize structure featured a grand prize of $10,000 to $14,000, depending upon which line of the Zingo game the reader completed. Two cars were also to be awarded plus over a thousand gift certificates. The catalog cover announced the contest and top prizes. It showed a picture of a woman playing the game (see Exhibit 48).

Exhibit 48. Front cover of Zingo catalog.

Affixed to the back cover was the mini-computer message, but with a new twist. In addition to the prospect's name and address and an eight-line personalized message, the bottom portion of the label included five peel-off game tabs. Each one had a computer-printed Zingo number on it (see Exhibit 49).

The center of the catalog contained the contest details with the back of the order form serving as a Zingo game card. The reader placed her Zingo game tabs over the matching numbers on the game card. The line she completed determined how much she was *eligible* to receive if her name was drawn as the grand prize winner. A space at the bottom also allowed her to match a number to determine which car she would be eligible to win (see Exhibit 50).

The numbers programmed into the computer made it possible for each prospect to complete one line of the Zingo card. But, because the front cover of the catalog had emphasized a prize of $10,000 or more, most people were pleasantly surprised when they found out they were eligible to win an even bigger grand prize, plus one of the cars.

To help support the sweepstakes, the catalog also contained a space on the second page certifying that the prize money had already been deposited in a local bank and guaranteeing that all prizes would be awarded. Sprinkled throughout the catalog were photos of and statements by big winners in other recent Sunset House sweepstakes.

Special audience messages

While the mini-computer messages were brief, they were changed somewhat for each type of audience the catalog was mailed to. For mailings to prospect lists, the message said "we want you as a new friend." For mailings to inactive customers, the message urged them to order again. Mailings to active customers adopted still another message devoted entirely to the sweepstakes.

Remailing best customers

For years Sunset House and other large catalog mailers had realized that their buyer list contained some customer names that were worth a lot more than others. Specifically, these were persons who had bought most recently, most frequently, and spent the most and were more likely to order again. This top customer group not only received all eight catalogs that Sunset House put out during the year, those customers even got some of them twice!

Testing had shown that those best names could be mailed the same catalog about four weeks later with good response, perhaps maybe 75 percent of what came in on the first mailing. And, because these were the best-pulling names the first time around, one could live with a drop-off like that and still have satisfactory results.

But there was a trick to it. For this kind of result, the remail catalog had to look different, so customers would browse through it again and maybe spot an item or two they had missed the first time. This was usually accomplished simply by having the cover on the remail book changed, with all the inside merchandise pages left intact. Test results, however, indicated that the greater the difference in the appearance of the catalog, the better the results were likely to be.

Exhibit 49. Back cover of Zingo catalog with computer label.

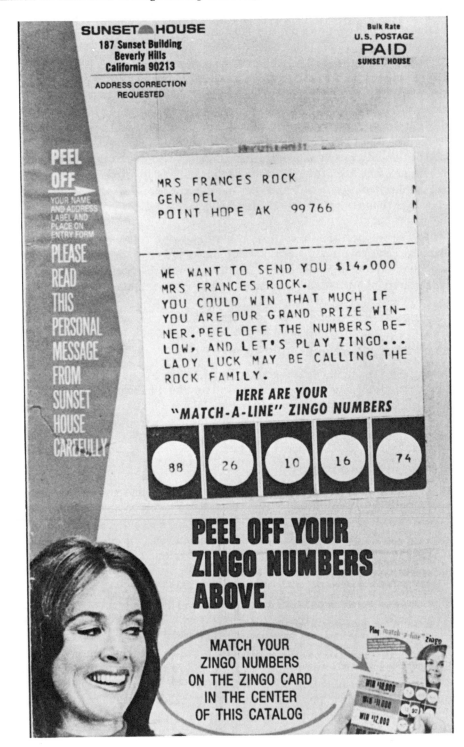

Exhibit 50. Zingo game card.

For the remail version of the January catalog, Sunset went to a cover illustration with an entirely different look. Instead of the Zingo game-playing illustration, the cover showed an attractive photo of one of the cars that was a runner-up prize (see Exhibit 51). In addition, the computer-personalized label message on the back cover was changed, the Zingo number tabs were printed in a different color, and design elements around the label message were rearranged.

Total promotion adds up to strong results

The total promotion effort on this catalog included a wide variety of items: the sweepstakes itself, the game-playing aspect, the computer-personalized labels, the special messages for each audience segment, and the remail book. The combination produced strong results. Although there had been more than thirty Sunset House catalogs in the interim, this one was the firm's most successful promotion since the Instant Winner Sweepstakes!

Common ingredients of a successful sweepstakes

In reviewing these two promotions plus others I've been involved in through the years, I think it's possible to isolate some of the main ingredients that go to make up a successful sweepstakes.

Large universe. Sweepstakes tend to be used more widely in the mail than in

Exhibit 51. Front cover of Zingo remail catalog.

space advertising, and you need a fairly large mailing universe. That's why you see sweepstakes used primarily by large catalog mailers and general-interest magazines. Unless you are mailing at least 500,000 to 1,000,000 pieces, it's hard to offer enough expensive prizes without overly increasing your promotion costs. A couple of specialized magazines have run effective low-budget sweepstakes, but they're the exception.

For example, let's say you plan a sweepstakes with a total prize budget of $25,000 and mail one million pieces. The prizes add $25.00 per thousand to your promotion cost, which should be more than offset by improved results. But the same prize budget on a mailing of 250,000 pieces would add $100 per thousand to your promotion and make it difficult for the sweepstakes to recover its cost.

Attractive prize structure. A good prize structure should feature a valuable grand prize, usually worth at least $10,000. Cash, cars, and trips have proved to be the most popular prizes with consumers. However, Publishers Clearing House has successfully used two new homes as a grand prize for a number of years. Even if you feature something other than cash as the grand prize, it makes sense to offer cash as an alternate choice. And the winners invariably choose the cash.

In addition to the grand prize, there should be a good quantity of attractive runner-up prizes. Color TVs and mink coats and cameras are always appealing. The idea is to offer enough prizes so the readers feel they have a fair chance of winning something. Most people are naturally attracted by the main prizes. But they probably figure, "I really don't have much of a chance to win that top prize, but there are enough other interesting prizes so maybe I'll win something."

For each prize level you can also offer a choice of two or three prizes of equal value. This allows you to show a wide array of items and still keep your prize budget within reason.

Prequalification. As shown by both of the Sunset House sweepstakes we reviewed, your results are better if you have the reader go through some prequalification process, so he or she feels that there is a better-than-average chance to win or a better chance to win a bigger prize than other people. You can accomplish this by having each respondent match his or her lucky number against a winning number list. Or, in the case of the Zingo contest, the respondent can find out how big a grand prize he or she will be eligible to win. This makes the reader more likely to enter and place an order.

One of the most successful sweepstakes concepts I ever developed included a seven-part grand prize: cash, car, trip, freezer, color TV, diamond ring, and sterling silver dinnerware. The prequalification device established whether the entrant would get four, five, six, or seven parts of that grand prize. But everyone qualified for the "big three" prizes—cash, car, and trip—plus one other. So the prequalification device established a pleasant surprise that led to a high entry and order rate.

Involvement. My experience has shown that the involvement aspect is as important as the prize structure itself, sometimes even more important. Getting somebody to open a mystery gift envelope, rub off a spot to find a hidden number, play a game, or just compare his or her number against a lucky number list all tend to increase contest entries and sales results. Naturally, you have to exercise some caution and not make the contest so complex it's hard to figure out. The instructions should be clear and should be repeated in two or three different places so the reader knows exactly what he or she has to do.

Strong creative presentation. Here is where you come up with the name or theme for the sweepstakes. The name is usually tied in with the prize structure or involvement device, such as an around-the-world theme for a contest featuring a trip as the grand prize, or a buried-treasure theme for one that uses a treasure map as the involvement device. It's also important to show all the prizes as attractively as possible, using good photography or illustrations. In most cases the prize manufacturer can supply suitable photographs for his or her merchandise. But, in the case of a top prize which will often be featured on the front cover of a catalog or brochure, it can be worthwhile to do your own photography and get the precise illustration you want to dramatize the entire promotion.

If you have a large universe and do put together a sweepstakes with an attractive prize structure, prequalification, involvement, and a strong creative presentation, your effort can add up to a very successful promotion.

An insider's viewpoint

The following comments about Sunset House's sweepstakes program were provided by Roy Hedberg, the firm's chairman of the board.

> My first comment: I wish we could come up with another Instant Winner type of sweepstakes that would actually triple response. While we haven't had a "tripler" lately, we do find that these contests continue to be a very important promotional device for us.

> The trick is to properly blend an interesting prize structure with some element of customer involvement that's not too tedious plus a strong creative presentation. It's the delicately arranged mixture of all these elements that seems to determine the degree of success.

> We intend to continue using sweepstakes at Sunset House. Our customers, via their letters—and more importantly, their orders—prove to us that they enjoy them. And I must admit it does our otherwise cold hearts good when someone who has just received a prize check for $10,000 writes to tell us it's been a lifesaver for paying piled-up medical bills, overdue mortgage payments, and so on.

> Our experience has shown that it's not only fun for customers to participate, it's fun, too, to try to come up with innovative approaches. Perhaps some day there will be a viable alternative for us. In the meantime, *Viva la Sweepstakes!*

13

Franklin Mint:
Turning Book Lovers into Collectors
with Limited Edition Offerings

Let's go back to early 1974 and listen in as two publishers have lunch together. The conversation soon turns to:

First publisher: Did you happen to see that mailing from American Express last week which offered leather-bound books?

Second publisher: I sure did—the one put out by the Franklin Library. I think the series was called the "100 Greatest Books" or something like that.

First publisher: It's the craziest thing I've ever seen! Can you imagine anybody in their right mind signing up for a series of 100 books shipped one a month? Why, it would take over eight years to get the whole series.

Second publisher: Not only that, but at 28 bucks a volume, you're talking about almost three grand for the whole series! And you can't even think it over. They claim you have to sign up by a certain date and the series will never be offered again.

First publisher: What also amazed me is that they mentioned only a few actual book titles. You don't even know what these great books are that you're supposed to sign up for.

Second publisher: Well, I guess The Franklin Mint has done pretty well with their limited edition coins. But they sure don't know anything about publishing or how to sell books.

This conversation is fictional, but I suspect it's quite typical of some conversations that actually did take place in the publishing world about that time. The subject that caused so much discussion was the first offering from The Franklin Library, a then newly-created division of The Franklin Mint. And the offer was destined to become one of the single most successful promotions in the entire history of direct marketing!

This chapter will be devoted primarily to The Franklin Library, starting with its initial promotion and tracing what the Library did for an encore. To help put the firm in perspective, let's start with some background information on the Mint.

An overview of the Franklin Mint

The Franklin Mint is the undisputed leader in the field of limited edition collectibles. An executive recently described their business as "recognizing, stimulating, and satisfying the human desire to possess works of beauty, importance, and lasting value.''

The firm's first official offering was made in 1967—a series of 36 presidential medals cast in sterling silver. Many other commemorative medals and coin programs followed in the next few years. Subjects ranged widely from historic events to famous artists to antique cars, with a series often co-sponsored by prestigious organizations like the International Olympic Committee or the National Audubon Society.

Each series was offered on a limited edition basis. Rather than follow the tradition in the collectibles field of restricting the edition to a predetermined number, however, Franklin limited its editions according to orders placed by a specific deadline. This meant the firm could literally produce the exact number of coins or medals that were subscribed with virtually no inventory or unsold production.

Minting dies were then destroyed to ensure no further production of the item. Moreover, Franklin Mint built a reputation for integrity by faithfully adhering to its deadline policy. During one year, the firm reportedly rejected $20 million in orders that came in after the deadline.

By the end of 1976 the firm had reached an annual sales volume of over $300 million. Despite a slowdown in its historic 35 percent growth rate early in 1977, which lead to reduced sales and profits, the product mix had been expanded to include ingots, collector plates, stamps, art prints, sculptures, and, of course, books. About 150 different collectible programs were offered each year. Franklin Mint had also developed a substantial international division which accounted for more than a third of total sales.

Besides its fine reputation, Franklin Mint had another outstanding asset in its customer list. In just ten years the firm had built a list of established collectors totaling over 1.7 million names worldwide. The list was growing at a compounded growth rate of 33 percent, and was promoted heavily throughout the year on new offers (see Exhibit 52).

Exhibit 52. Growth of Franklin Mint established collectors.

Year	Quantity
1971	425,000
1972	575,000
1973	810,000
1974	1,115,000
1975	1,359,000
1976	1,765,000
1977	1,868,000
1978	2,013,000

Source: Franklin Mint Corporation Annual Report, 1978.

The Franklin Library

The Franklin Library was established late in 1973. Here's how it came to be, as told by former publisher Robert Vincent O'Brien:

> By 1973 it was clear that we were doing a good job of serving the collector market for such items as medals, foreign coins, ingots, and etched sterling silver plates. To broaden the company's horizon, we evaluated a number of other areas of known collector interest which seemed susceptible to The Mint's expertise in marketing to existing collectors and to actually creating new collectors. Out of this study came our activities in books, graphics, philately, porcelain, and crystal as well as some other products which have not yet been marketed.

Speaking at a seminar on the economics of direct response publishing, sponsored by the Association of American Publishers, O'Brien, said:

> Experience in the planning and marketing of many other collectibles had shown the importance of not underestimating the size of the market. The fact that no one had done it did not mean that the market was not there.

Charles Andes, board chairman of Franklin Mint, continued the story in a talk at New York Direct Marketing Day:

> We started with a basic idea that people admire fine books. We didn't have specific books in mind, and we had no special expertise in bookmaking. But we did see an opening for a product that wasn't being offered at the time. Our first idea was to build a collection of classic literature, called "The 100 Greatest Books of All Time." With that idea in mind, we began to create a marketing plan and a unique product to match.

The 100 Greatest Books of All Time

The first test mailing went out on January 2, 1974, to 200,000 names. Only two lists were used: Franklin Mint collectors and American Express credit cardholders. A January 31 ordering deadline was established for the test mailing. But the copy clearly pointed out, "Another group of American Express card members, along with selected Franklin Mint collectors, will receive their invitations later and will have until March 31, 1974 to subscribe."

Elaborate mailing package

The mailing package was an elaborate one—to match the product. It consisted of a 9 × 12 outer envelope, a two-page letter printed on separate sheets, a 16-page, four-color booklet, a subscription application, and a business reply envelope. For the American Express list, an additional one-page letter on the firm's letterhead was included (see Exhibit 53).

An expert later estimated the cost of the mailing at $500 per thousand, or 50¢ each. The letter set the tone for the package and these opening paragraphs explained the product concept:

Exhibit 53. Mailing package on 100 Greatest Books.

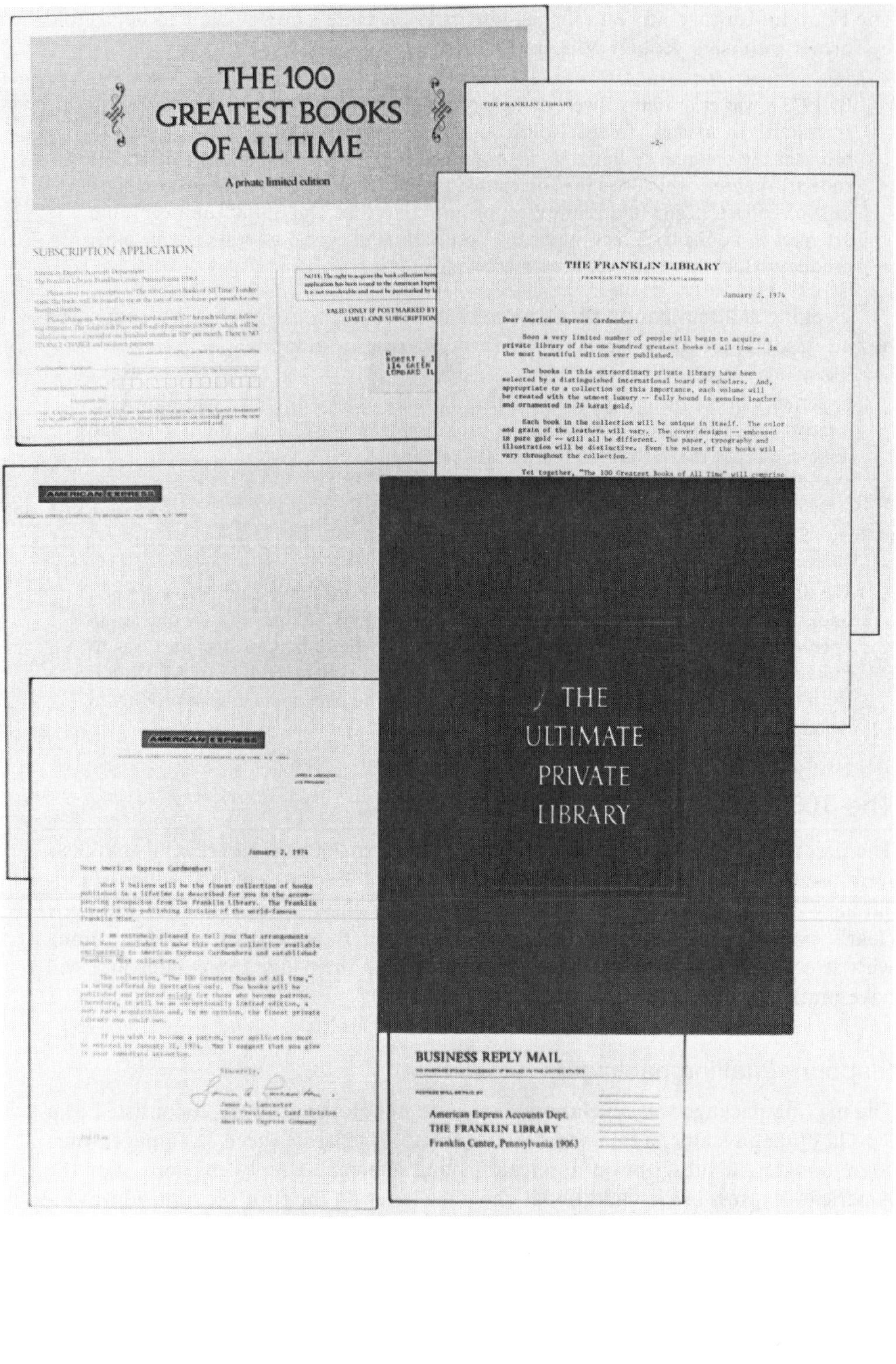

Dear American Express Card Member:

Soon a very limited number of people will begin to acquire a private library of the one hundred greatest books of all time—in the most beautiful edition ever published.

The books in this extraordinary private library have been selected by a distinguished international board of scholars. And, appropriate to a collection of this importance, each volume will be created with the utmost luxury—fully bound in genuine leather and ornamented in 24 karat gold.

Each book in the collection will be unique in itself. The color and grain of the leathers will vary. The cover designs—embossed in pure gold—will all be different. The paper, typography, and illustration will be distinctive. Even the sizes of the books will vary throughout the collection.

Yet together, "The 100 Greatest Books of All Time" will comprise a complete and harmonious collection—the kind of library that would be difficult to assemble even if you were a rare book collector with unlimited time and resources.

Unlike ordinary volumes which are printed in many editions, the books in this collection will be published in *only one edition*. The limit of that edition will be determined by the exact number of subscribers to the collection, and the books will be custom-printed and bound *solely* for those who subscribe in advance. The collection will not be available through book dealers, nor will the volumes be sold singly.

The booklet portrayed the quality and details of the series as well as the details of the offer. The cover was printed separately on heavy stock and simply titled, "The Ultimate Private Library." The four-color section inside included a number of product photographs. Some provided atmosphere with the books shown in the setting of a private library; others provided close-ups of the illustrations, leather binding, and gold ornamentation (see Exhibit 54).

Copy was set in a large, readable typeface. Only a few of the actual book titles were mentioned, but the copy skillfully sold the concept of the series and the unique offer. These selected paragraphs give us a feel for how it was done.

On the books themselves:

Out of the thousands of books written over the centuries, a small number stand out as the supreme source of knowledge and inspiration. These are the great works of literature—the ultimate achievements of the world's most brilliant writers and thinkers.

On the leather binding:

Today it is increasingly rare for books to be bound in genuine leather. Even the most costly editions are usually published only in cloth or synthetic bindings.

But each book in this collection will be *fully bound in leather*—as were the most beautiful editions of the past. To produce the bindings, only the finest leathers will be used—including calf, cowhide, kid, and sheepskin. Hides will be purchased throughout the world, wherever the finest leathers are available. Each volume will thus have the beautiful lustre, the sumptuous feel, and even the rich smell characteristic of such leathers.

On who might enjoy them:

This invitation is extended to those who appreciate great writing and the beauty of finely-made books—and who seek a superb heritage of literature to give to their children and grandchildren.

Exhibit 54. Product illustrations from the 100 Greatest Books booklet.

On the subscription plan:

> Each subscriber will be billed for his collection on a monthly basis—at only $28 per volume. Genuine leather-bound books of comparable quality are typically priced at $40 to $80 each—and limited editions are often priced higher. The favorable price of $28 is made possible because "The 100 Greatest Books of All Time" are offered only as a complete collection.

The brochure also pointed out that the original price per volume would be guaranteed for the life of the program, which is an important point for a series destined to stretch out over eight years. Names and biographies were provided for the scholars who were selecting the actual works to be offered.

Successful test leads to quick roll-out

The test proved successful. As soon as the January 31 deadline was past and results analyzed, the roll-out mailing was planned. Within a month, about three-million pieces were in the mail to the entire American Express list and about 800,000 Franklin Mint collectors. By the March 31 deadline, 38,000 orders had been sent to the Franklin Library—a response rate of over 1 percent! Because each subscriber who completed the series would be spending $2,800, this represented a *potential* sales volume of $106,400,000! Virtually overnight, the Franklin Library had become one of the largest book publishers in the world.

Allowing for expected attrition, Franklin Mint management has recently attributed $65 million in orders to that single promotion. This is only a 39 percent attrition or drop-off rate. Considering the length of the series and the big ticket involved, this is almost as amazing as the front-end response.

The only major problem encountered was in finding the bindery capacity to handle the quantity of leather-bound books that had to be produced. As a result, only the first three volumes were actually fulfilled in 1974. But, before long, Franklin had installed its own book binding facility designed specifically to produce leather-bound volumes.

Other book series follow same formula

To build on its success with "The 100 Greatest Books," Franklin Library began planning other limited edition book collections. The first to follow was the "Pulitzer Prize Library." Mailings were again limited to Franklin Mint collectors and American Express cardholders, with April 30, 1975, as the final subscription deadline for the roll-out (see Exhibit 55). The price was again $28.00 per volume, although several other prices were tested. The series was only half as long, with one volume for each of the 49 novels that had won a Pulitzer Prize. Over 22,000 subscribers signed up with the program ultimately expected to generate more than $25 million in sales.

To tie in with the U.S. Bicentennial, the "100 Greatest Masterpieces of American Literature" was tested in the spring of 1976. The book titles were nominated by universities throughout the U.S. and issued under the auspices of the American Revolution Bicentennial Administration. Each volume was priced at $35.00.

Another elaborate and tasteful mailing package was used. In addition, the mailing booklet was adapted into an eight-page, four-color newspaper insert complete with bind-in application and reply envelope. Inserts were used in Sunday newspapers and had the same July 31 deadline date as the roll-out mailing (see Exhibit 56). A total of 31,271 subscribers signed up.

Later that year, Franklin Library offered the "Collected Stories of the World's Greatest Writers." This series was limited to fiction with a total of 100 books in the series and a price tag of $35.00 each.

The roll-out promotion had an October 31, 1976, deadline. The campaign included mailings to Franklin Mint collectors and Diners Club cardholders (see Exhibit 57). In addition, about 40 million newspaper inserts were used in the United States and international promotions were slated for Canada, England, and Australia.

Exhibit 55. Pulitzer Prize Library booklet.

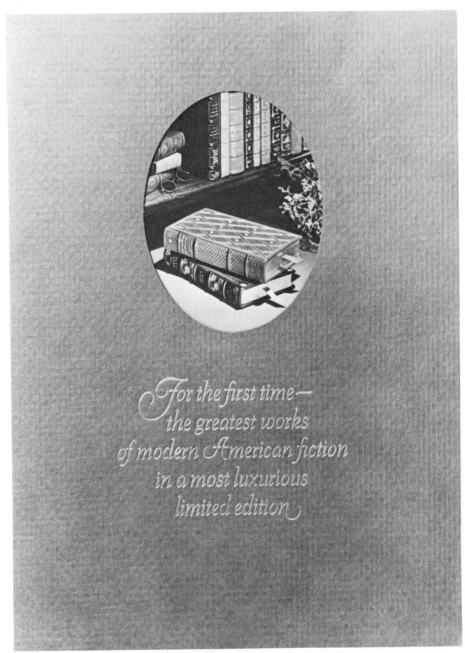

Exhibit 56. Newspaper insert for 100 Greatest Masterpieces of American Literature.

Exhibit 57. Mailing package on Collected Stories of the World's Greatest Writers.

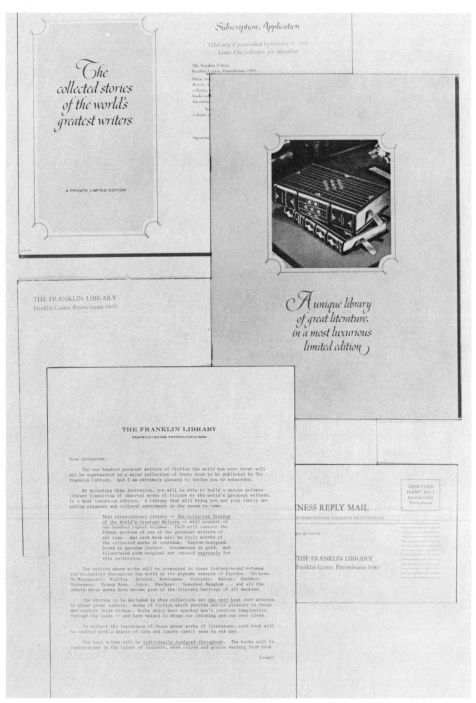

According to the *Guidebook of Franklin Mint Issues* (Krause Publications, 1978), subscribers to the "Collected Stories of the World's Greatest Writers" numbered 30,550.

First Edition Society adds new twist

Despite the great success with its initial offerings, the Franklin Library was working under one handicap not faced by other publishers or book clubs. Namely, that the nature of their limited edition product concept required a complete new book series for each promotion. They couldn't promote a series continuously and see a steadily building membership. Each series was, in effect, "sold out" when the final enrollment deadline passed.

Would they have to live with this problem? Or was there a way to retain the nature of the limited edition appeal but, at the same time, offer a permanent or continuing book program? To find out, Franklin Library put together a program called the First Edition Society. While it still offered deluxe leather-bound books, the new program differed in a number of respects from its previous offers. First, instead of featuring classic books from the past, the offer was built around brand-new titles. Arrangements had been made with leading authors and publishers to issue privately printed first editions of their next work.

Second, the fact that the books would be first editions added a stronger investment appeal. Franklin Library could cite figures on how previous works by the same authors had appreciated in value. For example, first editions of works by Arthur Miller and Truman Capote were valued in rare book dealers' catalogs at five to six times their original price.

Third, the commitment required from members was less rigorous. They were asked to sign up for a three-year period with no more than twelve books to be issued each year.

Fourth, this was a permanent program that could be promoted continuously year after year. To retain the limited edition appeal, the firm decided that membership would only be promoted for a short time annually. Each promotion period would have a deadline date and new members would start with a current selection. Copy could thus point out, "Those who enroll in The First Edition Society later on will be able to acquire *only* those volumes offered during the period of their membership, at prices then prevailing. No back titles will ever be available."

Charter membership offer used for initial test

The First Edition Society was tested early in 1976 with direct mail and newspaper inserts. Both featured a charter membership offer and a price of $35.00 per volume (see Exhibit 58).

The value of owning first editions was brought out in the copy as well as the convenience of the membership plan: "Never before in the long history of publishing has it been possible to *systematically* acquire specially designed first editions of major new books like these as they are completed." The names of 18 major authors scheduled for publication were listed. And benefits of charter membership were emphasized, including the fact that only charter members could acquire the complete collection from the very beginning.

Exhibit 58. Newspaper insert on First Edition Society (first inside spread).

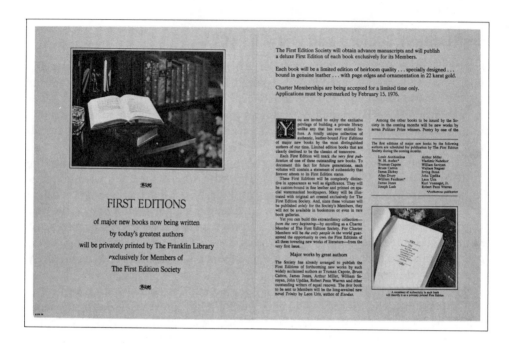

The first annual promotion

The initial test on the First Edition Society was successful. But one more question remained to be answered before the concept was proved: Would the annual promotion of new memberships have sufficient appeal without the benefit of the charter offer? A small test was made in September 1976, announcing the opening of membership for a limited time. The copy mentioned the book titles and authors whose works had already been offered to members as well as some of those scheduled for the near future. And the price per volume was raised from $35.00 to $37.00 (see Exhibit 59).

Results were good. The first annual membership promotion was launched in November using direct mail, newspaper inserts, and magazine ads. The First Edition Society closed out its first year of promotion with over 22,000 members signed up.

Product quality—and something extra

An important ingredient in the Franklin Library success story shouldn't be overlooked. It is product quality combined with a corporate philosophy of giving the customer more than he or she expects. Here's how the Mint's chairman, Charles Andes, explains it:

Exhibit 59. First Edition Society mailing.

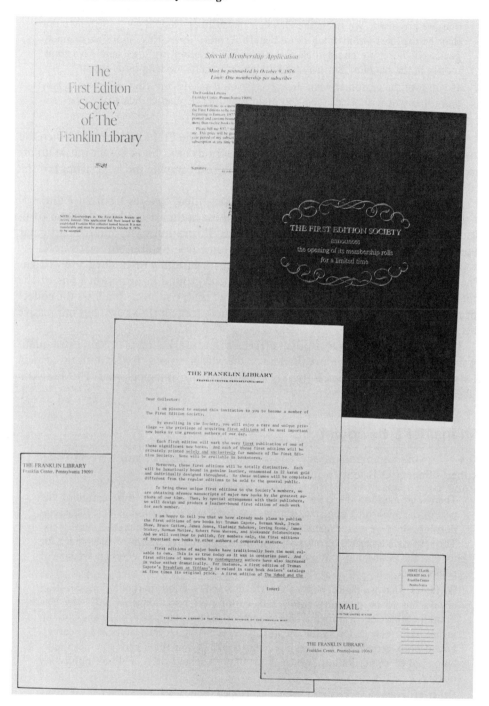

Our emphasis on quality doesn't stop once we have the order. It continues right through the production process. More often, the products we ship are superior to the ones we promised. We stress the idea that the customer should get something more than he expected—something more beautiful, more interesting, more handsomely packaged. Sure, we could stick to what our promotion promised and save some money in the bargain. But why trade short-term gains for long-term growth?

If you give the customer what he expects, you'll satisfy him. But, if you give him *more* than you promised, then you build *enthusiasm*. And enthusiastic buyers are repeat buyers.

How was that philosophy applied in the case of the Franklin Library? When the customer opens the shipping carton, he or she finds each book is sent out in an attractive presentation folder secured with a gold seal carrying the logo symbol of the Library.

Accompanying the book is a 24-page booklet titled, "Notes from the Editors." It provides historical material on the book and the author as well as a number of illustrations. It also explains the paper, typeface, illustration style, and the particular type of leather the designer chose for that volume (see Exhibit 60).

All Franklin Mint collateral material like this is carefully researched and written. The objective is to give the collector enough background information so he or she can become something of an "instant authority" on the subject. It allows the collector to show off the collection to friends and quote some little-known but impressive facts.

It all adds up to a unique product offer, a sound marketing plan, and extra quality that gives the customer more than he or she was promised. It also adds up to such a strong success story that I frankly find it hard to imagine what The Franklin Library will do for an encore.

An insider's viewpoint

The following comments about The Franklin Library program were provided by Robert Vincent O'Brien, former publisher of the Library:

There's no question there was a good deal of skepticism about this venture on the part of the publishing industry. But this has given way to a mutually beneficial relationship, since we secure many of the titles for our collections from other publishers. The very visible success of our programs has earned a high degree of acceptance for us with the publishing community. And, as one might expect, a certain amount of competition.

So far as what we do for an encore is concerned, a good marketing organization always has to be planning ahead and working on new things. That's why The Franklin Mint Corporation has always emphasized the planning process and built an inventory of new concepts for use in future years. We recently launched a leatherbound book series that features the great books of our time, each one personally autographed by its author, which is an unprecedented offer in book publishing history.

Other programs are constantly being developed, which will be marketed for many years to come.

Exhibit 60. Book presentation folder and Notes from the Editors booklet.

14

Haband Company
**The Men's Clothing Sale
That Never Ends**

Which of the following men's clothing items do you think could be sold successfully by mail: Ties? Shirts? Shoes? Sox? Hats? Jackets? Sweaters? Leisure suits? Gloves? Slacks? Belts? Business suits? You might think it would be difficult to get men to order some of these by mail with only standard sizes to choose from and no alterations. But they've *all* been sold successfully by Haband Company. The firm has been at it for over a half-century. The company mails 30 million pieces a year, has over 2 million men on their customer list, and does an annual sales volume of $50 million. Yet, despite the firm's size, Haband has managed to maintain the impression of being a rather small family business.

Two things I think are especially interesting about the Haband story. First, how they've added a personal feeling to shopping by mail with chatty, skillfully written letters that have become a Haband trademark. Second, the firm's shifting emphasis from direct mail to space advertising, which reflects the changing economics of the business. We'll go into both of these in depth, but first a bit of history.

Haband's early history

Back in 1925, a $50.00 investment was all it took to launch the firm. The location was Paterson, New Jersey. Large silk mills had made that city the necktie capital of the world. The two young partners were Max Habernickel, Jr., and John Anderson. The former had learned the necktie business in one of the large local mills. The latter was a banker who was selling ties on the side to fellow workers.

They formed a moonlighting partnership choosing a firm name that was a contraction of their two last names. Habernickel knew how to buy silk remnants and get ties made inexpensively. Anderson handled the sales efforts, soon covering every bank in Paterson.

To expand, they decided to go after out-of-town banks by mail. Habernickel wrote some sales letters, and, before long, they were mailing to banks from coast to coast. For a few years they continued to moonlight with a spare bedroom serving as an office. But, eventually, Habernickel had to quit his job and take over Haband full time. Anderson followed a few years later, serving as treasurer.

Exhibit 61. Early tie mailing package.

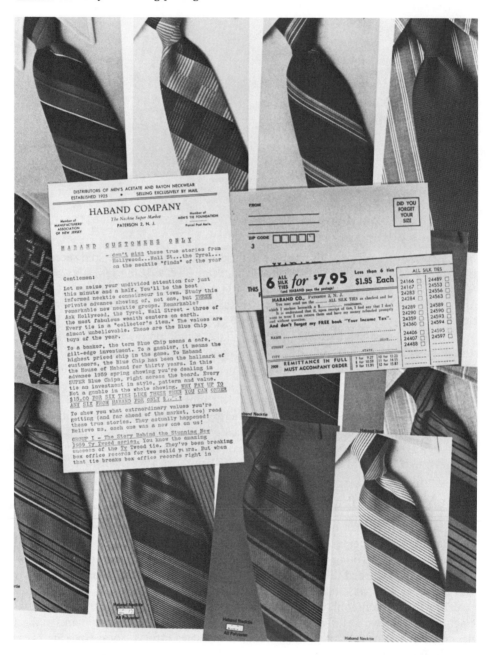

Tie mailings establish a pattern

After trying various approaches through the years, the tie mailings evolved into a fairly consistent format. The firm used a small outer envelope, measuring about 3¾ by 6¾ inches. When it was opened, out tumbled a dozen or more little slips plus an order form, letter, and return envelope (see Exhibit 61).

Each slip showed a single tie design and was printed in full color. There was no copy on it, just the style number of the tie. The customer could pick any six ties at a special price. The standard offer, for example, during the fifties was six ties for $6.75.

The order form was a simple one. The customer simply checked off the tie numbers he wanted, filled in his name and address, and enclosed his remittance. There were no billing privileges or free trial, but the back of the order form contained a strong money-back guarantee.

The letter was usually only a single 8½ × 11 sheet. But it was folded in half and printed as a small four-pager with a black letterhead and blue body copy. And, because there was little other copy in the mailing, the letter had to do the main selling job.

Letters add personal feeling

Many direct marketing firms have tried to add a personal touch to their promotions by featuring the name or photo of the founder who acts as a spokesperson. But none have done it any better than Haband. Through the years, the letters going out over Max Habernickel's signature have been a unique blend of nostalgia, history, jokes, personal family references, and sell copy. One might refer to "Miss Feeney, my secretary for the past 25 years." Another to the fact that his son, Duke, has joined the family business. Still another to a typical father/son disagreement.

To really appreciate how skillfully the human interest is interwoven with the selling story, you have to read a letter in its entirety. Here's one of my favorites, dating back to 1967:

Dear Sirs:

I once heard my son Duke mutter, "I'm sure glad my old man doesn't sell top hats."

What he meant was this: I sold ties. And when Duke was a kid I insisted that he wear one. Always. Breakfast, Dinner and Supper. And Tennis. In fact his standing orders were, in case of fire and before he fled, first put on his tie and then wake me up.

I would like to tell you that this stern upbringing inculcated lasting virtues. But the fact is that it may have been a flop. Ture, he always makes a good appearance. But lately I notice some rather peculiar things about Duke. The fact is he's an addict. He's hooked. On Polly-Ester. Let me tell you how I found out:

One night this summer the wife and I were over to Duke's for dinner. Duke and his wife were bathing the kids and putting them to bed. We were marveling at how quickly they get it done. (They've got it down to a science—Gael washes, Duke wipes.) When all of a sudden Duke came bustling out of the bathroom with his tie wringing wet, showed it to me and said, "Look at that! No damage. That's why I've ordered the whole season's production to be Polly-Ester." ("Dacron" to you.)

A father-son relationship is a delicate thing. So I responded gently. "Duke," I said sweetly, "How long have you been with the company, not counting tomorrow?"

I was really flabbergasted. I'm semi-retired now. Duke is running things. But a decision about the whole season's production is not to be made by some thirty-three year old whippersnapper who's President of his old man's company, without consulting said old man. So I said so. Told him if he didn't mind his P's and Q's he'd find himself right back where he started ten years ago. As Vice-President.

It was then that he conned me. My own Son. And did it by quoting one of my own stories.

It seems that many years ago we were down Maine on vacation and came across this General Store. I took the kids in for ice cream. Duke wanted chocolate. The proprietor said he never stocked it. "Because as soon as I get it in the dang kids clean it all out."

Now, twenty-five years later Duke was pointing out a parallel. Every time we have included "Dacron" ties in our collection they are the first to go. You guys clean us out. So why not sell "Dacron" ties exclusively. Give 'em what they want! Anything else, Duke said, was simply standing in the way of Progress.

Now don't get me wrong. I am not against Progress. You take these new miniskirts, for instance. I'm not against them. For one thing, they tend to make men more polite. Have you ever seen a man get on a bus ahead of one?

But this exclusively "Dacron" thing was too much for me. All our eggs in one basket. So then Duke started quoting facts. Like the fact that "Dacron" ties a superlative knot. Like the fact that it holds a dimple perfectly. Like the fact that no matter how tight you tie your tie the wrinkles just fall out. Like the fact that "Dacron" not only makes tie cleaning *really* possible—the stuff can even be washed. And above all, like the fact that "Dacron" ties are simply beautiful.

Well, if there's anything I can't stand it's somebody who disagrees with me and is right. So I was getting a little miffed. Nevertheless, I elected to reason with him.

"Shut up," I explained.

But the fact of the matter is, Duke *was* right. I woke up the next morning hooked on the stuff myself. So it's "Dacron" for us. As it should be. It is better in every conceivable way. So the ties in this year's collection promise to be so good I may even take to wearing them myself.

I thought that would stop you. But it's true. I seldom wear our ties myself. For a simple reason. Our reputation for style setting is such that the competition watches everything I wear like a hawk, trying to get a line on what our collection will be. I like to keep them shook up. That way our collection remains secret until you get it.

The way I pick our ties is simple. I shop everywhere from the posh Fifth Avenue shops to those reject/remnant shops looking for those really exceptional 12 styles which will make up our collection. Do it all year 'round. So I can tell you a few things. The real smart ties are few and far between. You've got to find them. Watch out for bargains. Some of the dollar ties ought to be against the law. Out-and-out swindle. It's really a crime. But gee whiz, you can't get any tie that's halfway decent for less than $2.50, $3.50, or even $5.00.

Except from us. Our prices are incredible. Which may be why we've been successful for so long. The fact is I've been writing you these letters for so many years that many of our customers today are the sons who remember when Dad bought Haband ties.

Now a word about quality.

Our quality is superb. Take a look, for instance, at our #25032, the blue one with the Scotties woven right into the cloth. Not printed. Every two inches an extra "Light Blue" shuttle makes 12 separate trips back and forth across the loom to weave in the Scottie. Still another shuttle makes 4 more round trips to add Scottie's white collar. Here's the best of that old-fashioned Jacquard weaving which put Paterson on the map, now combined with the finest 1967 "Dacron" miracle yarn. We haven't been as proud of anything since we put the nylon drawstring on the year's new nylon Snuggler.

But Jacquards are only one string in our lyre. Look at the regimental stripes. The pin-dots. The all overs. Everything all "Dacron." Now hear this. You pick five and I'll guarantee that you'll be picking your all-time favorite neckties. The ones you wear day after day, forsaking all others, because they are "Dacron" and the cream of the "Dacron" crop.

Then look at the price. Five for $6.75. Impossible to beat. What's more you select these ties at your leisure. Not with some salesman breathing down your back. Perhaps your wife will help. (Or perhaps not. I don't know your wife.) Either way, it's a wonderful way to shop. And economical. Five "Dacron" ties for $6.75. Five "Dacron" ties for $6.75 when the going price is $2.50. Each.

So, pick your five, slip your check into the mail and we'll have them off to you pronto. Postpaid. You'll be absolutely delighted.

In closing, I would like to thank those of you who wrote in about my recent accident. Everything's Jake and prospects are excellent.

> Your old friend,
>
> M. Habernickel, Jr.
> (Signature)
> Haband Company

MH/FS

P.S. The lady next door to me is one of those nuts who always has her Christmas shopping done by July 1st of any given year. While she is a fanatic, I have to agree that *some* preparation is not a bad idea. And how many days are left till Christmas?

On a first reading, you might think this letter has more personal or "story copy" than it does selling copy. But if you reread it carefully, you'll find that most of it does deal with the tie designs, the Dacron fabric, or Haband's institutional story. The over-all effect is one of credibility—it sounds as if the letter was written by a real person.

Same copy approach for other products

In the fifties Haband started to offer other men's clothing items. Like slacks. The mailing format would be similar to that used for selling ties, except that a simple folder replaced the product slips, some small swatches of the material were added, and often a paper tape measure was enclosed for checking measurements (see Exhibit 62).

In addition, special offers were frequently used. A prospect mailing might include a little one-color slip offering a 5 percent discount to those who ordered promptly. And somewhere along the line, the firm started offering customers a free gift with any order from its annual Christmas mailing.

After reviewing a rather large collection of Haband mailings and letters that span a 20-year period, we can see some common themes emerging over and over. One of these is the fact that Haband has often featured new developments or materials in

Exhibit 62. Mailing on men's slacks.

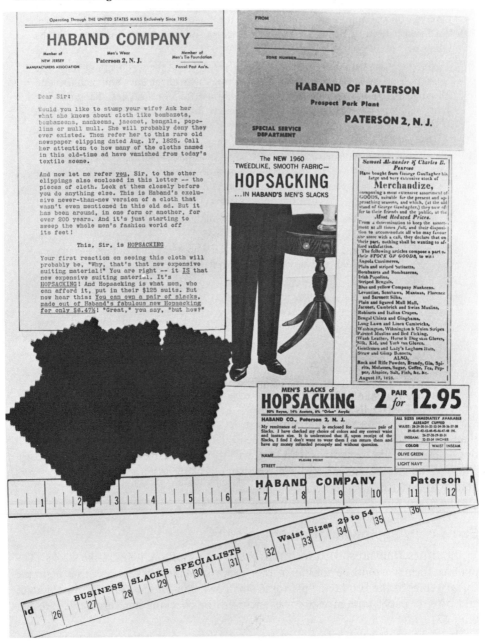

men's clothing. Here, for example, is how they introduced Haband customers to Scotchgard-treated slacks:

> The Missus and I were on one of those giant new Jet planes. The young airline stewardess, in her spick-and-span sky-blue uniform, was just passing me a few of those free snacks they give out, along with a Coke—when blam! The big plane went into one of those sudden dips and over went the whole thing, Coke and all, right down the poor gal's spotless blue uniform! You never saw such a mess!
>
> To me it looked like a major problem for a professional dry cleaner. Those stains looked like they were there for keeps. But that stewardess opened our eyes—fast. (The Coke ran right off her uniform like magic. No sign of it 10 seconds later.) She took a couple of tissues and gently blotted off the rest of the stuff. In about 2 minutes HER UNIFORM LOOKED AS SPOTLESS AS IT WAS BEFORE! NOT ONE SINGLE DAMP, WET, OR STAINED PLACE. *NO TRACE OF A SPOT OR STAIN OF ANY KIND!*
>
> She saw our eyes popping and she cleared up the mystery. The uniforms worn by the trained personnel of this great airline are tailored of goods treated with an amazing invisible "chemical shield" called "Scotchgard" Stain Repeller! An amazing stain-resistant discovery that actually repels waterborne and oil-borne stains—and resists dust, dirt, and dry soil, too! We figure that any textile finish that will do that can cut down your cleaning bills to almost a nubbin!

Another common theme is the emphasis on little-known product features that help establish Haband's knowledge and expertise in the men's clothing area. The following copy is from a mailing on men's shirts:

> But fabric is not the *only* thing to look for in a quality shirt. There are some things only the pros know. Comparison shoppers, for instance, judge a shirt as top quality if they see that the pocket stripes line up perfectly with the body stripes. That's like giving the Congressional Medal of Honor for neatness.
>
> Sure, *anybody* can make the stripes line up. (Although many don't. It costs a few cents more.) But the criterion is misleading. It's what you can't see in a shirt that determines quality.
>
> I mean things like 100% Dacron collar inner *linings.* Permanent Nylon collar stays and cotton (*not* Dacron) thread used to set on the collar to eliminate that tell-tale pucker that can ruin Permanent Press appearance. And then, of course, long tails that stay down. I hate those skimpy things.

Perhaps most important of all is Haband's strong emphasis on bargains. The firm encourages impulse orders by using a low price per unit. At the same time, Haband avoids handling orders that are too small by using "twofer" prices. Here's how the offer was described in a recent slacks mailing:

> But whoa, wait a minute! Maybe you think the price for such an improvement is going to be way out of reach! Not so. There is no catch. Prior to this offer, if anyone had asked me how much slacks with an Indelible Crease would have to cost, I would have ventured $30 a pair! I see some very ordinary slacks going for $30 per pair these days, plus alterations. But hold on to your pants. Our price is less than $20! *Two pairs* for less than $20. You get TWO PAIRS of our slacks with the Indelible Crease for $19.95 postpaid!

Customers get multi-product offers

Haband continued to test other men's clothing items throughout the sixties. The company soon found that slacks and shoes were the most successful for prospect mailings. And they worked so well they eventually replaced the tie offers. But when it came to customer mailings, Haband executives discovered their offers didn't have to be limited to slacks and shoes. Customers would buy a wide variety of other clothing. So Haband began mailing its customer list at least six times a year with multiproduct packages.

The format was similar to their solo item mailings: small outer envelope, four-page letter, and return envelope. But the mailing would contain 15 to 20 different offers. Each item would be featured on a separate slip or folder with its own self-contained order form. Swatches might be included for two or three of the offers.

One recent package, for example, included all the following: double-knit sport jacket, sweater, leisure suit, sport shirts, suede boots, nite shirt, slipper socks, knit slacks, vinyl jacket, vested suit, dress shirts, shoes, belt, insulated vest, knit sport shirts, socks, more slacks, more dress shirts, and a sport coat (see Exhibit 63).

The familiar Haband letter relates a family disagreement about the sale, works in some personal references, and romances the bargains offered. But this time the letter is from Duke Habernickel, the founder's son. Which is a pretty good indication that Haband's copy style probably won't change too much in the years ahead.

Shifting emphasis to space advertising

Haband first started flirting with space advertising years ago when *Life Magazine* came on the scene. Max Habernickel dreamed of running a full-color double spread in the new photo-journalism publication. He and his partner finally got up enough nerve to do it—and spent $43,000 for that one insertion. They sold enough neckties to pay for it and made it pay out again the following year. But as *Life*'s circulation and advertising rates grew, the same spread was up to $70,000 two years later. Haband tried it again and lost money.

In subsequent years, the company tested a number of other publications on a lesser scale. Some paid out. Some didn't. While direct mail volume grew steadily through the years, space was always a rather nominal part of the total ad budget.

A $2,000 investment is pyramided

After Duke Habernickel had been in the family business for a few years, he saw the handwriting on the wall. Postage increases were coming along with a disturbing regularity. He thought the firm should be looking at space advertising as another alternative to bring in new customers. His dad finally gave him $2,000 as a test budget. He spent it all on one ad and it produced a handsome return. So he carefully reinvested it year after year, pyramiding the original investment. The accompanying chart (Exhibit 64) shows how that budget has continued to grow in recent years. In 1972 Haband spent about $875,000 in space. By 1976 the firm was spending at the rate of more than $4,000,000 per year, making Haband one of the largest direct response space advertisers in the country!

Exhibit 63. Multi-product customer mailing.

Exhibit 64. Haband's growing space advertising expenditures.

Year	Magazines	Sunday Supplements	Total
1972	$155,446	$ 720,714	$ 876,160
1973	$117,971	$1,110,911	$1,228,882
1974	$127,372	$2,147,715	$2,275,087
1975	$120,423	$3,428,143	$3,548,566
1976	$104,405	$3,928,782	$4,033,187

Source: Publishers Information Bureau, Inc.

Haband's space program

What did that $4,000,000 budget cover in 1976? Mostly full-page, four-color ads like the one on the "slacks with the indelible crease." (See Exhibit 65.) Where did they run? The budget was concentrated in relatively few publications. In the magazine area, a couple of publications had only single insertions. But *Elks Magazine* was used consistently with a total of more than 15 pages for the year. Haband usually gets a cover position in this publication. While a coupon is included in the ads, the firm recognizes that some readers don't like to tear apart the cover of a publication they might wish to save. So, Haband runs another small coupon in the mail order section and uses a line below the cover ad directing the reader to the second coupon.

The bulk of the budget—97 percent to be exact—is accounted for by the Sunday supplements. One regional supplement, the *New York News Magazine,* was used regularly. But the big dollars went to the leading national supplements. The space in *Parade* was the equivalent of almost 22 full-run pages, and *Family Weekly* was not far behind with over 18 full-run pages (see Exhibit 66).

How Haband makes space work

What makes Haband's space program work? In my opinion, it's a combination of several factors:

A different creative approach. Obviously, Haband's space ads are quite different from the long folksy copy that has characterized the firm's direct mail efforts. But, when people are reading a publication, they usually skim over the ads rather rapidly. You have to grab their attention fast. Haband does it with ads that come across as rather hard sell. But they use strong graphics to display the merchandise as large as possible and still crowd in the necessary copy details. The over-all effect is what they want—ads that shout "bargain."

Attractive price points. To carry out that bargain feeling, most Haband space ad offers are currently priced at $24.95. But that's a "twofer" price that covers two pair of slacks or shoes. Some items, like a leisure suit, are priced higher. Some close-out offers are even lower. In any case, the price point is an attractive one for impulse sales. And Haband sometimes throws in an extra incentive like a matching belt with an ad for shoes. (See Exhibit 67.)

Exhibit 65. Space ad on slacks.

Heavy use of Sunday supplements. Supplements provide good color reproduction, which is important for fashion-oriented offers. But even more important, supplements provide large-number circulation at an attractive cost per thousand. Which means, if you can make them pay out—as Haband has—they can deliver a large number of new customers.

Transference of direct mail techniques. While Haband's space ads might look a lot different from their direct mail pieces, the firm has actually built on many things learned in the mail. Haband features and romances, for example, many of the new synthetic materials. And unlike a men's clothing store, the firm limits the number of styles and color choices to simplify the inventory.

When you get into their ad coupons you find another similarity. Offers are usually cash-with-order. While this undoubtedly reduces response, it virtually eliminates credit problems. (By contrast, one of Haband's competitors who sells clothing by mail on a free-trial basis has to set aside almost 5 percent of sales as a provision for doubtful accounts.)

Exhibit 66. Haband's 1976 space program.

Publications	Number of Pages*	Expenditure
Elks Magazine............	15.34	$ 98,830
Time Magazine...........	.04	$ 2,825
A. D. Magazine..........	1.00	$ 2,750
Parade..................	21.95	$2,502,519
Family Weekly...........	18.46	$1,138,655
New York News Magazine..	14.20	$ 287,608
Totals	70.99	$4,033,187

*Represents the amount of space used with regional insertions and ads of less than a page figured as the fractional equivalent of a full-run page. Thus, 1.00 equals one full page with full or national circulation.

Source: Publishers Information Bureau, Inc.

Haband today—and tomorrow

What Haband is doing today is probably a good indication of what its marketing program will be like in the years ahead. It boils down to the fact that the firm is finding it increasingly difficult to use direct mail for prospecting. Instead, Haband has turned to space advertising to bring in a steady flow of new customers. And chances are good, the space budget will remain at a significant level. Mail, on the other hand, is becoming more and more important for going back to those same customers and sell them other things to round out their wardrobes. Which means the firm's total mail volume may shrink, but direct mail will always make a significant contribution to the profit picture. And it's a pretty good bet that those folksy letters will be read by Haband customers for years to come.

Exhibit 67. Space ad on shoes with matching belt.

Space advertising to get new customers. Direct mail to resell them. It's a formula I think many other direct marketers will be following in the years to come.

An insider's viewpoint

Haband's founder and board chairman, Max Habernickel, rarely speaks in public about the firm or its marketing activities. But here's some of what he said about their ad program in a recent speech (to the Mail Order Nurserymen's Association, reprinted with permission from *Direct Marketing*).

> I know of no mail order business that can survive without repeat business. As I see it, most of us spend the biggest part of our advertising dollars to pick up new customers and rely on subsequent repeat business to bring in the profits.
>
> What a stroke of luck it was that we did get into space advertising. You all know what happened to the Post Office. Direct mail opportunities and possibilities have been dying fast for us. We can't get our money back from third class mailings anymore. That is, to do prospecting. The markup simply isn't there.
>
> When I started 50 years ago, postage was a penny a piece. Now as you know just as well as I do, it's 8.4 cents to mail a circular.
>
> If Haband didn't have its space program, we couldn't afford to dig for new customers, and, without new customers, our business would be dead in four or five years.
>
> The life of a Haband customer is at best three or four years, and while they are alive, they've got to be promoted, which we can only do by third class mail. But expire they will, and new names must be found. And that's not only for Haband, that's for everybody.

15

Lanier Business Products:
How Multi-phase Testing Produced a Cost-Efficient Sales Lead Program

"I believe a salesman should spend his time doing the one thing he does best—selling!"

That quote from chairman Gene Milner typifies the philosophy that has made Lanier Business Products one of the largest firms, certainly the fastest-growing, in the dictating equipment field. From being a regional distributor a few short years ago, Lanier has become a leading national manufacturer in a market estimated at more than $150 million in annual sales.

A large part of Lanier's success must be attributed to the sales-oriented attitude that pervades the entire management team. For this is one company that doesn't just leave the selling up to its salespeople, even though the company has over 1,000 of them in 75 distributorships and branch offices throughout the country.

Every member of Lanier's management and marketing team has to spend a minimum of four weeks a year in the field making calls with the local sales force. They not only provide additional human resources for the firm's sales emphasis weeks, they learn first-hand about market conditions, selling problems, competition, and product reception.

Naturally, a sales-oriented firm like this knows what its selling costs are. Management knows that industry figures show it costs over $96.00 to have a salesperson make a single sales call. They know a salesperson can be more productive when he or she's working sales leads rather than making cold calls. So it's only natural the firm would use direct mail to develop a sales lead program.

A direct mail program with problems

Based on some initial success, Lanier developed an extensive mailing program that totaled almost two million pieces annually. But, before the first year was even over, the direct mail program began running into problems.

First of all, Lanier's list universe was limited to less than 700,000 names. Which meant, to meet its mailing quota, the firm had to mail to the same names three times a year. In an effort to maintain response, Lanier turned to premium offers.

But there was no testing built into the program. The premium offer was arbitrarily changed from one mailing to another. Putting too much emphasis on the premium drastically cut response. Before long, salespeople were not even bothering to follow up as many as half the leads they received!

A major revamp of Lanier's direct mail program was clearly in order. The firm started by appointing a direct response ad agency with a proven track record for success in the business market. Then a major testing program was budgeted to start in 1975.

The strategy: concentrate on qualified leads

The new agency spent more than a month analyzing Lanier's direct mail program and results. The account team pinpointed the areas that were working best as well as those that were least productive. Then they recommended a detailed mailing and testing program designed to build a steady flow of qualified leads. The marketing strategy behind the program was outlined in a letter from the agency's executive vice president to Gene Milner at Lanier:

> This year's program places more emphasis on the solid benefits of switching to Lanier dictating systems and less on the free gift. As a result, each lead is an open-door invitation for your salesman to demonstrate—and *sell*—the product. The premium becomes what it *should* be: just a little extra "nudge" to get the already-interested prospect to let us know he's interested.
>
> We've secured some of the most *proven-productive* lists of mail-responsive, affluent businessmen presently available: lists like American Express, Carte Blanche, and *Business Week* and *Fortune* subscribers.
>
> We're recommending that you mail more heavily to those specialized market areas that showed the most active interest and sales results last year, such as legal, medical, educational, and government administrators.
>
> Looking at the other side of the same coin, we've recommended that you cut back on mailings to areas that we now know were not productive, so that all of your salesmen's time is spent following up on the most qualified prospects and closing the greatest possible number of sales.
>
> And we've structured a meaningful series of tests to establish the ideal mailing package for producing the maximum number of top-quality leads at the most efficient cost. This involves testing premiums, formats, and copy.

Selling the new program to dealers

The strategy and new program were accepted by Lanier management. But they knew that before the first prospect mailings could go out they had a tough hurdle to cross. Namely, to sell the program to their dealers.

Unlike the case with other media advertising, which was paid entirely by the home office, dealers were asked to pick up the cost of mailings made into their local territories. Lanier would charge the dealers 19½¢ each, or $195 per thousand.

The poor results and quality of the leads generated the previous year had turned off a lot of the dealers. So resistance to the new program was not only expected but anticipated. The budget for the announcement mailing to dealers was only $1,700, but the universe was small. A dramatic mailing went out to Lanier's 40 dealers in 32 states outlining the 1975 program (see Exhibit 68).

Exhibit 68. Mailing to Lanier's dealers.

The key element of the mailing was a natural. Because Lanier's line of dictating equipment was built around cassette tapes rather than belts or discs, a real cassette tape was tipped onto the cover of the presentation folder. It contained a personal message from Gene Milner that acknowledged the problems with last year's mailing program, explained how Lanier had brought in a top direct response agency, and promised the new program would live up to its name and deliver "Solid Gold Leads for '75."

Milner also mentioned that the mail campaign was being backed up by Lanier's $3 million ad budget for newspapers, magazines, radio, and television. While those media were important in reaching the target audience, Milner said it would be up to direct mail to generate the leads.

Inside the presentation folder was a two-page letter from Milner. To make the program more attractive, he announced that Lanier would be doing substantial testing throughout the year and that dealers would not be charged for these additional mailings. Therefore, they would not only get bonus leads at no extra cost, but the continual testing program would help to further improve lead quality.

To bring out the strategy behind the campaign, the folder included a full reprint of the ad agency's letter to Milner. This dramatized the professional help that Lanier had got for the program, and, by mentioning some other well-known clients with whom the agency worked, it tended to reinforce Lanier's decision.

In addition, the mailing included a simple four-page folder with an outline of the entire year's plan. Plus an agreement form that indicated the total prospects in the dealer's area that would be mailed and the total investment for the program.

It added up to an impressive package—all designed and produced for just 40 dealers. And it worked: 38 of the 40 dealers signed up, committing themselves to a total investment of more than a quarter million dollars!

The lead-getting mailing program

The mailing plan divided the full year's program into three separate cycles. Each cycle lasted between 12 to 16 weeks and had a different objective:

Cycle 1. Started in January and was designed for the major testing of new offers, package formats, and list possibilities. Concentrating the testing in this first cycle would allow the results to be utilized that much sooner.

Cycle 2. Started in May and was planned to refine and expand the list selections that showed promise on the initial tests.

Cycle 3. Started in September and would be used to roll out the maximum quantity using the best offers, package formats, and list selections.

Within each cycle the mailings were spread out as evenly as possible on a week-by-week basis. Because a new cycle began the week after the previous one ended, the schedule provided continuous mailing and lead flow throughout the year.

Naturally the mailing quantities established for each area were realistic ones so the salespeople would not have more leads than they could handle. Procedures were set up to monitor the lead flow in each area and permit adjustment in mailing quantities and drop dates, if necessary.

Cycle 1 offer tests

A new control package was established for the mailing program—against which all other new approaches would be tested. The package included the following elements all printed in two colors: a number 10 outer envelope, a two-page letter on executive-size stationery, a reprint of an article on the rising cost of producing a business letter (with marginal notes handwritten by Gene Milner), and a business reply card. The detachable stub of the reply card and the PS on the letter provided the only mentions of the premium offer; the balance of the package was devoted to the benefits of dictating and Lanier's VIP desktop unit (see Exhibit 69).

Lanier had just completed development of a new shirt-pocket-size dictating machine that was tested against the VIP control package. The product was called the Pocket Secretary. It measured only 2½ × 5½ inches and utilized a new microcassette that could record for up to one hour and provide excellent sound quality.

Exhibit 69. VIP control package.

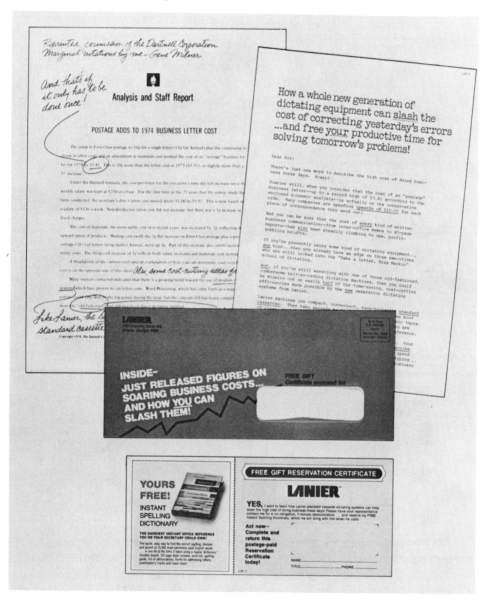

Naturally, a dramatic product like this was suited to a dramatic mailing package. The result was a 6 × 9 package with an outer envelope that invited an "audition of an extraordinary new executive tool." The two-page letter had a flap on the right which included an actual-size reproduction of the product. The reply card showed a hand holding the product to further dramatize its small size and used a flap at the top to cover the premium offer. As in the control mailing, the premium was also covered with a PS on the letter (see Exhibit 70).

Exhibit 70. Test mailing on Lanier's Pocket Secretary.

   The Pocket Secretary package proved to be a big winner. It produced over 50 percent more leads than the VIP control package. Later analysis showed that the average sale from this mailing was almost as high as for the control, even though the Pocket Secretary sold in the $200 price range compared to $800 for a standard VIP system. This meant that the Pocket Secretary was an effective door opener, but, in most cases, the salespeople would still end up selling the more expensive standard system.

   Another important offer test in the first cycle was a free-trial offer. Feedback from the sales force indicated that many potential prospects were reluctant either to try using dictating equipment for the first time or to try newer dictating equipment with which they would be unfamiliar. So this package put heavy emphasis on a five-day free trial which would allow the prospect to "get acquainted" with the Lanier equipment.

The free trial was tested against the control mailing with the premium in the hope that this free offer would pull as well as using a free gift. It didn't. The control mailing pulled 20 percent more responses.

Tests were also planned in the first cycle to determine which premium would be most effective. Four different premiums were tested, which covered a broad spectrum of business and personal appeal. The first one was an Instant Spelling Dictionary which could be used by either a business executive or a secretary. The second was a Sheaffer pen, suitable for business or personal use. The third was a miniature Dymo labeler, which was basically a personal or "take home" item. And the fourth was a helpful booklet titled "How to Get More Done." (See Exhibit 71.)

Exhibit 71. Tests of different premium offers.

Which item was most appealing? Compared to the Instant Spelling Dictionary as a control, the booklet pulled 27 percent worse. The Dymo labeler pulled 26 percent better. And the Sheaffer pen pulled 39 percent better.

The pen was clearly the winner—But!—reports from the field indicated the salespeople were overwhelmingly in favor of the Instant Spelling Dictionary. They felt that this product-related premium produced better-quality inquiries, and the sales conversion figures seemed to bear them out. Lanier's management was smart enough to realize that this could have been strictly a psychological thing. In other words, a salesperson perhaps felt more professional delivering a product-related premium than, say, a pen or labeler and therefore did a better selling job. But the human element had to be taken into consideration, and it was decided that future mailings would stay with the Instant Spelling Dictionary as a premium.

Cycle 1 package tests

Format variations of the basic VIP control mailing and the new Pocket Secretary mailing were also developed for testing. One such package was a Reply-O type of format in which the letter and reply card are combined. The pre-addressed card showed through a die-cut window at the top of the letter and could be easily pulled out for responding to the offer (see Exhibit 72). While this format has often done well in lead-getting situations, it turned out to be 10 percent worse than the control in this case.

An involvement device, however, produced better results. The device was tested on the Pocket Secretary package, which featured an actual-size product illustration on the letter. Instead of just printing the illustration, a gummed stamp picturing the micro-cassette was tipped on the letter. The copy directed the reader to "lift off this cassette stamp and paste it on the enclosed Reservation Card for your Free audition of the Pocket Secretary." When affixed properly, the stamp "completed" the product illustration on the return card (see Exhibit 73).

The involvement device improved response 20 percent over the identical package without the gummed stamp. Some direct marketers have always believed that certain response techniques such as involvement devices only work in the consumer market. Their theory is that it's fine for homemakers to play with stamps and tokens, but a business executive is too busy or sophisticated for things like this. This particular test, however, with an involvement device used to dramatize one of the product features, seems to prove otherwise.

Additional package testing showed that a two-page letter pulled better than a one-pager, the addition of a brochure did not improve response, and a third class stamp on the outer envelope didn't work any better than a printed indicia. But several tests showed that adding a telephone response option as a means of getting quicker action consistently increased results.

Cycle 1 list tests

Lanier had always used compiled lists, traditionally the most effective in the business products market. But, as indicated earlier, response was falling off because the firm had to go back to the same limited universe three times a year.

Exhibit 72. Reply-O test mailing.

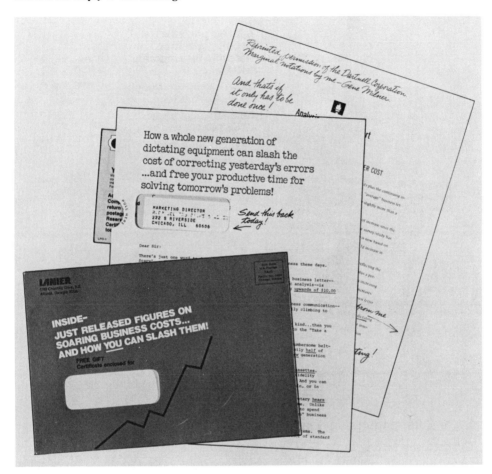

In an effort to open up the mailing universe, Lanier tested direct response lists in four specific categories: business mail order buyers, business equipment inquiry lists, travel-and-entertainment cardholders, and subscribers to business publications. Besides their history of being mail responsive, these lists provided names of individuals rather than the title addressing that was necessary for reaching top and middle management executives on the compiled lists.

About half the direct response lists that were tested paid out. Looking at the over-all list results for Cycle 1, the average return on the direct response lists was 49 percent higher than that for the compiled lists used during the same period. And the sales force reported the quality of leads from these new lists was as good or better than that of other leads.

Exhibit 73. Pocket Secretary mailing with stamp as involvement device.

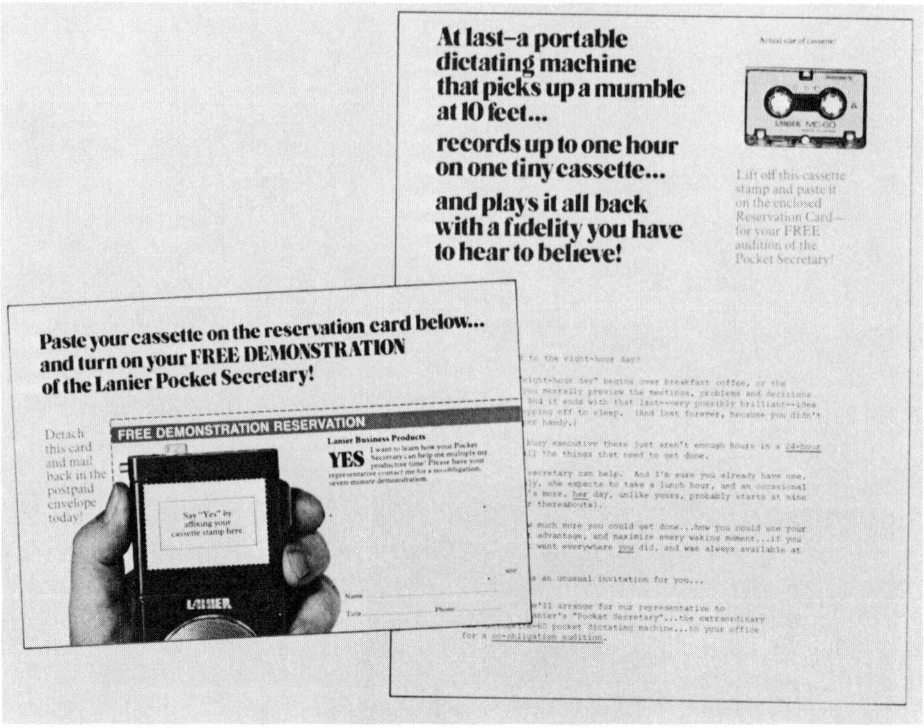

Cycle 2 list expansion

The extensive testing in the first cycle provided a new control mailing for cycle 2. The mailing consisted of the Pocket Secretary offer, with the stamp involvement device and the Instant Spelling Dictionary as a premium, plus the phone response option. In addition, only direct response lists were used for this cycle. The lists that had performed well on the first test were ordered in larger quantities, and a variety of similar lists were tested.

The total mailing quantity for the second cycle was about the same as the 500,000 pieces mailed in the first cycle. But the winning mailing package, coupled with the direct response lists, virtually tripled response from 0.50 percent to 1.47 percent. This, of course, brought the cost per lead down to about one-third of what it had been. And, at the same time, the sales force felt there was an improvement in lead quality, which was reflected in their sales closure rate.

Cycle 3 roll-out

This was destined to be the real test of Lanier's new direct mail lead program. This was because 1,250,000 pieces had been scheduled—more than the first and second cycle combined. And, during the third cycle, a postage increase brought the in-the-mail cost to a new high.

The third cycle included additional continuations of direct response lists (about 14 different ones had now proven effective), the best or most-responsive segments of the compiled lists used in the past, and Lanier's own customer list.

For maximizing response, testing was limited to a couple of new packages which were being pilot-tested in the hope of producing another winner for the 1976 mailing program. One of these was a full-line package. The mailing used an oversized illustrated letter with photos of the Pocket Secretary and three other best-selling models. While the appearance of the package was much different, it incorporated some of the success elements of earlier efforts, such as an Instant Business Dictionary as a premium and the use of a Free Audition stamp as an involvement device (see Exhibit 74).

And the over-all results of the third cycle not only held up, they improved slightly to 1.50 percent. So, despite the postage increase, the increase in the cost per lead was less than 5 percent. Results of the new full line package showed a slight decrease in response but a substantial increase in the average sale, thus providing an even more effective package for the following year.

Special market mailings

While the mailings we have just reviewed represented the main thrust of Lanier's program, a number of specialized mailings were also made throughout the year. These went to market segments that had produced good results in the past including legal, medical, educational, and government administrators.

Each mailing was slanted to that specific market and featured a Lanier product or dictating system which was particularly suitable. Although individual mailings were relatively small, the total effort provided a good supplemental source of sales leads.

The year in review

Looking back over Lanier's year-long 1975 mailing program, I see four major accomplishments that stand out:

1. The firm signed up 95 percent of the dealers to participate in the program, despite the poor results of the previous year.

2. The biggest breakthrough was in making direct response lists work. This expanded the universe of proven lists from 700,000 to about 2,000,000 names, thus providing enough potential leads to support the sales force without heavy remailing of the same lists.

3. A reduction in lead cost, made possible by multiphase testing of products, offers, packages, and premiums. The result: a control mailing piece that was a steady lead producer.

4. A corresponding improvement in lead quality that resulted in more sales calls being made and more sales. According to *Direct Marketing* Magazine, the Lanier sales force converted 25 percent of the leads to sales with an average order of about $800.

Exhibit 74. Full-line mailing package.

The name of the game

For a sales-oriented company like Lanier, the real measurement of the success of this program is the effect it had on sales. The year 1975 was a recession year; most office equipment manufacturers were cutting back and licking their wounds. But not Lanier Business Products. The company chalked up a healthy 16 percent sales increase!

An insider's viewpoint

The following comments about Lanier's direct mail lead program were provided by Clifford Walker who served as the firm's advertising manager while the program was created and developed.

> The real instigator of Lanier's direct mail program and the prime person responsible for its existence is company chairman Gene Milner. He's always been a firm believer in direct mail, going back to the days when he was selling dictating equipment himself in Kansas City.
>
> A few years ago, Milner asked us to put together a national direct mail program that would produce some high-quality leads for our salesmen to follow up. One of his favorite sayings is, "Leads are the best way to get your salesmen out making calls early in the morning."
>
> Lanier has found that leads also help motivate the sales force and reduce turnover. A typical salesman making cold calls is faced with rejection on call after call after call. Leads break up this rejection. When a salesman gets some leads, he knows he's got calls to make today where he's welcome and has actually been invited into the prospect's office. Then, of course, the salesman can get referrals from these prospects, which further extends his prospect list and nonrejection rate.
>
> I'm very proud of the fact that our 1975 mailing campaign won the Henry Hoke Award for the most courageous solution to a difficult sales problem. After the poor 1974 campaign, it was a miracle we were able to sell our dealers again. But the announcement package to dealers did the trick. When they saw we were going to a top-flight ad agency and were promising "solid gold leads" they were excited.
>
> But the thing that really excited them most was the testing plan which had been prepared. And as you've learned, that testing plan really added up to improved response, better quality leads, and more sales for Lanier *and* its dealers.

16

Montgomery Ward:
Auto Club Attracts Large Membership
in Record Time, Despite Limited Universe

Why would Montgomery Ward start a new auto club when there were already 16 million members in the American Automobile Association plus a few million in other clubs? Why would Ward's executives limit memberships to their own charge customers, especially when 20 percent of them already belonged to another auto club? Why would Wards launch a club at a time when the economy was beginning to get soft and other clubs were actually cutting back on their promotion efforts? And how successful could Wards expect to be with things like this stacked against the company?

This chapter should provide the answers. Fact is, though, the Montgomery Ward Auto Club has been remarkably successful. Just two years after launching its first promotion, the club had zoomed to over a half-million members. A year later it topped the 800,000 mark with no slowdown in sight.

Pretest measures appeal

Back in 1973, Wards had started a new subsidiary known as Signature Agency. It was designed as a separate profit center with a broad-based charter to develop special services and products that could be sold via direct marketing. The firm's goals were to help retain and activate the 15.5 million customers who had a Ward's Charg-all account. (Over half of Ward's total sales were on credit, so this list of charge-account customers obviously represented a very important asset.) And, if possible, to attract new credit customers.

After its initial success with a credit insurance offer, the Signature Agency began to explore a wide variety of services. One of them was an auto club. Signature's president, Richard Cremer, wasn't at all sure he wanted to start another club at that point. But he felt its appeal could be tested rather easily by using the services of an existing club.

Three test objectives

The test was slated for Florida in spring 1973. A relatively small club known as the United States Auto Club was lined up to provide the necessary membership benefits.

Three objectives were then outlined for the pretest:

1. To determine the general appeal of an auto club to Ward's Charg-all customers.
2. To find the best or most appealing offer to get new members.
3. To determine whether the Wards name would have more appeal than the United States Auto Club name.

Most firms would have probably chosen a solo mailing to accomplish these objectives. But the vehicle Wards chose was a statement insert that would go out with the monthly Charg-all bills. This format had performed well in past on other offers to their credit file. And it provided an opportunity to test a number of versions or offer variations at relatively low cost.

Seven-way test provides answers

While the insert folded down to 4¼ by 7 inches to fit the billing envelope, it provided plenty of copy room. It opened up to 8¼ by 20¾ and was printed in three colors. The control insert announced that Wards had made arrangements with the United States Auto Club for its credit card customers to join the club and have the membership cost billed directly to their Charg-all account (see Exhibit 75).

Inside was a letter-type message from Ward's credit vice-president plus full descriptions of all member benefits including travel accident insurance, emergency road service, and trip routing service. The insert did not contain an application. Instead, the agreement copy was imprinted at the top of the Charg-all statement so the customer could just sign and return it when paying the bill.

While all the inserts were almost identical, there were naturally minor changes for the offer testing. The control insert offered the United States Auto Club membership at an annual fee of $24.00. Tested against it was a $2.00-per-month offer. While this came out to the same annual price, it did not have a minimum commitment period so members could cancel at any time.

Four offers or service variations were also tested. The first offered a free premium, a garment bag. The second offered one month's free membership with a commitment to join the club. The third offered a special six-month membership for $10.00. The fourth offered check-cashing privileges at Ward's stores as an extra membership benefit.

The final test was the one involving the name of the club. The front panel said, "Montgomery Ward is proud to announce our own brand-new Auto Club available exclusively to you as a Charg-all customer." Inside, it repeated the use of the Wards name but provided the same benefit descriptions and price as the U.S. Auto Club control version.

Because there was a considerable spread in the results, the test provided some firm answers. The club definitely had appeal to Charg-all customers—response was much better than the target. The $2.00 monthly billing was the strongest offer, even better than the free premium or other special offers. And the Wards name had the most appeal with response significantly better than the same offer from U.S. Auto Club.

Exhibit 75. Ward's statement insert announcing new auto club.

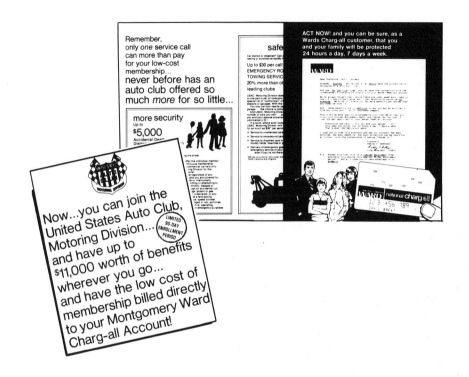

Montgomery Ward Auto Club launched

Wards now knew an auto club could be a winner, but it didn't yet have a real club. So the company used the balance of 1973 to plan and structure one. The first stage was research. Competitive research. Executives joined the 50 largest auto clubs in the U.S. to study their benefits and rates. Five were independents; 45 were affiliates of American Automobile Association whose benefits were different in each of their associate clubs. At the time, AAA had 16 million members nationwide. Amoco was second with 1.2 million members and Allstate third with 650,000 members. Research was also done with Charg-all customers. That's where it was learned that 20 percent were already members of an auto club with about 90 percent of this group belonging to AAA.

The marketing strategy for the Montgomery Ward Auto Club suddenly began to evolve. The best prospects were probably those Charg-all customers who already belonged to another club. The way to win them over—and also attract nonmembers—was to develop a better club. One with stronger benefits and favorable rates.

So Wards began an ambitious program to expand and improve the "traditional benefits'' offered by other clubs. Its accidental death and dismemberment insurance, for example, was designed with absolutely no exclusions. Members would be covered for any type of accident, not just travel accidents or accidents in commercial carriers. Car rental discounts were established. Hotel and motel discounts were provided for members, and a continuing campaign was developed that eventually led to discounts at 5,000 of the 18,000 U.S. hotels and motels.

Many other clubs charged an initiation fee or an extra charge if the person's spouse wanted to become a member. Wards decided to go with a flat $2.25 monthly charge, which included member and spouse, and no initiation fee. When translated to an annual rate of $27.00, the cost was quite competitive. (Average dues for other clubs ranged from $18.00 to $35.00; most AAA clubs were priced at the higher end of the range and still charged an extra fee for the member's spouse.)

In addition to developing its benefit/pricing structure, Wards developed a highly computerized system to handle the club billing. And its legal staff began researching and studying the state statutes that covered auto clubs and insurance offers.

February start for solicitation

The marketing plan called for announcing the Montgomery Ward Auto Club to all active Charg-all customers during 1974 and to start building awareness among the general public. The legal staff determined that 22 states had no auto club statutes on file, so those states were slated for the first release in February 1974.

Charg-all customers in those states were solicited with a statement insert almost identical to that used for the pretest the previous spring. But, in addition to describing the new benefits, a couple of other significant changes were made.

The country was then going through an energy crisis. Gas was scarce and expensive. Unnecessary auto travel was being curtailed. And other auto clubs were cutting back on their marketing efforts. Did Wards consider delaying the introduction of its club? No. Everything was ready to go. The company decided to proceed with the launch but tailor its benefit story to the times.

Thus, the letter built into the statement insert was designed to capitalize on the situation in the marketplace. Here's how the opening paragraphs read:

> Dear Preferred Credit Customer:
>
> In this time of severe energy crisis, with fuel so scarce and Sunday service at a bare minimum, everyone—everyone who drives a car—*needs* the protection of an auto club. Particularly, a club with benefits specifically designed to accommodate the problems which will be encountered as a result of the crisis.
>
> That's why we decided to start our own club, *exclusively* for you and for all Wards preferred Charg-all credit customers.

Because Ward's management still felt the best prospects were those customers who already belonged to another club, the company used one full panel inside the insert for a competitive chart. The chart compared the benefits of the Montgomery Ward Auto Club with three competitive clubs in the area being mailed. This eventually required 25 different versions of the insert to cover different parts of the country, but it did a strong selling job (see Exhibit 76).

The insert did well and brought in 60,000 new members. In June 1974, Charg-all inserts went out to 23 additional states where the club had been licensed and approved. Three more states were finally approved and solicited in October of that year. As before, the response was good.

Exhibit 76. Comparison of auto club benefits in Ward's statement insert.

Compare these major comprehensive benefits with three of the AAA Motor Clubs in Florida and you won't want to drive another mile without a MWAC card in your pocket!				
CLUB BENEFIT	**MONTGOMERY WARD AUTO CLUB**	**CLUB A**	**CLUB B**	**CLUB C**
Coast to coast toll-free "Hotline" for information and emergency service	YES	NO	NO	NO
Emergency road & tow coverage	$30 **not restricted to a special list of "authorized" service stations or garages.***	$10 if authorized station is not available.**	$15 if authorized station is not available.***	$25 if authorized **station** is **not** available.****
Legal defense reimbursement	To $500	To $200	To $500	To $300
Custom trip routing	YES	YES	YES	YES
Accidental death & dismemberment protection	Up to $5000 **not limited by length of membership**	Up to $2000 1st yr. (Gradually increases up to $3000 in 6th yr.)*****	Up to $2000 1st yr. (Gradually increases up to $3000 in 6th yr.)*****	Up to $2000 1st yr. (Gradually increases up to $3000 in 3rd yr.)*****
Is the above coverage limited to specified accidents?	NOT LIMITED	YES—LIMITED	YES—LIMITED	YES—LIMITED
Can accidental death & dismemberment benefits be optionally divided between you and your spouse?	YES	NO	NO	NO
Hospitalization benefits	NONE	Up to $15 per day per person insured toward hospital room charge for a maximum of 90 days for specified accidents **only** plus $60 for specified emergency expenses **only**.	Up to $14 per day per person insured toward hospital room charge for a maximum of 45 days for specified accidents **only** plus $130 for specified emergency expenses **only**.	Up to $10 per day per person insured toward hospital room charge for a maximum of 365 days for specified accidents **only** plus $80 for specified emergency expenses **only**.
Emergency travel expenses	$100	NONE	$100	NONE
Arrest bond coverage (Not available in California.)	$200	$200	$200	$200
Bail bond coverage	$5,000	$5,000	$5,000	$5,000
Professional travel bureau	YES	YES	YES	YES
Theft reward	$200	$200	$200	$200 (Plus $50 reward for hubcap stealing.)
Car rental discounts	YES—20%	NO	NO	NO
Hotel/motel discounts	YES—10%	NO	NO	NO
First year's membership fee for you and your spouse	$24.00	$37.50	$33.00	$35.00

Newspaper ads build awareness

Concurrent with the statement insert mailings, Wards launched a newspaper ad campaign. Its purpose was to start building consumer awareness for the club and reinforce the competitive thrust of the inserts.

Small ads were developed to highlight the MWAC benefits that were superior: higher tow reimbursement, $5,000 all-risk accident insurance, and 20 percent rental car discount—with one benefit headlined per ad. Larger ads, measuring 10¼ by 16, were also prepared. Each ad included a competitive chart similar to that in the inserts (see Exhibit 77). And headlines like these dramatized the marketing strategy:

> The only thing wrong with AAA is that our new auto club is better.
>
> After you compare our auto club with theirs, you'll want to join ours.
>
> Here's why AAA now rates second to Montgomery Ward's new Auto Club.
>
> If your AAA renewal date is about due, now's the time to join our club.

The ads went on to explain that club membership was limited to Charg-all customers who could join by signing the form that would come in the mail with their current statement. And non-Charg-all customers were invited to apply for charge accounts. Because statements were mailed throughout the month, the ads were spread out accordingly. Twenty-seven major newspapers were used for the campaign with one large ad appearing each week for four consecutive weeks. The small ads were interspersed through the week to provide continuity.

While there was no way to measure exactly how well the ads fulfilled their purpose, they stirred up a lot of interest. And Wards wound up 1974 with over 168,000 members in its new club. All this was achieved through an unusual multi-media combination—statement insert solicitations supported by newspaper ads.

Media mix expanded

1975 represented a year of important "firsts" for the Montgomery Ward Auto Club. They included the first use of solo mailing packages, television, outside mailing lists, and a star personality who would play a major role in the club's future.

During January 1975, statement inserts were again sent to the credit file. But this time some segments of the file received a solo mailing on the club 30 days later. A variety of copy approaches, formats, and premiums were tested. Multivariate Linear Regression Analysis (MLRA) was used to learn which segments of the list responded best to the insert and which responded best to the solo mailing.

The combination of the winning package and the MLRA system proved that a selective follow-up mailing would produce a satisfactory incremental response. The solo mailing also made it possible to solicit inactive Charg-all accounts, who were not receiving statements.

As the year went on, the club was promoted through various Wards channels including catalog inserts, in-store advertising, and inserts sent out with new charge plates. To enhance consumer awareness, the club became the official and exclusive U.S. ticket agent for the 1976 Summer Olympic games in Montreal. Advance ticket sales were promoted heavily and generated some excellent news publicity.

Zsa Zsa Gabor tested with TV support

To top off the year, Wards planned a major saturation mailing for November. One that would go to Charg-all customers as well as rented lists—including auto owners. Ward's executives believed that TV support could enhance results so a three-market test was slated for October. The first market received only the mailings. The second used a 30-second TV support spot, featuring an unknown professional announcer, in advance of the mailings. For the third market, TV support was also planned—but with a well-known personality. The choice was Zsa Zsa Gabor. While at first blush,

Exhibit 77. Large newspaper ad with comparison of auto club benefits.

The only thing wrong with AAA is that our new auto club is better.

There really is nothing at all wrong with AAA. And until now, it was about the best auto club you could belong to.

So when we decided to form an auto club, we decided we had to be even better than AAA. And we are. We don't think you can belong to a better auto club than ours at any price.

To join our auto club, you must be a Wards Charg-All customer. And if you are, all you do is fill out and sign a simple form that will soon be mailed to preferred Charg-All customers with their current statements. After that, you're billed just $2.25 per month . . . and get up to $11,000 worth of benefits.

And that's all there is to it.

You get $5,000 of all risk, no exclusion accidental death and dismemberment protection. Higher tow reimbursement — up to $30 per call for emergency and towing services.

Plus up to $200 arrest bond and $5,000 bail bond coverage. Plus $100 emergency travel expenses. Plus worldwide tour discounts that can save you up to hundreds of dollars, merchandise discounts up to 50%, up to $500 legal defense reimbursement, $200 theft reward.

And, 24 hours a day toll-free telephone "hotline" service. Also, 10% discounts for leading hotels and motels and 20% rental car discounts from Avis and National.

And these are just some of the reasons that make our new auto club a truly superior value.

So if you're already a Wards Charg-All customer, you can join our new auto club just by filling out the form that will come in the mail with your current statement.

If you're not a Charg-All customer, become one. It costs nothing, and you'll find your account is extremely convenient for identification, emergency purchases, check cashing and special offers. Simply apply for credit at your local Wards store . . . or call 000-0000.

And that's how you join the new Montgomery Ward Auto Club. We think you'll agree that it's just one great reason why you should have a Wards Charg-All credit card.

Compare ours to theirs.

Club Benefits	Montgomery Ward Auto Club	AAA— Louisiana Division
Coast to coast toll free "Hotline" for info and emergency service	YES	NO
Emergency road and tow coverage	$30 not restricted to a special list of "authorized" service stations or garages	Up to 10 miles maximum claims may be submitted for consideration if authorized garage not available.
Legal Defense Reimbursement	To $500	To $325
Custom Trip Routing	YES	YES
Accidental Death and Dismemberment Protection	Up to $5000 not limited by length of membership.	Up to $2,000 (gradually increasing to $3,000 in 3rd year).
Is the above coverage limited to specified accidents?	NOT LIMITED—NO EXCLUSIONS	YES—limited
Can AD & D benefits be optionally divided between you and spouse?	YES	NO
Hospitalization Benefits	NONE	Up to $10 per day per person insured for a maximum of 365 days for specified accidents only. Plus up to $80 for specified emergency expenses only.
Emergency Travel Expenses	$100	NO
Arrest bond coverage (not available in Calif.)	$200	$200
Bail Bond coverage	$5,000	$5,000
Professional Travel Bureau	YES	YES
Theft Reward	$200	$200
Car Rental Discounts	YES—20%	NO
Hotel/Motel discounts	YES—10%	NO
Mdse./Service Discounts	YES	YES
First year's membership fee for you and spouse	$27.00	$37 (includes $7 initiation fee)

'Common disaster protection pays additional sum of $5,000 only if member and spouse are killed (or die within 48 hours of each other) in the same accident covered under club policy, and have one or more surviving children under the age of 16 are covered for $1,000. Will also pay up to

$2,500 per insured member for certain specified accidents such as railroad, steamship, interurban railway, subway and elevated accidents.

The Montgomery Ward Auto Club

Zsa Zsa might not appear to be the ideal personality to endorse an auto club, research had shown she appealed to all age groups. And the spot provided some good rationale. She explained how all her 17 cars were covered for only $2.25 a month and how nice it was to have other people pay her bills for things like emergency road service (see Exhibit 78). As might be expected, TV support worked better than no television. And the spot with Zsa Zsa worked about 30 percent better than the spot with the unknown announcer.

Exhibit 78. Clip of Zsa Zsa Gabor from TV spot.

So the Zsa Zsa spot was used for a heavy national TV campaign preceding the November mailing. Ten million pieces went to Wards credit file and three million pieces to rented lists. While the response to the rented lists was somewhat disappointing, the over-all results were good. A total of 175,000 club members were added as a result of this single promotion, bringing the year-end membership in MWAC to almost 525,000 members!

Sweepstakes solves double-sell problem

To confirm Zsa Zsa's appeal, two other split tests were made early in 1976. One entailed the Donnelley Carol Wright co-op mailing; the other provided "take one" brochures distributed through supermarket literature racks. In both media the same insert was tested with and without Zsa Zsa. And in both cases she improved response substantially.

Meanwhile, another big mailing was made to the Charg-all list in the spring. The winning test package included a temporary membership card which was computer-personalized, and a five-page letter (see Exhibit 79). The copy built up the exclusivity of the club as indicated by these opening paragraphs:

Dear Mr. Jones,

I don't care if you own a Rolls-Royce, a Mercedes, *and* a Cadillac, you can't join us unless you are qualified.

That's what I have to tell individuals who think that they can muscle their way into our club just because they have money.

Word travels fast. There's no doubt in our mind that Montgomery Ward has created the *finest auto club in the country.*

Exhibit 79. Spring 1976 mailing including temporary membership card.

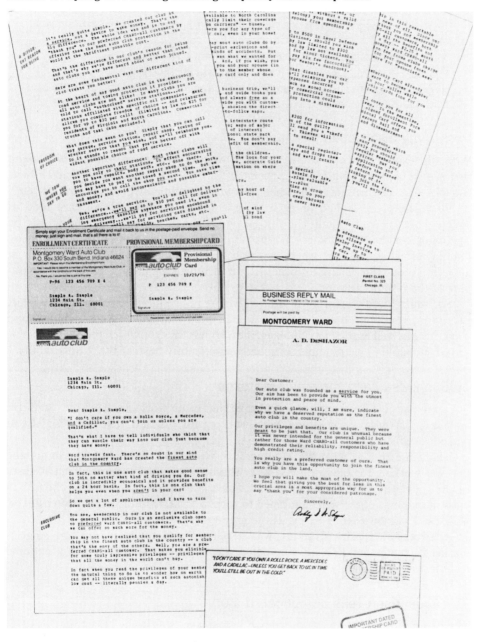

In fact, this is one auto club that makes good sense to join no matter what kind of driving you do. Our club is incredibly economical and it provides benefits on a 24-hour basis. In fact, this is one club that helps you even when you *aren't* in your car!

So we get a lot of applications, and I have to turn down quite a few.

You see, membership in our club is not available to the general public. Ours is an exclusive club open to *preferred* Ward Charg-all customers. That's why we can offer so much more for the money.

Exclusivity also poses problems

While the exclusivity copy strategy worked well when directed to the Wards credit file, it also highlighted a growing problem that Ward's management had to face. Namely, that any promotion aimed at the general public involved a "double sell."

First, the prospect had to be sold on applying for a Charg-all card (and of course, pass the credit qualification). Second, the new applicant had to be sold on signing up for the Montgomery Ward Auto Club. Going a step further, this meant that any effort aimed at prospects not only had to describe the MWAC benefits, it also had to describe Charg-all benefits and include a detailed credit application as part of the response device.

So, while Ward's efforts toward its own credit file had been almost universally successful, results of most outside tests had been marginal. These included auto owner lists as well as a variety of magazines. Unless the double-sell problem could be solved, it wouldn't be possible to expand significantly beyond the Wards family.

Solution: Zsa Zsa plus a sweepstakes

In creative problem solving, one technique that often works is called the "additive approach." You take something that's working for you and add something else to make it even stronger.

That, in effect, is what the Montgomery Ward Auto Club did. The something that was working for them was Zsa Zsa, who had produced good results in all three of the split tests. The additive element was a sweepstakes, a proven technique in mass marketing. These were combined to form a $100,000-Plus Super Sweepstakes, with Zsa Zsa's own Rolls-Royce as the grand prize.

A sweepstakes prize structure was developed and tested in the Los Angeles market in September 1976. It stimulated enrollments dramatically and a national roll-out was immediately planned.

TV Guide insert tells complicated story

The first major promotion of the Super Sweepstakes was in the December 18, 1976, issue of *TV Guide*. A six-panel centerspread insert appeared in editions with a total circulation of 17 million. The four-color insert was well designed to present its somewhat complicated story in a logical way. The front panel announced the sweepstakes and showed Zsa Zsa in front of her Rolls-Royce (see Exhibit 80). The next panel described the complete prize structure. Copy explained that Zsa Zsa's Rolls was valued at $61,000, but a brand-new one was available as an option, if the winner preferred.

Exhibit 80. Front panel of *TV Guide* insert.

Dahling... you can win my lovely
Rolls-Royce

Zsa Zsa

Enter the Montgomery Ward Auto Club
$100,000-Plus

Super Sweepstakes

**Win Zsa Zsa Gabor's Famous Custom-built
Rolls-Royce or a Brand New Rolls**

•

A Cadillac Seville or a Continental Mark V

•

Vacations in Hawaii

•

**1582 Super Prizes
PLUS
if your entry is received by December 31, 1976
you are eligible for a promptness prize
of One Thousand Dollars ($1,000) in Cash.**

To Introduce You To  and help you apply
for a Wards Charg-all
Credit Account

To take care of the double sell, the inside spread devoted one panel to the Charg-all credit card story and one to the auto club (see Exhibit 81). The sweepstakes entry form was prenumbered and had a built-in credit application. The back of the fold-over entry form contained the mailing area and sweepstakes rules.

The insert didn't exactly appear at the best time of the year, but then *TV Guide* centerspreads aren't that easy to get. Apparently the concept was so strong that it overcame the preholiday timing.

The club's president, Dick Cremer, told *Chicago Tribune* advertising columnist George Lazarus, "It's the most incredible success story I've been part of in direct response advertising." Final response to the sweepstakes was over 2 percent. And about a third of the entries—more than 100,000—either opened a Wards credit account, or joined the auto club, or both.

Exhibit 81. Inside spread of *TV Guide* insert.

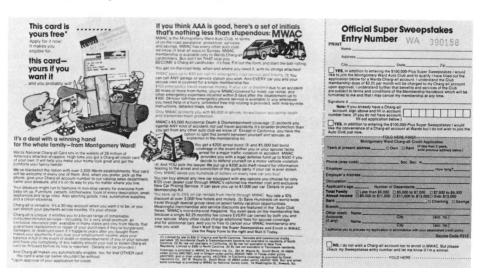

Three-year-old club tops 800,000 members

The Zsa Zsa Sweepstakes was continued into 1977. A 14 million-piece mailing started in late December and ran through February. Also in February, 11 million pieces were released in Donnelley co-ops, and some additional space advertising was scheduled.

By the end of the month, the club celebrated its third anniversary with over 800,000 members signed up. It had been just three years since the first batch of statement inserts went out to Charg-all customers in 22 states. As the chart shows (Exhibit 82), MWAC growth has been quite spectacular.

Membership benefits were steadily improved during this three-year period. *Montgomery Ward Auto Club News,* originally a two-color newsletter, had become an attractive full-color magazine that members received bimonthly. And in 1976 a new optional car pricing service was added, enabling members to get a new car at only $125 over dealer's cost.

Exhibit 82. Montgomery Ward Auto Club membership growth.

Month Ending	Number of Members
February 1975	244,730
May 1975	353,451
August 1975	358,507
November 1975	365,443
February 1976	563,140
May 1976	594,430
August 1976	623,358
November 1976	621,051
February 1977	803,238

Benefits to parent company

The Signature Agency (now known as Signature Financial/Marketing) can indeed be proud of its accomplishments with the auto club for it has provided a number of important benefits to Montgomery Ward in addition to the revenue and profits generated.

First, the club has offered a valuable service to Charg-all customers. And the $2.25 monthly billing has helped reactivate thousands of inactive accounts.

Second, the club has helped to attract new Charg-all accounts and thereby build up the credit customer file. One early group of new accounts generated by the auto club was reviewed a year later. It turned out that most members, besides belonging to the club, had purchased merchandise with their Charg-all cards. And their accounts had an average balance at least as high as accounts opened through other methods.

In addition, Zsa Zsa Gabor has been used for personal appearances at a number of Wards stores. Besides promoting the auto club, she has built excellent store traffic and received extensive publicity for Wards from local media.

Finally, the auto club has helped in the development of additional profit centers. The *Auto Club News,* for example, has become a valuable tool for the club in selling other merchandise and services to members. One recent issue included 45 different merchandise offers from the club.

All in all, the rapid growth of the Montgomery Ward Auto Club is truly remarkable. Especially when you remember that the rapid growth has come primarily from a limited universe of its own customers. I think this is a classic example of what can be done when a parent company is smart enough to see the potential for a new venture and give its management team the freedom to run with it.

An insider's viewpoint

The following comments and observations about the Montgomery Ward Auto Club were provided by Richard E. Cremer, its president:

It's true—the phenomenal growth of the Montgomery Ward Auto Club has come primarily from our own customers. But we've had three key factors going for us: the most sophisticated mailing list availabe in the direct marketing industry, an active testing program to help us get the most out of it, and enthusiastic professionals in key management positions. People like Peter J. Fioresi, vice-president and general manager, who has performed his unique switch from credit manager to direct marketer almost as if he had spent his entire career in direct marketing.

The format of the Charg-all master file was originally developed when we computerized our accounts, starting in 1968. That format contains many demographic characteristics on each of our millions of accounts. The extra input expense for compiling this data was millions of dollars, and it costs us $500,000 annually just to input data for new accounts and update existing ones.

But the subsequent promotional efforts of Signature Financial/Marketing, Inc., have proved this to be a sound investment. We've developed our testing programs for the Auto Club to the point where we've had a significant reduction in our over-all testing costs. By using Multivariate Linear Regression Analysis (MLRA), we've managed to identify and select parts of our master list file that are three to ten times better than others. Thus, we've been able to keep our test cells small enough to minimize cost and still maximize the returns on roll-out mailings.

I'm happy to report that Montgomery Ward Auto Club has topped the one million mark in members. That makes us not only the world's fastest growing auto club, but the third largest full-service auto club in the country—and we're gaining ground fast on Number Two.

17

Truman Library
**Building a Million-Dollar Endowment
through Direct Mail Fund Raising**

In July 1957 the Harry S. Truman Library and Museum was officially opened in Independence, Missouri. The complex was built and furnished entirely by private funds including pennies collected from thousands of school children throughout the country.

The library currently contains more than 10 million letters, memos, reports and documents. In short, all the official papers of the presidency. Papers that capture the spirit and accomplishments of the Truman administration. As President Truman himself said, "The papers of the presidents are among the most valuable source materials for history. They ought to be preserved—and they ought to be used."

With this thought, the Truman Library Institute was established. Its principal goal: Make the library a major research center by providing funds for study of the Truman era, encouraging authorship, and financing additional acquisitions.

For many years the Institute was funded primarily by personal contributions from President Truman, his associates, friends, and admirers. But as the Institute's activities grew and its expenses rose, Truman often expressed a dream. A dream that the Institute could build an endowment fund of $1,000,000 to ensure the continuation of its long-range programs.

The beginnings of a membership program

In 1966 the Truman Library Institute decided to broaden the base of its financial support. It established an Honorary Fellows Program. Those who enrolled committed themselves to giving $25.00 a year to support the Institute's activities.

A modest but successful direct mail program was used to attract Honorary Fellows. Total mailings averaged less than 17,000 pieces per year and were directed to small, but highly select lists. Within a few years, about 1,000 members had been attracted, and a high percentage renewed their membership year after year.

President Truman died in December 1972. The following year the wheels were set in motion to make his dream come true, to build a million-dollar endowment fund, which could be invested and provide a self-perpetuating income for the Institute.

The five-year plan

The Truman Library Institute approached a leading direct marketing agency to discuss the prospect for an ambitious fund-raising program. The Honorary Fellows Program with its contributions of $25.00 per year was discussed as was the solicitation of larger endowment fund contributions of $500 or more.

It was recommended that the larger contributions should be solicited primarily through personal contact on the part of the Truman Library Institute board members. But the Honorary Fellows Program could best be expanded by a large-scale direct mail effort. The idea of having the Institute's work supported by a relatively large number of small donors was appealing. And widespread mailings would also help to acquaint more people with the Library, even if they didn't respond, thus stimulating interest in and visitors to the Library.

Exhibit 83. Truman Library Institute five-year plan summary.

Year	Prospect Mailing Quantity	Promotion Expense*	Gross Income†	Net Income	Percent Expense Ratio
1974	1,000,000	$135,000	$ 135,000	—	100
1975	1,000,000	135,000	258,000	$123,000	52
1976	800,000	108,000	323,000	215,000	33
1977	600,000	81,000	269,000	188,000	30
1978	500,000	67,000	355,000	288,000	19
Totals		$526,000	$1,340,000	$814,000	39

*Includes mailing expense, incentives, and the cost of servicing a first-year member.

†Includes income from both new and renewal members with renewal expense covered by a separate operating budget.

A five-year plan was developed for the direct mail program, which projected a total net income after five years of $814,000 (see Exhibit 83). Like all projections on new programs, the plan was based on many assumptions. But these assumptions would provide the benchmarks against which the progress of the program could be measured. They included:

1. That the initial test mailing would prove successful in acquiring new members at a breakeven rate, roughly calculated at six new members per thousand pieces mailed. In other words, the first year income would offset the promotion expense, any tangible incentives that were offered, and the cost of servicing a new member for the first year.

2. That new members would renew almost as well as the small group of original Honorary Fellows. This group had been renewing at the rate of about 85 percent a year. An 80 percent renewal rate was used to project future revenue from the new members.

3. That a list universe of 500,000 proven names could be developed through list testing and that these lists could be mailed twice a year with a satisfactory response.

4. That the heaviest mail volume would be concentrated in the first couple of years to rapidly build up the base of new members subject to renewal. To allow for attrition from repeated exposure to the same lists and thus a shrinking list universe, Institute officers projected the mailing quantity for new members at a lower level in years three through five.

The economics of fund raising

Almost every fund-raising mailing program is based on the premise that it costs more to get the first contribution from a new donor or member than it does future contributions. But once you have built a mailing list of donors or members, you can secure those future contributions at a very favorable expense-to-income ratio. This is particularly true of a membership-type plan, where the annual renewal provides a structured program for repeat giving.

The five-year plan developed for the Truman Library Institute followed this formula. In securing new members at a breakeven rate, these prospect mailings would show a 100 percent expense-to-income ratio so there would be no net income from first-year members.

But renewals were a different story. Eighty-five percent of the Institute's members were renewing and the only promotion expense was an inexpensive three-piece mailing series. So the renewal expense ratio was running less than 10 percent of income.

The expense ratio shown in the five-year plan is a combination of the efforts to secure new members and renew old ones. As you can see, the expense ratio declines rapidly after the first year reflecting the increasing base of members that are available for renewal and the steady decrease in the quantity of new member mailings.

With these fund-raising economics as background, the five-year plan was presented to the Institute's board of directors. They thought the plan might be somewhat optimistic in expecting an 80 percent renewal rate, since large-scale mailings to a variety of lists might attract Truman supporters who were not as loyal as the hard-core original group. On the other hand, the five-year plan did not reflect the investment income that could be developed year-by-year as the fund started to build up. And, in addition, they would continue to receive renewal income from existing members and solicit endowments through personal contact. The five-year plan was approved. The first mailing tests were scheduled for spring 1974.

The initial Truman mailing

For the initial test, one basic mailing package was created. It consisted of a number 10 envelope, a three-page letter printed on two separate sheets (with the back of the second sheet used to list the Truman Library Institute officers and directors), a small return card, and a business reply envelope (see Exhibit 84).

The entire package was a simple one. There was no brochure or folder. No

Exhibit 84. Initial test mailing.

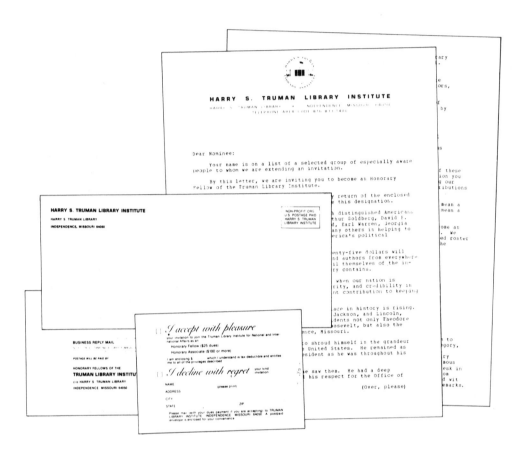

illustrations, other than the Institute's symbol on the letterhead. It was up to the letter copy to tell the story and move people to send their dues payment. I urge you to read it for yourself and see how well it does the job.

Dear Nominee:

Your name is on a list of a selected group of especially aware people to whom we are extending an invitation.

By this letter, we are inviting you to become an Honorary Fellow of the Truman Library Institute.

Please let us know within ten days, by return of the enclosed card, whether you wish to accept or decline this designation.

In accepting, you will be joining such distinguished Americans as Arthur Schlesinger, Jr., I. W. Abel, Arthur Goldberg, David E. Lilienthal, Hubert Humphrey, Clark Clifford, Earl Warren, Georgia Neese Clark Gray, William H. Hastie, and many others in helping to make the Truman Library a vital part of America's political heritage.

Your tax-deductible annual dues of twenty-five dollars will make it possible for students, scholars, and authors from everywhere to come to Independence, Missouri, and avail themselves of the incredibly rich resource materials the Library contains.

At this crucial point in our history, when our nation is groping for rededication to honesty, integrity, and credibility in government, you will be making a significant contribution to keeping alive the spirit of Harry Truman.

As time passes, President Truman's place in history is rising. To the eminence of Washington, Jefferson, Jackson, and Lincoln, historians now add as great American Presidents not only Theodore Roosevelt, Woodrow Wilson, and Franklin Roosevelt, but also the name of Harry Truman of Independence, Missouri.

Mr. Truman made no attempt to shroud himself in the grandeur of the office of President of the United States. He remained as unpretentious after he became President as he was throughout his career.

But he called the shots as he saw them. He had a deep reverence for history, and placed his respect for the Office of President far above his own ego needs. He made outstanding appointments to high-level positions and trusted them to do their jobs.

And he steered the nation with a steady hand through the dramatic days of winding up World War II . . . formation of the United Nations . . . quick recognition and warm support of the newly declared State of Israel . . . the Marshall Plan for rebuilding Western Europe . . . his 1948 "Whistle Stop" campaign and his stunning upset victory over Thomas E. Dewey in the face of seemingly impossible odds . . . the Berlin Airlift . . . bold American leadership of the United Nations' response to the invasion of South Korea by North Korea.

On his desk sat a homely sign given to him by an admirer. Its words have since passed into history, indelibly associated with President Truman's strong sense of personal responsibility for the actions of his subordinates: "The buck stops here."

When President Truman retired, he wished to preserve the papers and other historical material of his administration and make them available to all the people in a place suited for study and research. In addition, gifts from heads of state and ordinary citizens, as well as other items associated with him and his career, filled many rooms and needed a large museum facility in which to be properly displayed.

To realize this dream, The Harry S. Truman Library and Museum was built in Independence with funds contributed by thousands of individuals and organizations throughout the United States. The building and its contents were then donated to the U.S. Government. It is administered by the National Archives and Records Service as an integral part of the nation's record-keeping system.

But this does not provide any funds for encouraging research and authorship and for financing additional acquistions, two essentials to the continuing vitality of the Library in the stream of American history and culture.

So the Truman Library Institute was formed to provide funds for these worthwhile objectives.

About two hundred fifty deserving students, scholars, and authors have been able to come to the Library for research through grants-in-aid by the Library Institute for travel and living expenses. From these and other researchers have come hundreds of graduate papers and over 80 published books. But more funds are needed to continue and expand this program.

As an Honorary Fellow, you will receive recognition and appreciation for your support in the following:

1. An individually inscribed annual membership card, permitting free admission to the museum of the Library for you and your family accompanying you. Approximately three million people have visited the museum. Appointments may be made for a guided tour of the exhibit galleries and behind the scenes in the research area.

2. The Library Institute Newsletter, "Whistle Stop," published throughout the year to keep the Honorary Fellows informed of the fruits of their support.

3. A three-inch, half-pound, solid bronze Truman presidential medallion, obtainable only from the United States Mint, the Truman Library, collectors, and rare coin dealers.

4. Your name recorded in a leatherbound Register of Honorary Fellows, as one of the exhibits viewed by the millions of Americans who will visit the Library museum for generations to come.

5. Unexpected little privileges of Fellowship from time to time will include invitations to special programs and addresses and to receptions at the openings of new exhibits, or the printed programs of a Truman memorial occasion which you cannot personally attend.

But, of course, far more important to you than any of these tokens of appreciation will be simply the inner satisfaction you will have in keeping the Truman spirit alive and enriching our political process with a better understanding of his contributions to the American democratic tradition.

We do hope you will accept this invitation. It will mean a great deal to us if you do so, and we are certain it will mean a great deal to you.

But whether you wish to accept this invitation to become an Honorary Fellow or not, please let us know within ten days. We want to "close the books" on the next edition of our printed roster containing the names of Honorary Fellows. Thank your for the courtesy of your reply.

Sincerely yours,

W. Averell Harriman
(Signature)

John W. Snyder
(Signature)

PS: For those whose good fortune or achievement permit them to contribute $100 or more, we have created a special category, Honorary Associates. New members in this category will receive, in addition to all of the privileges of Honorary Fellowship listed above, (1) an exact replica of the famous sign, "The Buck Stops Here," that sat on Mr. Truman's desk in the Oval Office of the White House, and (2) "The Man from Missouri," a little book of memorable words, wisdom, and wit of Mr. Truman, culled from his speeches, letters, and remarks.

The only package variation in the initial test was a computer letter. The copy was identical to the basic mailing with the individual's name and address added at the top of the letter and a personalized salutation. In addition, a window envelope was used so the letter would serve as the address vehicle. One hundred thousand pieces were slated for the initial mailing, with that quantity spread out over the two package variations and ten different test lists of political donors and likely prospects.

The marketing strategy behind the mailing

Even a mailing that appears to be a simple one can have a lot of thought and effort behind it. Here's how the Institute's ad agency described the marketing strategy for the initial mailing:

Heightening the prestige appeal. Members are asked to donate $25.00 a year and are designated as Honorary Fellows of the Institute. They already include many of America's most distinguished citizens. Our letter points out this prestigious association and emphasizes the nomination and invitation aspects of the appeal, even down to the salutation, "Dear Nominee."

Making the appeal timely. With Watergate and the impeachment crisis so predominant in the news, we felt such could not be ignored, yet it would have been tasteless to refer to this directly. So we confined our copy to a one-sentence reference to "this crucial point in our history," and suggest that, in a curious way, contributing to the Institute means doing something about Watergate.

Re-selling President Truman. Mr. Truman is undoubtedly far more popular in memory today than he was when he retired from office. We feel it is important to remind the reader of the elements of his greatness.

"Tangibilizing" the prestige of belonging. So often a giver gets nothing in return except a momentary intangible feeling of satisfaction. We feel that much more satisfaction can be offered if the reward is a tangible permanent reminder of the giver's generosity and importance. So we developed an important program of membership benefits ranging from a Truman medallion to having the giver's name recorded in a leatherbound register to be kept in the Library.

Providing a "deluxe option." Experienced direct marketers know that a deluxe option, such as a leather-bound edition of a book you are selling, will almost invariably be chosen by about 10 percent of the respondents. To provide such an option, we created a new membership category, that of Honorary Associates, "for those whose good fortune or achievement permit them to contribute $100." Members in this category are promised two additional tangible benefits, including a replica of the famous "The Buck Stops Here" sign.

Requesting a yes *or* no *decision.* In keeping with the invitation nature of the copy, the return card provides two check boxes. The recipient can check off "I accept with pleasure" or "I decline with regret." We feel this is a logical extension of the letter, which calls for a decision in ten days. By asking people to make an immediate decision, we expect to pick up enough additional affirmative responses to justify paying the return postage on the negative replies.

Regional segmentation of lists. We suspect that people living in the Midwest will have stronger feelings of identification with Mr. Truman and are more likely to visit the Museum. Thus the membership benefits of free admission and having their names recorded in a leatherbound membership roster could have more appeal. So a special list test is recommended to measure the response from Missouri and its five bordering states against a national sample of the same lists.

Encouraging results

Apparently, the marketing strategy was sound; the results of the initial mailing were highly encouraging. When the test mailing was costed out in quantity runs, the breakeven turned out to be a little less than five responses per thousand. As shown by the summary below, which uses an index of 100 for breakeven, the control mailing exceeded this target on seven out of ten test lists.

Democratic political donors.................... 129
McGovern donor list.......................... 142
Affluent contributors........................ 38
Social scientists............................. 35
Forum for Contemporary History............. 214
Center Magazine subscribers.................. 163
Vista Magazine subscribers.................. 222
New Republic subscribers..................... 115
Law Journal subscribers..................... 108
Wealthy individuals......................... 34

About 8 percent of those who accepted membership contributed at the higher $100 level designated for Honorary Associates. This resulted in an average contribution of $34.22. Even the negative responses were substantial with a ratio of seven *no's* to every one *yes*.

The computer letter was split-tested on eight of the ten lists. While it showed some improvement on a couple of the lists, the over-all results were almost identical to the control. The regional segmentation test, however, was another story. On the three lists where the midwestern states were tested against a random sample of the same national list, results increased over 50 percent!

The first roll-out mailing

Based on the encouraging results from the initial test, the Truman Library Institute released about 575,000 pieces in September 1974. The mailing included a number of refinement tests on the basic control package, plus over 45 different list tests.

Over-all results were disappointing, with an average response rate of less than four new members per thousand. Only about a dozen of the lists produced results at or near breakeven. The poor response on the other lists pulled the over-all average down to less than breakeven. It was felt later that results had been hurt by mailing in a pre-election period, when many candidates and political organizations were seeking funds by mail and the competition was severe. Then, too, most fund raisers reported poor results that fall as inflation increased and the economy began to take a turn for the worse.

The package tests did, however, prove interesting. The highlights of these tests included:

• The same letter printed on one side only of four separate sheets did 28 percent better than the original letter, which was printed front and back on two separate sheets. And the four-sheet package added only about 10 percent to the in-the-mail cost.

- Deleting the negative option on the return card cut positive response by 25 percent. The strategy of requesting a *yes* or *no* decision did help bring in more affirmative replies.
- Asking the prospect to supply his or her own postage on the return envelope (instead of providing business reply prepaid postage) did not reduce the *yes* responses, but it did cut the *no* responses by 50 percent. So this offered a chance to save some money on return postage.
- Adding a temporary membership card as a stub on the return card boosted response 17 percent and added less than 5 percent to costs. This larger return card also allowed the package to be mailed in a window envelope with the return card pre-addressed (see Exhibit 85).

Exhibit 85. Return card with temporary membership card on stub.

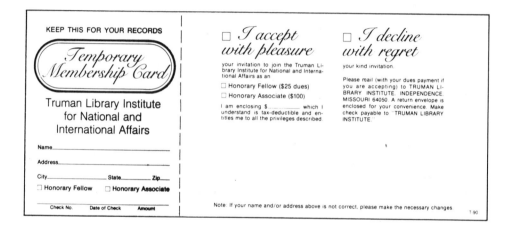

An assessment of first-year results

Final results after the first year's mailing program were mixed. The Truman Library Institute had an established control mailing which had been modified and improved somewhat by the fall tests. But its list universe appeared to be rather small; only about a dozen lists had paid out. Fortunately, a couple of these were pretty good-sized lists with a substantial number of names.

Because the fall mailing had been much larger than the spring test and the results poorer, the over-all program for 1974 did not produce new members at the break-even goal that had been established. Expenses actually exceeded first-year-member revenue by 13 percent. But on the "plus" side of the ledger, the two mailings had produced over 3,000 new Truman Library Institute members and more than $100,000 in income. The real key would be how the renewal turned out the following year. So it was decided to proceed with the new-member acquisition plan the following year but on a more cautious or limited basis until a renewal history could be built up.

Exhibit 86. New member welcome package.

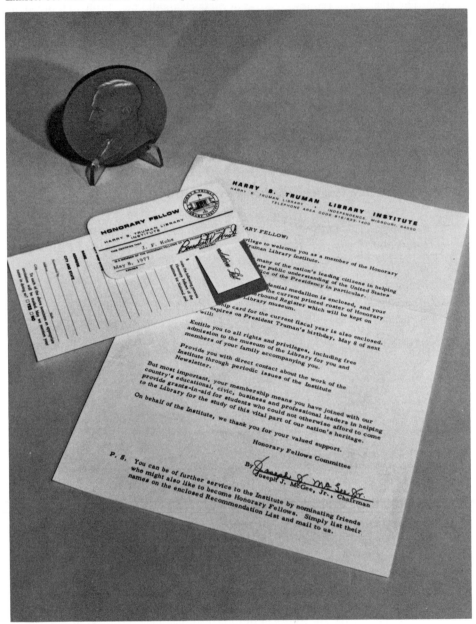

The renewal program

For an effective renewal program, you begin laying the groundwork as soon as a new member is signed up. That's what the Truman Library Institute does. New members receive their bronze Truman presidential medallion, a personalized membership card, and a welcome letter pointing out that all memberships expire on May 8, the date of President Truman's birthday. A referral card is also enclosed so new members can send in the names and addresses of friends who might be interested in joining (see Exhibit 86). And, of course, the Honorary Associate members also receive "The Buck Stops Here" sign and a book. After the welcome package, members regularly receive the "Whistle Stop" newsletter to keep them in touch with the activities of the Institute.

The new members acquired in 1974 were due for their first renewal in May 1975. The renewal series included four separate mailings for the $25.00 regular members with variations of the same mailings used for the $100 associate members.

The first mailing went out April 8, a month before the May 8 expiration date. It included an outer envelope, one-page letter, renewal invoice card, and an enclosure slip explaining the different membership categories (see Exhibit 87). The letter

Exhibit 87. First renewal mailing.

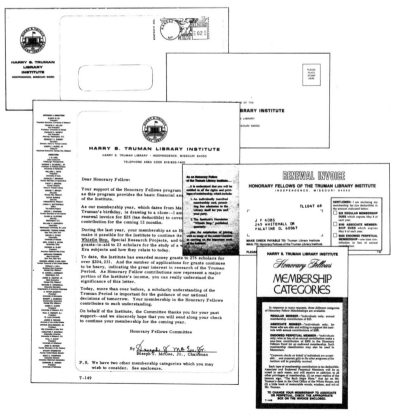

pointed out some of the Institute's accomplishments in the past year and urged members to continue their support. A postscript indicated there were two other membership categories for consideration—the $100 associate membership category and a $500 perpetual membership—and directed the member to the enclosure slip.

The second mailing went out a month later to those who hadn't yet renewed. The mailing contained all the same elements as the first renewal effort plus an "important notice" slip that pointed out another copy of the letter and invoice were enclosed (see Exhibit 88).

Another month later, early in June, the third mailing was released. It included a somewhat more hard-hitting letter, stressing the importance of each member's renewal to the success of the Truman Library Institute program. At this point, the strategy was shifted from trying to upgrade the member, if possible, to merely getting a renewal of his or her $25.00 dues (see Exhibit 89).

The final renewal effort followed a month later and pointed out this would be the last reminder a member would receive. It mentioned that a new membership roster would be going to press shortly, and the member's contribution had to be received soon to make sure his or her name would be included (see Exhibit 90).

Exhibit 88. Second renewal mailing.

Exhibit 89. Third renewal mailing.

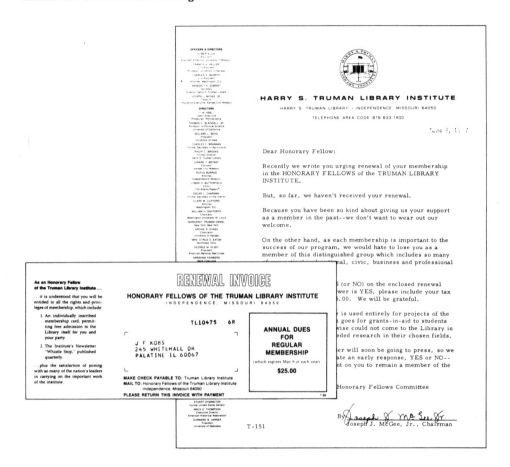

The renewal series received by Honorary Associates was similar. However, the slip covering the different membership categories was eliminated from the first two mailings. Only the final mailing mentioned the $25.00 category in an effort to salvage the member by downgrading him or her, if necessary, to a lower dues level.

When the renewal series was completed 56 percent of the regular members and 50 percent of the associate members had been renewed. While these percentages were considerably lower than the historical 85 percent renewal rate of old members, it still provided very satisfactory results. The expense-to-income ratio was about 10 percent. If the renewal percentage would continue to improve year by year, a new five-year projection showed that the combined income-to-expense ratio for acquiring *and* renewing new members would come in at less than 50 percent. This was considered a satisfactory rate for continuing the program to build a million-dollar endowment fund.

Exhibit 90. Fourth and final renewal mailing.

Later test highlights

The Truman Library Institute continued to solicit new members throughout 1975 and 1976. While the mailing universe was smaller than had been hoped for, the more limited mailings produced members at an acceptable cost. While one or two new copy approaches or formats were tested each year, it wasn't until fall 1976 when a new control package was established.

This package used the same basic copy as the original control but presented it in a more formal invitation package (see Exhibit 91). It produced over 20 percent better response than the control with no significant difference in the mailing cost.

Meanwhile, the second-year renewal of the new members acquired in 1974 showed a substantial improvement. Regular members, who had renewed at 56 percent the first year, jumped to a 75 percent renewal rate the second year. And associate members showed a corresponding increase, from 50 percent the first year to 71 percent the second year.

After three years—80 percent of goal!

The Truman Library Institute is typical of many direct marketing programs I've seen. Some of the original assumptions did not turn out as planned and a number of changes and adjustments have been made in the original mailing plan. But if the concept itself is appealing to enough people, one can still build a viable program.

Exhibit 91. Invitation mailing package.

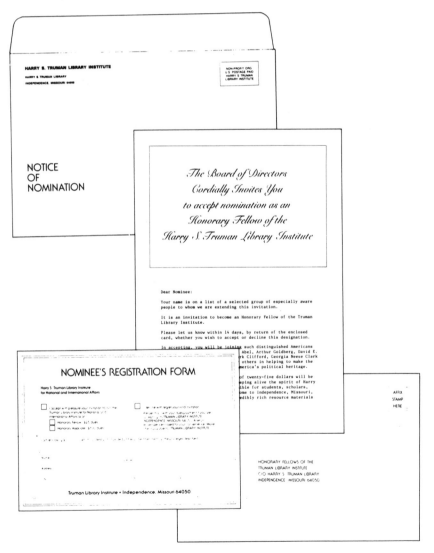

At the end of only three years, the Institute had reached 80 percent of the $1,000,000 goal for its endowment fund. And it passed the goal in May of 1978, seven months ahead of schedule!

Both the personal effort to secure large contributions and the direct mail effort had proved successful, with the Honorary Fellows program playing a key role in helping President Truman's dream for the endowment fund become a reality.

An insider's viewpoint

The following comments about the Truman Library Institute's fund-raising program were provided by Joseph J. McGee, Jr. Mr. McGee is treasurer of the Institute and chairman of the Honorary Fellows Committee. He is also president of Old American Insurance Company, and his extensive direct marketing background provided the inspiration for the Truman mailing program.

> Accomplishing President Truman's dream that the Institute would one day be made financially secure through the establishment of a fund of at least $1,000,000 is now assured, thanks to the expansion of the Honorary Fellows direct mail solicitation program.
>
> Although the Institute's experience prior to the expansion of the program provided a certain degree of assurance, it was the broad experience and confidence of the experts at our ad agency, particularly Bob Stone and Tom Collins, that gave us at the Institute the courage to test-mail those first 100,000 pieces in 1974.
>
> I well recall the day that Tom Collins, who wrote the original copy, came from New York to visit the Truman Library and home in Independence. Although Tom was renowned for his direct mail fund-raising successes, he wanted to see and feel firsthand what he was to write about. The sign of a true expert.
>
> While initially we were concerned with the concept of just breaking even the first year, the renewal projections made it clear to us that, in the final analysis, the cost-benefit ratio made the expanded program feasible.
>
> We now have reached our initial goal. But, as this goal was set almost 20 years ago, we must continue until the purchasing power of our fund in today's dollars is at least equivalent to what the initial goal anticipated. Indeed, a continuing challenge, but one I'm confident we can meet.

18

Fingerhut Corporation:
How the Leading Mail Order Merchandiser
Reversed Its Growth to Revive Profits

In 1975, one of the leading mail order merchandisers chalked up a sales volume of $243,861,377—and lost $7,451,887 in the process! The company was Fingerhut, one of the fast-growing giants of direct marketing. After years of solid growth, the firm was approaching a quarter billion in annual sales volume. Its product offerings included home furnishings, apparel, recreation and travel items, small appliances, and automotive accessories. Aside from the giant catalog firms like Wards and Sears, it had become the nation's leading mail order merchandiser.

Then the bottom fell out. Results dropped. Costs increased. Profits vanished. Here's how Fingerhut's aggressive management faced up to the problem and overcame it.

The beginnings of a family business

In 1948, Manny Fingerhut was manager of a used car lot. He became dissatisfied and decided to join his older brother, William, who had a small business producing seat covers. In those days, most Detroit automobiles came with car seats that weren't too durable. They could be torn or stained rather easily. Owners kept their cars for a longer period of time so it was fairly common to buy seat covers, either to protect the original car seats or cover them up when they became worn.

The business was located in a Minneapolis garage. The brothers divided the management duties with William handling production and Manny taking over the sales and bookkeeping. There were only four other employees in those days, and the business was grossing less than $100,000 a year.

A year later, in 1949, the Fingerhut brothers came up with their first breakthrough idea. The inspiration came in the form of a mailing from a firm selling neckties by mail. Why couldn't we sell seat covers by mail, they thought, and expand our sales beyond the local Minneapolis-St. Paul market?

The obvious market was car owners. The Fingerhut brothers found a mailing list of new car buyers and bought a small quantity of names in areas surrounding Minneapolis. An advertising agency was used to develop a circular. They sent out the mailing and waited. The mailing pulled an incredible 8 percent response and Fingerhut was on its way.

The firm naturally expanded to lists of new car buyers from other states. Four years later, by 1952, the fledgling company had been converted entirely to mail order. Its sales volume had expanded ten-fold, and was close to $1 million annually.

Surviving the first crisis

In the middle fifties, the firm faced its first real challenge. Most of the car interiors coming out of Detroit had been upgraded. The car seats were now covered with vinyls and nylons that stood up much better than cloth. And a variety of attractive patterns and colors were offered to the car purchaser. In short, not the kind of car seats you'd want to hide under inexpensive seat covers.

The second big idea came at this point and it probably saved the business from going under. Fingerhut's seat cover line was switched to a transparent plastic. The clear plastic allowed the car owner to show off the attractive pattern that came with the car, and at the same time provide protection.

Formula established by early mailings

Through experimentation and testing, Fingerhut's seat cover mailing package soon evolved into a basic pattern that was a forerunner of things to come.

A typical mailing package from 1960, for example, featured the following elements: A number 10 envelope, a one-page letter, a four-page brochure, a two-sided gift slip, a large swatch of the seat cover material, and a combination order form/return envelope (see Exhibit 92). Both the letter and envelope included hand-written notations to add a personal touch. And the package was mailed first class. The brochure had a four-color front cover, with a glamour shot of a car interior. The headline promised "Now your car interior can look this lovely—*for life!*" The inside and back panel of the brochure were only two colors, but they emphasized a strong offer: Free 30-day inspection, three months to pay, and a lifetime guarantee for repair or replacement of the seat cover.

A lot of people associate Fingerhut mailings with multiple free gift offers, which is something they were doing even back in 1960. One side of the gift slip offered a free pair of visor covers, the other a free pair of door panels. The order form offered a free litter bag. And all three free gifts were in a transparent plastic that matched the seat covers. The order form provided a choice of front seat covers only for $11.95—or front and rear for $19.95.

Two decades of expansion

The crisis that caused that switch to transparent seat covers had an important long-range impact on Fingerhut's growth. For it led to expanding the product line into other areas.

The company first tested other merchandise in 1957, when it was approached by a syndicator who represented a number of different manufacturers. A variety of offers were test-mailed to the Fingerhut customer list. Three emerged as solid winners the first year—drills, dishes, and towels. More were added the following year to start a steady expansion of the product line.

Exhibit 92. Early Fingerhut mailing on seat covers.

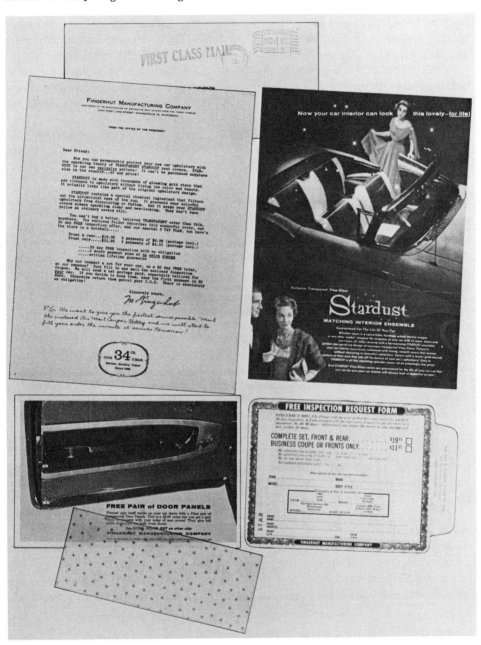

Car coat launches apparel line

In 1959, Fingerhut began diversifying its manufacturing operation. The first item it tackled outside of seat covers was vinyl car coats. They were merchandised in pairs as His 'n Her Car Coats—the mailing offered both for $19.95 (see Exhibit 93).

The coat package did so well to the customer list that it was soon being mailed to cold prospects. Before long, it replaced seat covers as the main offer to bring in new customers. And the coats went on to become the single most popular item Fingerhut has ever offered.

In 1967, for example, they sold 2.8 million coats. The following year they sold 3.5 million coats, and with the price up to $24.95 a pair, generated almost $44 million in revenue.

Continued growth of product line

Spurred by the success of the syndicated merchandise offers and its own car coats, Fingerhut embarked on a steady program of new product testing. Here's how Meyer Nemer, who was in charge of merchandising for 17 years, once described the selection process:

> New product discovery and development is a constant challenge requiring continual searching and test mailings. Although literally thousands of products are offered to us and as many as a hundred tested each year, the task is made somewhat easier by the fact that we have established screening criteria.

> We look for products which are basic rather than faddish. Products which are used in and around the home and whose benefits and value can be easily seen and demonstrated in our advertising material. Some physical constraints are imposed by the fact that most of our products are delivered by mail. A few years ago we had no more than a handful of regular items; today we are at 40 and hope to add more each year.

What type of products passed this selection process and were successfully tested? Over three-dozen are shown in the accompanying chart, broken down by apparel, tool and auto accessories, travel and leisure, home furnishings, and high priced merchandise (see Exhibit 94).

As the Fingerhut product line expanded, so did its manufacturing capabilities. Before long, the items it made represented about half of the firm's sales volume, including luggage, power tools, dinnerware, apparel, and seat covers. Because there are obvious economies when a firm manufactures its own goods, these items provided a better profit margin. And this better margin, in turn, made these items favorites for prospect mailings, since Fingerhut could afford a higher selling cost per order.

Low-priced offers for prospects

While Fingerhut built an extensive line of proven products, only about six to eight items were consistently used for prospect mailings to bring in new customers. Besides being items that were Fingerhut-manufactured, they were low-priced, in the $19.95 to $29.95 category.

A typical example was the firm's Master Craft power saw. The outer envelope had the look of a blueprint, with white rules and numerals reversed out of a blue

Exhibit 93. Circular from early mailing on car coats.

Exhibit 94. Fingerhut merchandise offers (38 products that passed Fingerhut's screening process and were offered successfully).

Apparel	His 'n her car coats, his 'n her ranch coats, shirts, slacks, men's clothing, women's fashions, robe and gown, shoes
Tool and auto accessories	Drills, grass shears, paint guns, hand tool sets, saws, clear seat covers, auto tune-up kit, power vac
Travel and leisure merchandise	Safari lantern, luggage, radios, sport goods, cassette recorder, coins
Home furnishings merchandise	Cooker-fryer, food grinder, iron, dishes, flatware, stoneware, floor polisher, vacuum cleaner, bedroom ensemble, comforters
High priced merchandise	Microwave oven, movie cameras, sewing machine, typewriter, 8-track stereo, char-b-que

background. The three-page letter had gummed *yes* and *no* stamps tipped on the top, and handwritten notations alongside the body copy. The four-color circular was simple but dramatic with oversize action photographs. An official-looking order form and a variety of gift slips rounded out the package (see Exhibit 95).

The saw was offered at $29.95. The addition of finance charges plus shipping and handling called for nine monthly payments of $3.93. The offer was sweetened with three free gifts: a 7-piece screwdriver set, a 17-piece socket and box wrench set, and a 16-piece dinnerware set.

What kind of prospects did Fingerhut seek out with offers like this? Primarily those in lower and middle-income categories. This of course, is a large market—an important consideration for a firm devoted to a high-volume operation. A recent list data card showed that 75 percent of Fingerhut customers earned less than $14,000, 70 percent were in the 45 to 54 age bracket, and 56 percent were women.

Customer promotions and testing formulas

As the firm continued to grow and promote its own products, Fingerhut was reportedly able to acquire new customers at a profit. But it didn't take long for the firm to recognize the value of its customer list.

A separate marketing department was formed for promoting the customer list, and it was mailed repeatedly. One source indicated a Fingerhut customer would get 35 to 40 mailings a year. These tended to be somewhat higher-priced items, with $45.00 as the average ticket and a few items getting up into the $300 to $400 range. The customer list was soon generating more than 50 percent of the firm's total revenue.

Exhibit 95. Mailing package on power saw.

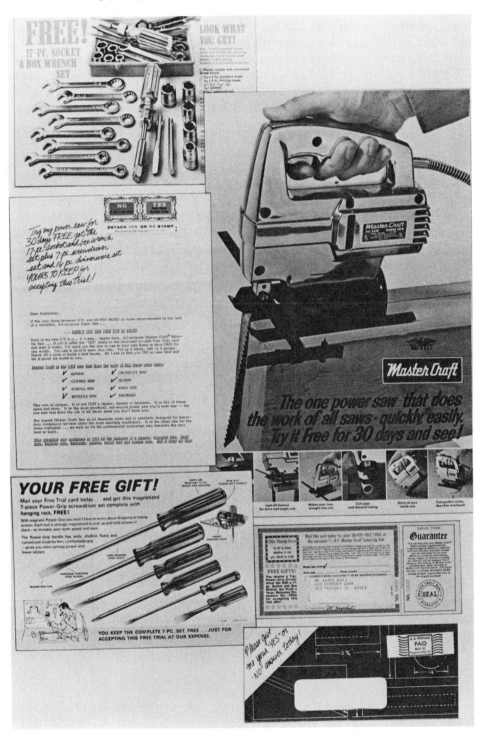

Fingerhut's typical testing pattern on a new item was to select 10,000 to 20,000 names from its customer list. While the front-end response would be known in a few weeks, returned merchandise and bad debts would also be monitored closely. So a test would not be considered complete until nine months had passed.

If the first test proved successful, a continuation mailing would be made of up to 200,000 pieces. If results held up, the item was added to the product line for regular customer promotions. Once Fingerhut had established a large stable of proven products, it was not unusual for them to have to test twenty items—just to find one winner.

Fingerhut in the early seventies

From the time Fingerhut started to broaden its product line in the late fifties, it chalked up a steady record of sales increases (see Exhibit 96). In 1965, it was still doing a volume of less than $50 million a year. The firm completed 1973 with total sales of $219,765,000—a 358 percent increase in just nine years. (While a public stock offering had been made in 1970, the Fingerhut family still controlled the majority of the stock.)

Exhibit 96. Fingerhut's nine-year growth record (in thousands of dollars).

Fiscal Years	Total Net Revenues	Percentage Increase Over Previous Year	Net Earnings
1965	$ 47,923	—	$3,126
1966	71,409	49	5,375
1967	92,314	29	6,519
1968	117,143	27	4,333
1969	112,243	(4)	4,646
1970	124,362	11	4,755
1971	141,242	14	4,811
1972	173,880	23	6,581
1973	219,765	26	8,391

Source: Fingerhut Corporation's 1973 Annual Report.

At this point the firm was mailing over 250 million pieces a year. Which meant that about a million pieces of Fingerhut promotion mail were being released each working day. And the firm filled more than five million orders in 1973.

Fingerhut's product offerings had become well diversified, falling into four main categories and two smaller ones:

Product Category	1973 Sales Volume	Percentage of Total Sales
Home furnishings	$72,522,323	33
Home entertainment, recreation, and travel items	39,557,631	18
Portable tools and home appliances . . .	57,138,800	26
Clothing	39,557,631	18
Automotive accessories	8,790,585	4
Products being tested	2,197,646	1
Totals	$219,764,616	100

The automotive accessories were, of course, the seat covers that had started the whole business about 25 years earlier. The mailing package naturally looked quite different now, but was still being mailed regularly to new car buyers.

By the early seventies, Fingerhut had become one of the largest direct marketing firms in the world. It had a number of major accomplishments to its credit and was still exploring other changes. Notable ones included:

First, the company's direct mail promotions had been switched almost entirely to computer-personalized formats. A typical one was its luggage offer. It was mailed in a brown kraft envelope, that had become a Fingerhut favorite. The computer letter was in a four-page format, with a detachable, personalized order card at the top of the first page. Naturally, there was an attractive four-color circular and a variety of free gift offers including a surprise or mystery gift (see Exhibit 97).

Second, Fingerhut had built an enviable reputation for list sophistication. All lists were carefully screened before they were even tested. And it was one of the first firms in the industry to develop its own duplication elimination system.

Third, while solo direct mail packages were still its mainstay, other promotion avenues were being developed. A 36-page mini-catalog was tested for the first time in 1973, which later lead to semiannual customer mailings. Space advertising was being tested. Television selling was tested and expanded. And package inserts were being used extensively in shipments going out from other direct marketing firms.

Fourth, foreign markets were being explored. The firm had been operating in Canada for a number of years, but in 1972 it made its first test mailing in France. This led to the establishment of a French subsidiary in 1973, while other test mailing programs were launched in England and Germany.

As Fingerhut reached the end of its first quarter century of direct marketing activity, it naturally looked forward to continued growth and expansion.

Two years of problems

The years 1974 and 1975 saw problems developing for business in general, and direct marketers in particular. The U.S. economy was suffering from galloping double-digit inflation, shortages of merchandise, and towering interest rates—factors that would lead to a recession in 1975.

Exhibit 97. Computer-personalized mailing package on luggage.

Fingerhut suffered the first major reversal in its history. Its 1974 sales rose 20 percent to a record $264 million. But profits plunged from $8.4 million to $1.2 million. And things got worse in '75 when sales dropped 8 percent and the company recorded a loss of $7.5 million. While there were many contributing factors, let's just examine some of the main ones.

Product shortages bring cost increases

There was a general shortage of many raw materials, but the Arab oil embargo brought about the worst ones for Fingerhut. Petrochemicals, used in making seat covers, luggage, and car coats, were almost impossible to obtain. And those that were available had tripled or quadrupled in price in the space of a few months.

Besides its own manufacturing problems, many of the firm's oldest and most reliable suppliers were unable to fulfill shipping commitments. This increased expenses in terms of customer service and correspondence, and caused order cancellations from impatient consumers.

Promotion costs also increase

In March 1974 there was an across-the-board postage increase. Third class rates had the biggest impact on Fingerhut with a 26 percent increase to 6.3¢. In addition, it faced a 25 percent increase in first class rates and a 6 percent increase in fourth class or parcel post. Other mailing costs were also increasing sharply, especially paper, which was in short supply.

Despite both product and promotion cost increases, Fingerhut was not able to immediately pass along its higher costs to consumers. The government's Cost of Living Council did not allow the firm to raise prices until its '74 fiscal year was almost over. And even then, it first had to do price-test mailings to make sure the higher prices wouldn't kill its response rates.

Interest rates and bad debts

Because Fingerhut was offering extended payment terms on virtually everything sold, it was normal to maintain a large line of credit. But the record high interest rates substantially boosted the firm's interest costs, the expense of financing its consumer credit. Worse yet, consumers—faced with the same inflationary economy—were taking longer to make payments. And some weren't paying at all. Fingerhut's allowance for bad debts was 8.1 percent in 1973. It jumped to 11.1 percent in '74 and hit 13 percent in '75.

Here's how one Fingerhut top executive explained it: "Inflation has taken away a lot of the income our customers thought they had when they ordered the merchandise. We found there were a lot of accounts where the customer made some payments, but then lapsed. They made an honest attempt, but they were having difficulty in paying."

Foreign operations become unprofitable

Despite a promising early start, Fingerhut's foreign operations contributed to its financial problems. The firm's French subsidiary suffered through a six-week postal strike and was never fully able to recover the lost revenue. The European economy then began to duplicate the problems experienced in the States. Customer response dropped off and bad debts increased.

The Canadian operation experienced similar difficulties, though not as severe. Intermittent postal strikes, a high rate of returned goods, bad debts, and rising operating costs all added up to a $1.7 million loss in Canada for 1975, while the European operations lost $3.4 million for the same period.

Planned sales reduction keys recovery

Manny Fingerhut was still active in the business at this point. But some years before the problems developed, he had turned the main task of running the company over to other family members. As the problems built up in 1974, one of the firm's vice-presidents, Theodore Deikel, was moved up to president. A year later, he was named chief executive officer and began assembling a young, progressive management team. Some of the problems the company faced almost solved themselves as the economy improved. But Deikel didn't wait for it to happen. Some drastic measures were taken to reverse Fingerhut's decline.

Concentration on customer list

The first step in the planned sales reduction program was to cut back on prospect mailings and concentrate on promotions to the customer list. This meant a larger percentage of sales would be made to credit-worthy names who had bought from Fingerhut before.

In addition, new credit scoring techniques were installed for prospect mailings. The combination resulted in a significant reduction in bad debt losses, from 13 percent in 1975 to 8.9 percent in 1976 and 6.8 percent by 1978. The decrease in accounts receivable also meant a reduction in borrowing and interest expense.

Wide-ranging cost economies

Deikel's team did the obvious things like reducing the number of employees, postponing pay increases for salaried employees, reducing compensation of senior executives, and temporarily shutting down certain manufacturing facilities.

But Deikel went beyond that. Through organizational changes and improved control systems, his management team reduced inventories on both raw materials and finished goods. This led to a further reduction in borrowing and interest expense.

Advanced computer systems were installed to speed fulfillment and reduce order processing expense. The computer-personalized order forms included in each mailing became turn-around documents and, when they were returned, they were fed directly into the computer via optical scanning. Other computer systems covered everything from on-line order accessibility, for better handling of customer inquiries, to a computerized postage system to calculate postage and address package labels.

Foreign operations terminated

In 1975 Fingerhut established a reserve for the disposition or liquidation of its European subsidiaries. The following year the operations in England and Germany were suspended, and ownership of the subsidiary in France was transferred to two French nationals. Because of the continuation of significant losses in Canada, plans were also made to dispose of or liquidate that operation.

Product emphasis shifted

While Fingerhut continued to promote products in the same categories as before, there were a couple of major shifts. First, the apparel line was diversified and appropriate manufacturing capabilities developed. While apparel had accounted for 18 percent of sales in the firm's 1973 fiscal year, it climbed to 30 percent by 1976 and 35 percent in 1977 (see Exhibit 98). These clothing products provided more potential for repeat purchases.

Product testing was also increased and, by 1976, represented almost 10 percent of sales. A number of new products were successfully added to the line. And a long-range program was begun to upgrade product quality and help build customer satisfaction.

Exhibit 98. Fingerhut's shifting product emphasis (in percentages).

Sales by product category	1977	1976	1975	1974	1973
Home furnishings...................	30	23	31	36	33
Home entertainment, recreation, and travel items...................	9	15	24	21	18
Portable home appliances and tools...............	14	20	14	20	26
Clothing.........................	35	30	23	16	18
Automotive accessories..............	3	3	3	3	4
Products being tested...............	9	9	5	4	1
Totals.......................	100	100	100	100	100

Source: Fingerhut Corporation's 1977 Annual Report.

Looking ahead

No direct marketing executive in his or her right mind would willingly ask for the kind of problems Fingerhut faced in '74 and '75. But as it turned out, they may have been the best thing that happened to the company since the big idea for transparent seat covers.

In 1976, the planned sales reduction program cut sales by 25 percent to $183 million. But profits did a real turnaround, from a $7.5 million loss in 1975 to a $5.4

million gain in 1976. The upward trend continued with profits reaching $9.2 million in 1977 and a record high of $11.5 million in 1978.

And the streamlined operation, that started selling seat covers in a Minneapolis garage, is now looking for steady and controllable growth in the years ahead.

An insider's viewpoint

The following comments about Fingerhut's direct marketing program were provided by Theodore Deikel, president and chief executive officer:

> We have become increasingly aware of the need to improve further the quality of our products and the service we give to our customers. We plan to emphasize a policy which will demonstrate our concern and which will improve our reliability through the implementation of a policy of "Satisfaction Assurance," letting our customers know that we stand behind our products and will, without question, resolve their problems and meet their needs. At the same time, we intend to make better use of customer selectivity techniques and will tailor our offerings to the characteristics and interests of our customers.

> In addition, we will begin to devote our efforts to specialized segments of the marketplace utilizing our broad marketing capability. We intend to make significant commitments to develop identified market potentials.

> We will invest more of our profit dollars in product development, market research, customer analysis, and operational and strategic planning to create a clear course for future growth. While it will take time for these investments to produce measurable results, we believe that, in the long run, they will pay for themselves many times over.

> With the plans now being developed, I believe we can steer the company in new directions while continuing to earn profits at a satisfactory level.

19

Skeptic Magazine
A Structured Creative Process Develops
a Breakthrough in Space Advertising

If you're tired of being hustled, hyped, and conned . . . if you've been taken in once too often by those who want to line you up on one side or the other . . . SKEPTIC will come as a refreshing change.

It's a new magazine designed to *inform* rather than to persuade . . . to help you understand the most important issues, problems, and controversies by giving you both the pros *and* cons.

Those are the words that helped launch a new magazine. For they formed the heading of a subscription solicitation letter that offered a charter issue of *Skeptic*. The first issue came off the press in Spring 1974.

Unlike most new magazines, *Skeptic* wasn't launched from a standing start. It evolved out a a series of published letters sponsored by the Forum for Contemporary History. While there had been good reader interest in the Forum Letters, its format limited the amount of editorial material and points of view that could be expressed.

So Jim Bartlett, the Forum's president, and Hank Burnett, its editor, decided a magazine would be the next logical step. Although new ideas are often being tried in the magazine field, the publishers started out with some precepts that must be regarded as rather unusual.

First, the editorial concept was that each issue would be devoted to a single subject. The publishers' idea was to concentrate on major topics like crime, pollution, energy, spying, and inflation. Second, they would cover the topic in depth, present as many points of view as possible, and aim for open-minded, intelligent readers who could draw their own conclusions. Third, they would build an editorial product that would be supported primarily by readers and, therefore, would not plan to solicit advertising until the magazine was well established.

The first issue of *Skeptic* was devoted to the subject of impeachment. It fulfilled its promise with 64 pages of articles and opinions and a $1.00 price on the cover. The topic was a timely choice, since the Nixon controversy was then boiling to its inevitably dramatic conclusion.

Exhibit 99. *Skeptic's* **first mailing package.**

skeptic CHARTER SUBSCRIPTION ORDER

Please forward for my critical appraisal my free Charter issue of SKEPTIC. If I like it, send me the subsequent issues and bill me at the Charter rate of just $7.50 for the year. If I don't like it, I just write "cancel" across your bill and that's that. No obligation, no commitment, no cost, and the sample issue is mine to keep free.

812 Anacapa Street, Santa Barbara, California 93101

Send no money! Return this card.

Send me a dollar's worth FREE

to receive the charter issue of SKEPTIC ... pay it if you like it!

5114

812 Anacapa Street, Santa Barbara, California 93102

Send me a dollar's worth FREE

skeptic
THE FORUM FOR CONTEMPORARY HISTORY

Dear Friend:

     You are being lied to.

     I had heard rumor after rumor, and finally decided to find out the truth for myself. So I chartered a boat and sailed into Mexican waters, to Baja California. There must be at least 50 oil tankers anchored here in the fog, just outside U.S. territorial waters. They could be here for only one reason: they have been ordered by their owners -- American oil companies -- to hold back their shipments to the Port of Los Angeles until the prices we pay for gas and oil have soared even higher.

                    *   *   *   *   *   *   *

Dear Reader:

     Of course this is not an actual account; but in times of crisis, when rumors fly, how do we know what to think? The experts claim to understand why the energy crisis happened, but they don't agree on the reasons. In fact, they don't even agree on whether the crisis is authentic. Even high level administration policy makers argue in public about its severity and extent.

     What do you believe? Who do you believe? What are the facts? The truth? What kind of plans are you supposed to make if your job is heavily dependent on energy? After all the scrimping on fuel and paying outrageous prices, how would you feel if you learned that there really wasn't a legitimate crisis after all, that you were just playing the pawn to grand master power blocks?

          There is a way to reduce the level of confusion. Now, in a convenient form, a new communication that helps you under-stand the most urgent issues, problems and controversies of our time (there are already enough people trying to con you about them, to persuade you to line up on one side or the other).

          It's called SKEPTIC. If you've been taken in once too often ... if you've developed a healthy skepticism yourself ... if you want information that can help you make sense out of the '70's and make important decisions with greater confidence ... SKEPTIC is for you.

          This is your invitation to become a Charter Subscriber and receive a FREE issue under terms that obligate SKEPTIC, but not you.

     SKEPTIC was created to alleviate one of the most critical shortages of

812 Anacapa Street, Santa Barbara, California 93102

Direct mail builds subscriber base

Skeptic's first mailing effort was an unimposing-looking package. A number ten envelope provided the teaser copy. It said, "Send me a dollar's worth *Free,*" a reference to the value of the free charter issue.

The four-page letter posed some of the questions that were troubling people in the early seventies. And, of course, the letter offered *Skeptic* to help sort out the answers to those troubling questions. To back up its claims, the letter urged readers to send for the charter issue (see Exhibit 99). The offer was easy to accept. No payment or signature was required. The reader merely had to detach the stub and mail back the postpaid reply card. If the reader liked the free charter issue, he or she would simply pay the invoice; if not, he or she would cancel.

This is what publishers often call the complimentary copy offer. It's regarded as a rather "loose" offer because the reader is not making a definite commitment. But, if the magazine itself lives up to its promises, about half the respondents will usually pay the bill and become subscribers. For a new publication, the offer provides the opportunity to get exposure and build circulation more rapidly. In *Skeptic's* case, both the response rate and the payment rate were satisfactory.

The first year of testing

While some minor testing of different packages was done, the main thrust of the early mailing program was testing prices and lists. The frequency of the magazine was every other month. Which meant that the full price for a year's subscription was $6.00. Historically, most magazines feature cut-rate offers to attract new subscribers with a bargain price. One advantage of a bimonthly publishing schedule is that a full-price offer seems more like a bargain because it entails only a nominal annual expenditure.

Skeptic conducted a number of price tests the first year. Some were cut-rate. Some were higher-price offers for longer terms. But a full-price offer of six issues for $6.00 was the clear winner in the first round of tests. After a later round of tests, the cover price of the magazine was raised to $1.25, with $7.50 the subscription price.

The testing was equally extensive in the list area. Although a number of list categories were tried, subscribers to other publications proved to be most responsive. And *Skeptic* found it could make many of them pay out. Mass circulation books like *Time* and *Esquire.* More specialized magazines like *New Times, New Republic,* and *Rolling Stone.* Even some business publications like *Harvard Business Review.*

The evolution of a control mailing

Throughout its first year, *Skeptic* continued to mail the initial package that launched the magazine. A couple of packages done by top direct response writers were tested but failed.

The first package to replace the control was done by its own editor, Hank Burnett, who had long been regarded as one of the best copywriters in the business. The format was similar to the old package—number 10 envelope, four-page letter, and reply card with detachable stub.

But a token involvement device was added to the card to dramatize the value of the free issue. A window outer envelope was used with the token showing through. A postpaid return envelope was provided for sending back the token card. The letter copy, while not dramatically different from the original package, included the quote at the beginning of this chapter.

Skeptic started its second year with about 77,000 paid subscribers. It was fall 1975 before a more elaborate package was tested, and it became a convincing winner. It featured a 6 × 9 envelope, four-page letter, simple two-page folder, token order card, and return envelope.

The token device was a question mark like that used to replace the "p" in the *Skeptic* logo. It also showed through a window on the outer envelope. The folder explained the kinds of articles the magazine had included in a recent issue on America's survival, and followed up with reader testimonials (see Exhibit 100).

The letter copy took a hard-hitting approach. It started out as follows: "Distrust some of the stuff you hear on the news? Disillusioned with public officials?" It then went on to tease the reader with thought-provoking questions based on actual topics covered in *Skeptic's* early issues.

Specialized promotions supplement mailing efforts

Skeptic had started newsstand distribution its first year. While the magazine was not a runaway success, there was steady sales growth. Newsstand sales also provided exposure to potential new readers who were encouraged to subscribe through house ads and loose "blow-in" cards in the magazine.

In 1975 *Skeptic* started a program to sell bulk subscriptions to high school social studies teachers. A teacher's guide was developed for each issue of the magazine. A typical mailing package included a sample issue of the magazine. The package offered the teacher his or her own subscription free with a minimum of 10 subscriptions at the special classroom rate. A telephone follow-up was used after the mailing, and the phone-mail combination produced good results.

In addition, postcard publications were successfully used to bring in new subscribers. Radio and television spots were tested, both without success. And back-issue sales provided an additional revenue source. Up to 10,000 copies were sold each month, and a number of issues actually had to be reprinted, which is a rare occurence in the magazine field.

Structured program followed for space advertising

As the end of 1975 approached, *Skeptic's* management faced a quandary. Circulation was growing steadily, issue by issue, but the magazine still had less than 100,000 subscribers.

Direct mail was working well. Extensive testing had uncovered a solid list universe of about a million names. But *Skeptic* was already using virtually all the names available, and it was unlikely they would find many more that paid out. How could they maintain their growth rate, or even increase it?

Space advertising appeared to be the answer. Virtually nothing had been done with this medium except for the postcard publications and house ads in the magazine itself. But *Skeptic's* management team, from their collective experience with other publishers, knew that space advertising was a real gamble. While virtually all magazines were using direct mail, only a rather small percentage of them were able to make space work well enough to bring in a meaningful number of new readers.

The publishers were willing to take the gamble. But to cut their risk, they decided to employ an ad agency with a good success record in using space for other publishers. The agency recommended a highly structured testing program to find the best creative approach.

Eight ads developed with hypothesis method

Two reasons called for testing a variety of creative approaches rather than the traditional one or two. *Skeptic* wanted to learn quickly whether space was viable for them. Equally important was the fact that testing more ads maximized the odds of coming up with a breakthrough.

The agency suggested that eight black-and-white page ads be split-tested. And it used an interesting two-step approach to develop them:

1. The agency first developed a list of hypotheses about the magazine, its readers, and the benefits readers got from it.
2. After narrowing down the list to the eight hypotheses felt to be most significant, the agency created an ad to prove or disprove each one.

On the following pages, you'll find the eight ads that were created, along with the hypothesis for each and the rationale behind it.

Time magazine slated for telescopic test

In addition to those eight ads, a bind-in business reply card was to be tested. The two-color card played up the free-issue offer (see Exhibit 109).

The technique used to test the eight ads plus bind-in card is known as telescopic testing. In the mail it's always been possible to split-test a number of things simultaneously so long as the list is large enough. But in space advertising, an advertiser is usually limited to just testing one ad versus another with an A/B split test. This is simply because many magazines are printed two-up; so ad A runs in half the copies and ad B in the other half.

The obvious disadvantage of this approach is the length of time it takes to test a series of ads. You would have to schedule the first two ads, prepare them, wait for the magazine to come out, find out the winner, and then repeat the whole process to test another new ad against the winner. *Skeptic* was able to telescope this long drawn-out testing process into a single issue of one magazine and get a quick answer on its whole series of ads.

How? By using *Time* magazine which has a number of regional editions with split-test capabilities. While a general-interest magazine like *Time* was not expected to produce the lowest cost per order for *Skeptic,* it was suitable for finding the best creative approach. And the agency's experience with other clients showed that results of creative tests in *Time* were transferable to other more specialized publications.

Exhibit 100. *Skeptic*'s control mailing.

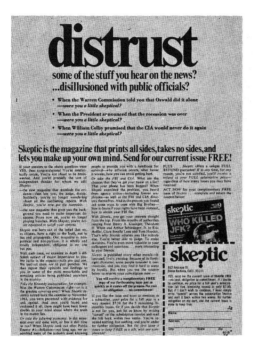

Exhibit 101.

Ad A—"Distrust"

Hypothesis: An ad using the same creative approach as *Skeptic's* most successful mailing package should likewise be a strong approach in space.

Rationale: The 6 × 9 mailing package shown earlier had become the control, based on beating a number of other mailing packages. It should, therefore, be adapted as a space ad, using the same heading as the letter and as much of the body copy as possible.

Exhibit 102.

Ad B—"5 Reasons"

Hypothesis: *Skeptic* has a number of things that make it different from other magazines. If all these key reasons are presented, one or more is likely to "strike home" and get the reader to respond.

Rationale: Most of the other ads zero in on just one aspect of *Skeptic's* story. This was an attempt to combine all of the main product differentials in a single ad.

Exhibit 103.

Ad C—"Decide for Yourself"

Hypothesis: A hot issue has more appeal than an editorial concept, and "Who Killed JFK?" has been the hottest newsstand issue in the magazine's history.

Rationale: All of *Skeptic's* previous promotions sold the concept of the magazine and offered to start a subscription with the next issue on an unspecified subject. It was felt readers would be more interested in starting their subscription with a specific and appealing issue.

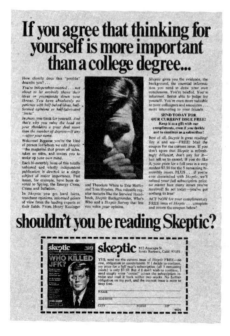

Exhibit 104.

Ad D—"If You Agree"

Hypothesis: The prime prospect for *Skeptic* readership is someone who prides himself on his intellectual independence, whether or not he has a college degree.

Rationale: Research showed that the magazine had a high percentage of college graduates among its readers. But it was felt an ad aimed solely at college grads could be too limiting. So this approach addresses itself to independent-minded graduates, as well as nongraduates.

Exhibit 105.

Ad E—"Captures History"

Hypothesis: *Skeptic's* primary appeal lies in the fact that it becomes a running contemporary history of our times, and its back issues have a permanent value.

Rationale: There are thousands of history buffs in the United States. This approach positions the magazine for them and dramatizes its uniqueness with a "guaranteed buy-back" offer like that often used for collectibles.

Exhibit 106.

Ad F—"Are You Fed Up. . .?"

Hypothesis: A large segment of the population believes that the presentation of various issues by the news media is inevitably slanted, and *Skeptic's* greatest appeal lies in its impartiality.

Rationale: Most people don't like the idea of others telling them what to think and should respond positively to a magazine that is not trying to persuade them one way or another.

Exhibit 107.

Ad G—"9 Examples"

Hypothesis: Using a numbered list of subjects from past issues is the best way to introduce potential subscribers to the range and character of *Skeptic*.

Rationale: This approach has been effective for a number of other magazines through the years, and was therefore one of those ideas that almost had to be tested.

Exhibit 108.

Ad H—"Ever feel invisible. . .?"

Hypothesis: People are more interested in appearing knowledgeable in public or at social gatherings than they are in the issues themselves.

Rationale: While the immediate benefit of the magazine is to make the reader more knowledgeable or informed, the idea of being able to impress one's friends might be considered the ultimate extension of that benefit.

Exhibit 109. Bind-in reply card.

The control, ad A, would be tested against a different ad in each regional edition used. The testing configuration would be ad A versus B, A versus C, A versus D, and so on. This meant that all the test ads would be measured against a common control ad, and percentage improvements would be compared to find the winner.

The media plan called for using eight regional groups with the circulation of each group ranging from 170,000 to 205,000. Seven of the regions were used to split-test the ads. The eighth region was not split-tested but had a bind-in card added to the control ad. The total plan called for a circulation of 1,460,000 with a media budget of about $25,000 including printing of the bind-in card. Ads were scheduled for *Time's* March 1, 1976, issue (see Exhibit 110).

Six out of seven ads beat control!

The "Distrust" ad had been established as the control because it was adapted from the control mailing package. Rating the control ad with an index of 100, here's how the results came in:

Ad A—"Distrust"........................... 100
Ad B—"5 Reasons"........................... 125
Ad C—"Decide for Yourself".................. 253
Ad D—"If You Agree'....................... 142
Ad E—"Captures History".................... 70
Ad F—"Are You Fed Up. . .?"................ 122
Ad G—"9 Examples"........................ 156
Ad H—"Ever Feel Invisible. . .?".............. 125

Not only did all but one of the ads beat the control, the winning ad—"Decide for Yourself"—beat it by two and a half times! The bind-in reply card, which was tested in the Boston region with the control ad, pulled six and a half times as well as the same ad in other regions without a card. So, even taking into account the extra media and printing cost for the card, results indicated it could bring in orders at one-third the cost of a page ad with coupon.

Everything that could affect response was taken into account in the result analysis including ad position, time of year ads were run, the geographical response differences by region, and the conversion or payment rates on the individual ads. But the big payoff was the bottom line. It indicated that even *Time* magazine would come close to producing orders at an acceptable cost per order. Because special interest magazines had been expected to do even better, more testing of space advertising was clearly indicated.

From this single insertion in *Time* magazine, *Skeptic* had learned which creative approach was strongest in space—the efficiency of a bind-in card—and had a good over-all indication that space held potential for them.

Exhibit 110. *Skeptic* **telescopic test media summary.**

Ads	Edition	Circulation	Cost
(A) "Distrust" (B) "5 Reasons"	Ohio	185,000	$ 2,892
(A) "Distrust" (C) "Decide for Yourself"	Philadelphia	205,000	2,667
(A) "Distrust" (D) "If You Agree"	Minneapolis, Denver, and St. Louis	175,000	4,419
(A) "Distrust" (E) "Captures History"	Atlanta and Florida	170,000	3,445
(A) "Distrust" (F) "Are You Fed Up. . ."	Texas	170,000	2,512
(A) "Distrust" (G) "9 Examples"	San Francisco	185,000	2,478
(A) "Distrust" (H) "Ever Feel Invisible?"	Chicago	200,000	2,613
(A) "Distrust" with bind-in card	Boston	170,000	4,309*
		1,460,000	$25,335

*Includes cost of printing bind-in card.

Confirming results in space

The publishers decided the balance of 1976 would be used for retesting and a cautious expansion of the space program. Another regional edition of *Time* magazine was slated for June 1976. The objectives were to confirm the results of the first test and compare response between the two top ads when run with a bind-in card.

But there was a problem. Normally it is impossible to split-test two ads when you're using a bind-in card. Because of production limitations, you have to use the same card with each ad and you won't know which ad triggered the response.

The solution? Let the consumer key the reply card for you to indicate which ad they were responding to. A small boxed element was added at the bottom of each ad with the following copy:

> IMPORTANT: To help us record the response to this ad, would you please do us a small favor? In the appropriate space on the card, please write the letter A. Many thanks.

The other ad had the same copy but mentioned the letter B. And the reply card had copy that read, "See NOTE in adjoining ad. Please write the Ad Letter here." About 80 percent of the consumers did exactly as requested, and the self-keying bind-in card showed that the "Decide for Yourself" ad was still the strong winner.

Fall continuation of space campaign

To get some idea of how big its space universe would be, *Skeptic* scheduled full-page ads with bind-in cards for the October or November issues of five publications. All were chosen because their mailing lists had produced good results in *Skeptic's* direct mail program. The five were *Esquire, Psychology Today, Book Digest, Money,* and *New Times.* In addition, a small quantity of newspaper inserts was tested.

The newspaper inserts did not do well enough to pay out, but the magazines did. Every one of them hit quota. The magazines not only produced a cost per order better than the previous tests in *Time*, they produced a cost per order comparable to what *Skeptic* was getting in the mail. And the fall space campaign added more than 30,000 trial subscribers.

Based on this success—using a structured program to find the best creative approach and a careful expansion of its space universe—*Skeptic* began to map out an expanded space schedule for 1977. In the first quarter alone, the magazine scheduled two dozen publications with about 7,500,000 circulation. All featured the winning ad built around the "Who Killed JFK" issue.

Direct mail promotion was continued during the same period. And the combination of mail and space resulted in steady circulation growth throughout the magazine's second and third year (see Exhibit 111).

Exhibit 111. *Skeptic's* **subscription growth.**

Issue Number	Date	Subscribers
7	May/June 75	77,101
8	July/August 75	87,773
9	September/October 75	92,635
10	November/December 75	94,862
11	January/February 76	116,699
12	March/April 76	122,573
13	May/June 76	124,532
14	July/August 76	128,101
15	September/October 76	135,342
16	November/December 76	146,558
17	January/February 77	152,483
18	March/April 77	169,788

Update on *Skeptic*

While the space testing program was under way, a number of important changes were going on at *Skeptic*. Having completed two successful years, the publishers decided they would accept advertising. The ad sales program was kicked off with a four-page insert in *Advertising Age*, and ads were accepted for the first time starting in the November/December 1976 issue.

Also, some gradual but major changes were made in the magazine itself. At the outset, most of *Skeptic's* articles had been reprinted from other publications. Before long, it had done a complete turnaround and carried completely original editorial material. To go with that, the graphics were upgraded thanks to the addition of a top art director and a switch to four-color printing.

Starting in 1977, the magazine's editorial scope was expanded. *Skeptic* began to cover more than just one subject in each issue. But the magazine retained the basic principle of always providing in-depth coverage and a variety of opposing viewpoints.

The vitality of change

It's been said that a good publisher must keep one hand on the public's pulse and the other on his or her publication. Only by constantly monitoring the marketplace can the publisher deliver a consistently improving editorial product and find the most efficient way to sell it.

Forum Communications, the publisher in this case has done that. Perhaps the most dramatic change of all came early in 1978 when the name of the magazine was changed from *Skeptic* to *Politics Today*. It was a change designed to reflect the evolving editorial concentration on political issues and better identify the publication's contents to potential new readers. This management philosophy—to recognize the need for changes and make them—should lead to continued growth in the years ahead.

An insider's viewpoint

The following comments were provided by James L. Bartlett III. Besides being one of the magazine's founders, Bartlett now serves as publisher of *Politics Today.*

> The magazine business is like many other businesses. It requires hard work and a significant number of correct management decisions. The hard work must be supplied by each individual. But the use of a pragmatic marketing method, such as direct response advertising, can improve your ability to make accurate decisions.
>
> For example, initial direct mail tests for *Skeptic* revealed the best price to sell subscriptions, the proper mailing package to use, the correct lists, and most important—acceptance by the consumer. Further use of direct mail enabled us to grow at fairly predictable rates. As our initial success repeated itself through several major mailing campaigns of over one million pieces each, further direct response testing revealed success in other media.
>
> Most notable was *Skeptic's* participation in an eight-way test of space advertising that indicated enough response to support a major space campaign. The multifaceted test quickly revealed one winning ad from the original eight. This ad has since been placed successfully in over 25 national publications.
>
> *Skeptic* also tested direct response subscriber spots on radio and television. While the concept was exciting, the real key was the response from each of the media. Unfortunately there were not enough responses to support an extensive broadcast campaign. Once again, the pragmatism of direct response enabled us to curtail a program and save dollars and headaches.
>
> My viewpoint can be summed up in one word—test. Direct response is a challenging environment; proper testing can help you succeed.

20

A. B. Dick Company
How to Make Profitable Aftermarket
Sales without Making Sales Calls

Forms. Bulletins. Letters. Memos. Newsletters. Reports. Booklets. Schedules. Meeting notices.

Every working day, more than 200 million copies of papers like these are duplicated by A. B. Dick machines. The firm has been a leader in manufacturing and marketing office duplicating and copying equipment for over 90 years. Naturally there are a lot of A. B. Dick machines spread around the country—from church basements to giant corporations.

It's also natural that these offset printers, mimeograph machines, spirit duplicators, and electrofax copiers use a lot of supplies to turn out 200 million copies a day. Supplies like stencils, masters, inks and fluids, aluminum plates, plate etching solutions, cleaning materials, and, of course, paper.

The company had net sales of $329 million in 1977. According to its annual report, 54 percent of sales are represented by supplies and services. That means the aftermarket sales alone accounted for $178 million.

Consultant recommends market specialization

In 1973, A. B. Dick hired a top consulting firm to analyze its entire marketing and distribution system. The system then consisted of about 60 company-owned branch offices plus over 115 independent distributors and more than 400 independent dealers.

One of the major recommendations was a market specialization program. It called for a reorganization of the sales force. Sales reps would concentrate on selling business firms and the institutional market of schools and churches. Their efforts would be devoted to medium and large-size organizations which represented the best prospects for equipment and also used a substantial volume of supplies.

While the study recognized that a lot of smaller firms and institutions already have A. B. Dick equipment, it pointed out that it was not economically sound to have salespeople calling on those organizations regularly. Most of them probably had enough equipment, and their annual volume of supplies was relatively low. With a single sales call then costing over $66.00, the company simply couldn't afford to send a salesperson out to get a supply order that might average less than $50.00.

Instead, the consultant recommended that A. B. Dick Company consider a direct marketing program for aftermarket sales to low-volume customers. Customers buying less than $200 worth of supplies annually would no longer have a sales rep assigned to them but would be encouraged to order by mail or phone.

A timetable was developed to implement the new market specialization program. It called for starting with a pilot program early in 1974 in one branch office. If successful, the program would be expanded to other markets, with two years as the target period for completing the national changeover.

The potential and the challenge

The potential for the direct marketing part of the program was good. It was estimated that, throughout the country, over 100,000 of the firm's customers were in the low-volume category.

But developing a direct marketing sales program posed quite a challenge. Could A. B. Dick expect customers to continue ordering, even if nobody was calling on them? How could it contact them by mail or phone without making them feel like second-class citizens? Could each branch be left to develop its own mail or phone program? How could it offer a full line of almost 900 supply items without confusing the customer? Would it lose a good share of its profitable aftermarket business to local office supply stores?

Two things were clear to A. B. Dick management: First, they couldn't take a chance on these aftermarket sales coming to them "over the transom." It needed an aggressive direct marketing program to go after them. Second, the firm couldn't leave the job up to the branches. The home office would have to develop a direct marketing test program, work out all the details, and then turn it over to the branches for implementation. (A. B. Dick executives also envisioned that the program could later be made available to distributors, but, because they were independent, they would decide individually whether or not to activate it.)

The preferred customer program

The goal established was to provide small-volume customers with service at least equal to what they had been getting from a live salesperson. And to avoid implying that they were second-class citizens, the firm called the project Preferred Customer Service. The program that was originally developed outlined three stages.

Stage one: telephone announcement. Each small-volume customer would receive a personal phone call to announce the new way of ordering A. B. Dick supplies. The caller would also try to update the firm's records on what equipment the customer had and, if possible, obtain an immediate order.

Stage two: special offers. To build the customer's habit of ordering by phone or mail, the firm would use inexpensive mailings to announce special limited time offers such as free gifts or other incentives tied to an order.

Stage three: supplies catalog. Once the customer had become somewhat adjusted to ordering by phone and mail and once there was some indication of results to justify the investment, a new supplies catalog would be developed for the preferred customer program.

Phone announcement test in Boston

The A. B. Dick branch in Boston was selected for the first test of the preferred customer service plan. To give the program every chance for success, the firm engaged a direct marketing ad agency to plan the strategy. The agency, in turn, brought in a telephone communications firm to execute the test calls.

The basic strategy developed was to use a combination of live telephone communicator and a prerecorded tape message. The tape message would announce the new supplies-ordering program; the live communicator would update the customer's records and try for the order.

Tape messages were recommended to provide a consistent presentation of what the new service was all about. To localize the message, it would be recorded by the firm's Boston branch manager. Also, having the announcement come from A. B. Dick's top local executive would add credibility and authority to the announcement.

Here's the script that was developed, and then recorded by Branch Manager Walter Whalen:

> Hello, this is Walter Whalen. I'm taking this opportunity to talk to you about a new A. B. Dick customer service we've started with you in mind. The reason I feel it's important to you is that our new service will make ordering supplies easier, keep you informed about special offers, help you get the best possible copies at the lowest possible cost, and be of service to you in any way we can.
>
> A. B. Dick has organized a preferred customer service that we feel is going to make re-ordering a lot more convenient for you. Under this new plan you'll be able to order by mail or phone. And we'll call you periodically as a reminder and take your order if that's convenient.
>
> In short, we'd like to anticipate your supply needs and invite you to rely on *us* for a reminder. Stencils, inks, spirit masters, fluid, offset masters, and, of course, paper. Let us worry about them for you. When we call, we'll run right down a list of your supplies to ensure nothing gets overlooked, tell you about any new products so that you can take advantage of them, jot down your order over the phone, and take care of everything.
>
> Our customer service representative will be coming back on the line to answer any questions you might have, and, since this is really our first customer service call, take an order from you if you like.
>
> I know you'll find our new A. B. Dick customer service a convenience, and I hope you'll take advantage of it.
>
> Thank you for being an A. B. Dick customer.[1]

Communicator's message carefully scripted

A good script for a telephone sales program must be precise, yet flexible. The script has to anticipate the various ways a customer can answer each question and give the communicator specific directions on how to respond or what to do next. The same script can then be used by a variety of communicators with predictable results.

An important asset in launching the A. B. Dick test was its customer records. Information on all equipment and supply purchases from each customer and for each branch were maintained in a central computer system. The information included the

1. Copyright CCI, 1974.

customer's purchase history and dollar volume for the last four years. So it was relatively simple to get a printout of all Boston customers and segregate those customers with an annual supply volume under $200.

The system did not, however, include the customer's phone number or the name of the individual who had purchased. So phone numbers were looked up in advance for all the customers to be called. And the communicator's first task was to get in touch with the right person. Here's how the script handled that, as well as getting permission for the customer to hear the tape message:

> *Introduction to person answering the phone:*
>
> > This is _____. I'm calling for A. B. Dick Company. May I speak to the person who buys supplies for your duplicating equipment? (Note name on card.) That's Mr(s). _____? Thank you.
>
> *To prospect:*
>
> > Hello, Mr(s). _____. I'm calling for A. B. Dick Company. Are you responsible for the purchase of supplies for your duplicating equipment?
>
> *If no, ask who is and ask to be transferred.*
>
> > Mr(s). _____, I'm called with our first announcement of the A. B. Dick preferred customer program. Mr. Whalen, our Boston branch manager, describes this new program on tape. It takes just two minutes. May I play it now and answer any questions after you've heard it, Mr(s). _____?
>
> *If no or "what's this about," say:*
>
> > Mr. Whalen would like to tell you personally, Mr(s). _____. A. B. Dick is starting a new program that can be very important to you and your company. Mr. Whalen can tell you about it so much better than I. May I play it for you now, Mr(s). _____?
>
> *If says "no" to tape, go to summary and to question 1.*
>
> *If yes, play tape.*[2]

While the script obviously had to be written so as to anticipate those persons who would refuse to hear the tape message, past experience had shown this was usually a small percentage. In the A. B. Dick test, for example, it was about 5 percent.

After the tape message was played, the next objective was to update the records on the customer's current equipment, supply usage rates, and buying habits. A special preferred customer record card was prepared for this purpose. The four-page form was designed to serve as the master record for each account with plenty of room for recording future calls and order summaries (see Exhibit 112).

Here's the next section of the communicator script, beginning immediately after the tape message was concluded:

> > Did you hear the tape all right, Mr(s). _____? And may I take a minute now to check our customer file with you?

2. Copyright CCI, 1974.

If no, ask when you may call back (note on card).

Thank you. Goodbye.

If yes:

Our records indicate that you have _____ A. B. Dick equipment. Is this correct?

Yes _____ No _____ What equipment do you have? _____ Do you know the model number? (Note on card)

If yes and no:

What other types of A. B. Dick duplicating equipment do you have? (Note on card)

If the customer does have other equipment:

And what is the model number? (Note on card) How long have you had this? (Note on card) And can you tell me please, approximately how many copies do you make per month? (Note on card)

If don't know, ask:

Is is about—

500 to 1,000_____ 1,000 and over _____

For: (type of machine) _____

Mr(s). _____, what other brands of duplicating or copying equipment do you have? (Note on card)

The purchase record I have before me runs through December 31, 1973. Can you tell me if you've bought any A. B. Dick supplies or equipment since that time? (Note on card) And are you currently getting all your dupicating supplies from A. B. Dick, such as:

If has mimeo machine, say:

Ink, stencils, paper, or protective covers

If bought spirit duplicator, say:

Masters, fluid, or paper

If has copier, say:

Paper or toner supplies

If has offset machine, say:

Masters, ink, fountain solution, etch solution, blanket wash, or paper

If yes:

Ask from what location he or she is buying A. B. Dick supplies.

If no:

Can you tell me if there is some special reason why we haven't been able to serve your account for these supplies, Mr(s). _____? (Note on card)[3]

3. Copyright CCI, 1974.

Exhibit 112. First page of preferred customer record card.

PREFERRED CUSTOMER RECORD

Company —————————————————————
Address ——————————————————————
Name: Buying Influence ——————————————————
Title ———————————————————————————
Phone ————————————————————————————
Type of A. B. Dick Duplicating Equipment Owned
Mimeo ———— Spirit ———— Offset ————Copier ————
Model No. ———————— How old ————————

Other A. B. Dick Equipment Owned

Type	Model No.	How Old

Competitive: Duplicating Equipment Owned

Make	Model No.	How Old

No. of impressions made per month with all duplicating equipment
Under 100 ☐   100 to 500 ☐   500/1500 ☐   1500/5000 ☐   5000 ☐

The final phase of the script was designed to get a supply order, if possible. To make sure all orders would be accurately attributed to the test, the communicators used a special Direct Response Customer Order form (see Exhibit 113). Whether or not the communicators succeeded in getting an immediate order, they conditioned the customer to expect a future call in 30, 60, or 90 days (the customer's preference). And they closed with a name and number the customer could call if supplies were needed before hearing from A. B. Dick Company again.

Here's how the script covered this part of the telephone contact:

> Mr(s). ————, we're anxious to make this preferred customer program work best for you. Is there some special way that A. B. Dick can help you? (Note on card.)
>
> Do you have any immediate supply needs that you would like to fill with an order now?
>
> *If yes, fill out order form (Ask for P.O. number)*
>
> Thank you very much for your time, Mr(s). ————.

> Our plan is to call you on a regular basis to give you information about special products and to see how we may best serve you. What is the best day and time to call, and when should we call you again? (Note on card.)
>
> Fine. In the meantime, if you should have needs or questions, I'd like to suggest that you call our branch in Boston at 000-0000 and ask for Mr. Johnson. He will be happy to serve you. Goodbye.[4]

While the entire script may seem somewhat long on paper, it's good phone strategy to get the customer engaged in answering questions. Most customers were impressed with A. B. Dick's desire to serve them and were glad to answer the questions. And the average initial call only lasted about 10 minutes.

Preparation goes beyond scripts

Conducting a sound telephone marketing program entails a lot more than merely developing the tape message and communicator script. A quick reference product guide had to be prepared for the communicators listing the most common types of supplies for A. B. Dick equipment along with model numbers, quantities, and price lists. A list of expected customer questions and objections was also developed and professional answers were provided.

The last remaining "pre-flight check" was making some pilot calls. Of the 1,200 total calls that were scheduled for Boston, 50 were selected for advance calls. The objectives: get some immediate reactions to the over-all thrust of the program, determine the response patterns to the questions, and discover what details or problems might arise in taking orders and handling product questions. The advance calls took place in late February 1974. Here's how it went, according to a report prepared by one of the A. B. Dick representatives on hand:

> The initial script was working very smoothly and only required a little fine-tuning.
>
> All A. B. Dick customers contacted were very cooperative and quite pleased with the A. B. Dick products. Most of them spent an average of ten minutes on the phone with the communicator listening to the Whalen tape and answering questions.
>
> One reason the script seemed to be working so well was that it had a customer service approach in terms of gathering information for A. B. Dick Company. There was no high pressure selling and this helped greatly.

Boston test results

The balance of the calls to Boston customers in the $200-or-lower category were completed by mid-March. Although some customers had to be called back once or twice before the contact was completed, less than 10 percent turned out to be unreachable by phone.

For those who were reachable, the over-all results were better than expected (see Exhibit 114). Ten percent placed an immediate order and 46 percent more wanted future phone calls to check their supply needs. Less than a third did not want future phone calls, although many of these indicated they would order by mail. Another

4. Copyright CCI, 1974.

Exhibit 113. Special customer order form.

Direct Response Customer Order

A. B. Dick Company
130 Third Avenue Waltham Massachusetts 02154

Bill To: **Ship To:**

Billing Instructions   Ship Via

Date Received	Order Received by:	Date Delivery Requested	Invoice Number	Invoice Date	Credit Approved By:
Tax Code	Territory	Customer Number	Customer Purchase Order No.	C.O.D.	

Quantity	Unit	Product No.	Description	Unit Price	Extension	Net Total
			Delivery Charge			

ABDICK   **Total**

Branch Copy White   Niles Copy Yellow   74-57

group of 6.6 percent had either just sent an order or required some special follow-up like a service call.

But the real "sleeper" in the test was the 8.8 percent who requested that a salesperson see them. Most of these were interested in new equipment.

Only three weeks after the last phone calls were completed, these leads had already generated over $10,000 in equipment sales with many leads still being followed up. Over-all, 71 percent requested some specific action or future contact as part of the preferred customer program.

Roll-out starts with Atlanta market

As good as the Boston results looked, A. B. Dick decided to confirm them in one more market before a complete roll-out to all the branches. At the same time, the firm could test a couple of important variables.

The first test was to find out if inactive customers could be profitably contacted—firms who were known owners of A. B. Dick equipment but who had not purchased supplies in the last two years. A higher number of these proved to be unreachable or not interested in future calls, but a substantial percentage were interested in the supplies program or more equipment.

The second test was designed to determine the importance of having the phone message recorded by the local branch manager. So a tape message from the Atlanta branch manager was split-tested against one with a similar script done by a professional announcer. The latter proved equally effective, thus eliminating the need to record each branch manager and simplifying the plans for the roll-out. Over-all, the Atlanta results were almost identical to Boston and a timetable was developed for converting the rest of the branches to the program.

Exhibit 114. Boston telephone result summary.

Activity or interest	Percent
Immediate orders...	10.1
Want future calls....	46.2
Leads for salesmen..	8.8
Special handling....	6.6
Not interested in future calls.......	28.3
Total completed contacts.........	100.0

Phone manual spells out details

As A. B. Dick management had decided early in the game, all the details of the direct marketing program would have to be worked out before it was turned over to the branches. As a result, the home office developed its own manual on the telephone direct response program. The manual explained step by step how to set up the program—from identifying potential accounts through recruiting and training the telephone communicators.

The manual pointed out that, after the announcement phase, all customers in the program should be contacted at least quarterly. It was suggested that each communicator could make about 35 outgoing calls a day plus handle incoming phone orders. The manual also indicated that a single communicator could be expected to generate up to $200,000 in annual sales volume.

To make it as easy as possible for the branches to get started, the home office supplied a recorded cassette with the tape message as well as the necessary forms. Everything else was covered in the telephone manual including required equipment and a count-down timetable that showed how all the preparation could be done within one month before launching the program.

As soon as the test phase was completed, the Boston and Atlanta branches took over the telephone program for their markets. The roll-out began with a number of additional branches starting the program later in 1974 and the balance scheduled for the following year.

The results continued strong. By year end, all the branches on the program were paying out. Supply sales were not only retained but increased. One branch actually doubled its supplies volume through the phone program. And equipment leads and sales continued to provide an important bonus.

Recession delays mail program

Results of the phone program were so strong that it was decided that the special offer mailings, which had originally been planned to build the phone ordering habit, weren't really needed. But a new supplies catalog for the Preferred Customers Program had been planned for 1975.

Then came the recession. Like most other equipment manufacturers, A. B. Dick Company was affected and had to cut back in some areas. Result? The catalog was tabled for a year.

Early in 1976, the economy had improved and development of the catalog was started. It was a major project because the firm lacked an existing catalog representing all 800 to 900 items in its full line of supplies. Most of the items were covered in flyers or mini-catalogs. But these had been designed for use by the salespeople and did not contain enough product information to serve as a self-selling catalog the customer could use on his or her own.

Following good direct marketing catalog principles, the first step was to analyze and study supply sales, item by item. The decision was made that the catalog would feature only the "best sellers" in the supply line—about 20 percent of the items which accounted for about 85 percent of total supplies volume. Space for these items would be allocated on the basis of sales with the strongest sellers getting more catalog space.

Supplies catalog has unique features

The first Phone Order Supplies Catalog was a 24-pager printed in four-colors. It included an overwrap, two bind-in order form/envelopes, and a phone ordering check list (see Exhibit 115). To provide a complete selling story, as well as personalization for use by the local branches, the catalog included a number of unique features:

- While the four-color body of the catalog remained the same, the overwrap letter was changed for each branch. It contained the local address and phone number, and the letter message carried the signature of the branch manager.

- A number of helpful editorial tips were included with most major supply items to help the customer get better duplicating results. This was played up to boost readership and retention of the catalog (see Exhibit 116).

- Each supply section (mimeograph, offset, copying, and so on) was color coded and preceded by an attractive introductory page (see Exhibit 117).

- In addition to the most popular supplies, which were illustrated and described in detail, one of the pages listed all other supplies that could be ordered from the telephone representative. Another spread showed some of the most popular A. B. Dick equipment items.

Exhibit 115. A. B. Dick supplies catalog.

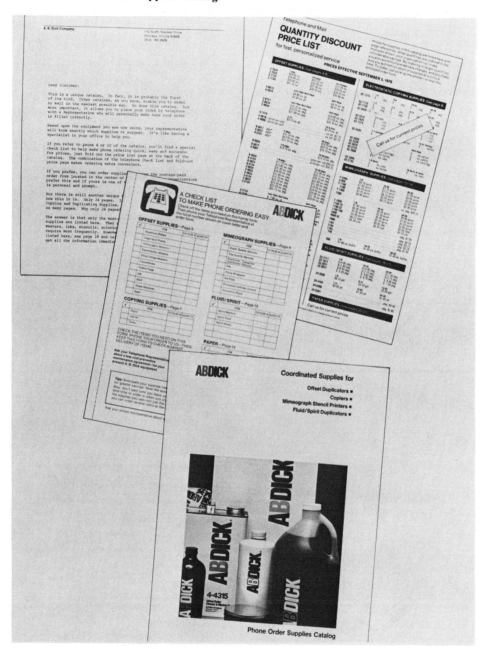

- The order form was personalized for each branch, again including the local phone number, and the tear-off business reply envelope contained the branch address.

Exhibit 116. Catalog page giving helpful operating tips to customers.

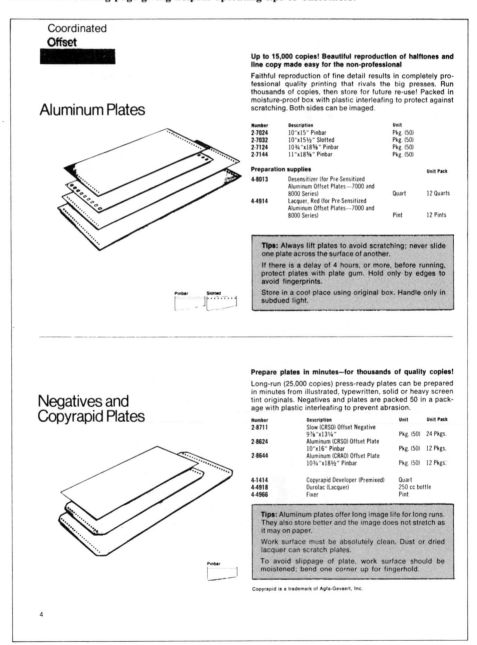

Coordinated
Offset

Aluminum Plates

Up to 15,000 copies! Beautiful reproduction of halftones and line copy made easy for the non-professional

Faithful reproduction of fine detail results in completely professional quality printing that rivals the big presses. Run thousands of copies, then store for future re-use! Packed in moisture-proof box with plastic interleafing to protect against scratching. Both sides can be imaged.

Number	Description	Unit
2-7024	10"x15" Pinbar	Pkg. (50)
2-7032	10"x15½" Slotted	Pkg. (50)
2-7124	10¾"x18⅝" Pinbar	Pkg. (50)
2-7144	11"x18⅝" Pinbar	Pkg. (50)

Preparation supplies		Unit Pack
4-8013	Desensitizer (for Pre-Sensitized Aluminum Offset Plates—7000 and 8000 Series)	Quart	12 Quarts
4-4914	Lacquer, Red (for Pre-Sensitized Aluminum Offset Plates—7000 and 8000 Series)	Pint	12 Pints

Tips: Always lift plates to avoid scratching; never slide one plate across the surface of another.

If there is a delay of 4 hours, or more, before running, protect plates with plate gum. Hold only by edges to avoid fingerprints.

Store in a cool place using original box. Handle only in subdued light.

Pinbar   Slotted

Negatives and Copyrapid Plates

Prepare plates in minutes—for thousands of quality copies!

Long-run (25,000 copies) press-ready plates can be prepared in minutes from illustrated, typewritten, solid or heavy screen tint originals. Negatives and plates are packed 50 in a package with plastic interleafing to prevent abrasion.

Number	Description	Unit	Unit Pack
2-8711	Slow (CRSO) Offset Negative 9⅞"x13¼"	Pkg. (50)	24 Pkgs.
2-8624	Aluminum (CRSO) Offset Plate 10"x16" Pinbar	Pkg. (50)	12 Pkgs.
2-8644	Aluminum (CRAO) Offset Plate 10¾"x18½" Pinbar	Pkg. (50)	12 Pkgs.
4-1414	Copyrapid Developer (Premixed)	Quart	
4-4918	Durolac (Lacquer)	250 cc bottle	
4-4966	Fixer	Pint	

Tips: Aluminum plates offer long image life for long runs. They also store better and the image does not stretch as it may on paper.

Work surface must be absolutely clean. Dust or dried lacquer can scratch plates.

To avoid slippage of plate, work surface should be moistened; bend one corner up for fingerhold.

Pinbar

Copyrapid is a trademark of Agfa-Gevaert, Inc.

4

- A fold-out price list was designed as part of the six-page overwrap. This allowed the customer to keep the price list open for reference while paging through the catalog. It also meant the price list could be updated, if necessary, without changing the body of the catalog.

Exhibit 117. Introductory page to a section of the catalog.

Coordinated Copying Supplies

Speed, economy, quality, ease of operation, consistency— are the outstanding features of A. B. Dick coordinated equipment, copy paper and supplies. Supplies and paper are coordinated with your equipment so that they work best together. The result is quality reproduction that is unexcelled in its class.

A total of 150,000 catalogs were mailed in November 1976. With orders going direct to field locations by mail and phone, it was difficult to develop exact figures on responses. But A. B. Dick Company management was very pleased with the program's results and has since developed a greatly expanded catalog. A line on the back of the catalog sums up the customer benefits: "Personalized service as close as your phone or mailbox." And the integrated use of phone and catalog selling provided A. B. Dick with a strong combination to maximize aftermarket sales.

An insider's viewpoint

The following comments about A. B. Dick Company's telephone and catalog direct marketing program were provided by Vernon R. Anderson, the firm's sales promotion manager, who is responsible for the program's development and implementation.

> It is not easy to launch a comprehensive direct marketing program successfully without the support of every level of marketing management, including field managers and salesmen—and our independent distributors.
>
> And this is especially hard to come by when an organization's products have been sold by salesmen for over 90 years. A salesman does not like to believe he can be replaced by a phone call or a catalog. We convinced him by pointing out the advantages of having extra time to build new accounts and customers—with no sacrifice of supplies commissions. We also emphasized the equipment leads he would get as a bonus and the increased supplies business, which would provide him with a growing "annuity."
>
> Our branch managers responded well to these same benefits plus the additional potential of increased service business and greater coverage of new business opportunities.
>
> Headquarters management agreed the program made sense because it was supported by the following facts: (1) Over 50 percent of the profitability of A. B. Dick products comes from supplies, (2) the total market for copying and duplicating supplies is now approaching one billion dollars annually, and (3) small accounts (those who buy less than $200 annually) could no longer economically be called on by a sales representative.
>
> Further support has come from our over 100 franchised independent distributors who have jumped on the bandwagon. Today, many of them are implementing the small-account telephone sales program and are enjoying the benefits of their own personalized Phone Order Supplies Catalog.
>
> We now know that telephone and catalog direct marketing techniques can be employed successfully and profitably for business and industrial products.

21

Time-Life Books:
How One Book Series Corralled More than
750,000 Readers and Two Top Industry Awards

Many awards are given annually in recognition of creativity and performance in the direct marketing field. Among the most prestigious is the Silver Mailbox which is awarded by the Direct Mail Marketing Association.

Time-Life Books may be the only advertiser in history who has won the DMMA Silver Mailbox award twice, for two different promotions on the same product! The product is a book series titled *The Old West*. The series captured the first Silver Mailbox award in 1973 for the best consumer mailing of the year. The honor was repeated in 1975 for the best television campaign of the year.

These two promotions, and other multi-media efforts, helped Time-Life Books sign up more than 750,000 readers for this continuity book series. It's one of the most successful series in their history. And how they captured the flavor of *The Old West* is quite a story.

The product and offer

Advertising Age columnist Bob Stone once devoted an entire column to the Time-Life Books success formula. At the top of his list were the products they offer. Stone wrote: "Success in any endeavor starts with the product. No business can long survive, no matter what the medium of selling might be, unless the product is *right*. On this score Time-Life Books rates extremely high. Its books are tops editorially. The bindings, illustrations, typography, and printing are among the finest."

This has no doubt been a key factor in the growth story of Time-Life Books. The book division was formally started in 1961. In 1977 the Time Inc. book publishing operations had sales of $258 million—over 20 percent of the corporation's total revenues. Time-Life Books sold about 24 million volumes during the year, and its books are printed in 28 foreign languages.

The Old West series was conceived by one of the Time-Life editors. The editor put together a proposal outlining an interesting series of books. Each volume would focus on the people who had played an important role in the development of our western frontier—the cowboys, the Indians, the railroaders, the soldiers, the pioneers, and so on.

The proposal called for books that would be impressive, even by Time-Life standards. The idea was to create an old-fashioned look and feel that would be in keeping with the subject matter: Large, 8½ × 11 volumes, bound in brown padded covers, embossed in a western saddle motif, and gold-stamped with a full-color cameo picture on the front. Each volume would contain about 40,000 words of text and 250 illustrations.

Time-Life Books' management was impressed with the proposal. They knew the series would represent quite an editorial project but believed there was definitely a market for it. The main concern was that the series would have strong regional appeal in the western United States and, perhaps, only limited appeal in the rest of the country. However, the over-all concept was so strong that the project was approved for testing.

Lead book and price determined

A typical Time-Life Book series ranges from 15 to 25 volumes depending on the availability of subject matter and market potential. Exactly how many books a series will contain need not be decided at the outset because an ad or mailing usually shows only six to eight volumes, and the reader is not asked to make a commitment for the full set.

Time-Life Books' standard offer is to feature one book—the lead book—which is the entry point to the series. The book is offered at full price on a 10-day free-trial basis. If the subscriber elects to keep and pay for the book, he or she receives another selection every two or three months. Each selection is sent on the same free-trial basis. There is no load-up shipment of the full set, and the subscriber can drop out of the series at any time.

The lead title selected for *The Old West* was "The Cowboys." The target selling price was set at $7.95 per volume plus shipping and handling. While the price was somewhat higher than that for most other book series the company was offering at the time, it would later be confirmed by price testing.

The Old West mailing program

Joan Manley, chairman of Time-Life Books, Inc., recently pointed out, "Because of its inherent selectivity, the most successful medium for selling our magazines and books has always been direct mail."

So naturally the firm started out with a direct mail promotion on *The Old West*, a promotion that would go on to win the DMMA Silver Mailbox.

Creative strategy for the package

The creative strategy that evolved was to capture the exciting western flavor of the books in the promotion package. The thinking behind it went something like this: Let's give the reader a taste of the interesting textual material. Let him or her see the wide variety of old photographs and illustrations used throughout the books. If we do that well, in a noncommercial way, the reader will sell him or herself on sending for the first volume.

Old newspaper serves as brochure

While the complete mailing package helped carry out the creative strategy, the most striking piece was the brochure. It was created in the style of an old newspaper. Almost the entire front and back panels of the four-page format were devoted to carefully selected samples from the books. Included were almost two dozen different items: Stories of the colorful language of the Old West, horses, cattle drives, and the search for gold and silver mines. Pictures of such varied people as Red Cloud, a Sioux Indian chief; Jim Bridger, a famous explorer; "Hanging Judge" Parker, who sentenced 172 men and women to the gallows; and Belle Starr, one of the legendary sirens of the Golden West. The brochure even reproduced such human-interest items as an old western song, a range quiz (complete with upside-down answers), and illustrations of well-known cattle brands. The brochure was all done in brown and black ink, to help create an old-fashioned look (see Exhibit 118).

When opened to its full 18 × 22 size, the inside of the brochure provided a real contrast. It was done in full color. A number of book covers were shown in large size to dramatize the impressive bindings. Three typical spreads of book pages were reproduced. In addition to the general copy on *The Old West* series, there was a whole section of partial contents from "The Cowboys," the lead book (see Exhibit 119).

Letter copy crackles with excitement

Complementing the brochure was a skillfully done four-page letter (see Exhibit 120). It used a narrative lead-in to relate the story of Joe McCoy, a livestock shipper who transformed Abilene into the first big-league cattle town. The first page included this fast-moving paragraph to introduce *The Old West* series:

> Its volumes are crackling with the excitement of men and women pushing out beyond the frontier, raising children and Cain, busting sod and staking out ranches in a land as wild and rugged as the open sea, hunting buffalo and bear, and finally becoming that marvelous blend of fact, legend, and myth that has fascinated us since two men named Lewis and Clark first crossed the country.

The copy went on to describe some of the cowboys the reader would meet in the first volume. It then included a separate paragraph on each of three upcoming volumes. Although the book series was aimed primarily at adults, the letter included some copy to bring out the family benefits:

> Introducing your family to the old West could be pretty worthwhile. They'll be meeting colorful people whose breed has become scarce these days; people with pluck, grit, and spunk whose times echo in our times. Your youngsters will be taken by these books because they'll discover that once life wasn't all cut and dried—men did the impossible because they didn't know any better or maybe because they had no choice.

The envelope, order card, and publisher's letter

Rounding out the package were the envelope, order card, and publisher's letter—each designed to help carry out the total theme of the package and each impressive in its own right.

Exhibit 118. Front of Old West brochure.

THE OLD WEST

TIME-LIFE BOOKS INVITES YOU TO JOIN ITS EXPEDITION ACROSS THE GREAT PLAINS

Counting Coup

The white man never understood many of the ways of the Plains Indians. Perhaps the most mysterious custom was "counting coup," an act of valor practiced by most Indian warriors. It meant administering a coup—French for stroke or blow—to an enemy, usually with a stick decorated with sacred "medicine" symbols. The degrees of coup varied from tribe to tribe, but the highest coup was touching an armed enemy in battle. A coup could be counted by the first brave to touch the body of a dead enemy. One warrior claimed a coup by lowering a rock over a cliff till it touched a foe. For each coup, a warrior could add a feather to his war bonnet.

A Four-Footed Friend

The horse and the West are inextricably bound together. Wiry Texas mustangs carried the ranch hands on their trail drives. Cowboys treasured their "cutting horses," which could separate from a herd cattle indicated by their riders. A "night horse" could find cattle in the dark. A "spoiled horse" was a badly trained outlaw. For the Indians of the Plains, the horse meant wealth, to steal or own him brought prestige. The Apaches owned horses first, but the Comanches, who called the horse "God Dog," were the best riders. The Nez Percé were the best breeders and responsible for the American stock of the famous Appaloosa.

The Windwagon

Men crossed the plains on foot, on horse, on mule, in covered wagons…and in the strangest vehicle of all, the windwagon. In 1853 Henry Sager constructed one of the first of these. It was a 12-by 25-foot wagon surmounted by a pilot deck and a 20-foot sail. Sager intended to use the nearly constant winds of the Great Plains for propulsion. On its maiden voyage, his windwagon was able "to take the horse in its teeth and show trim heels to a fresh breeze." But when the contraption tried to zigzag, the steering mechanism came undone. Succeeding windwagons did better, however; one covered 50 miles in one day and reportedly passed 625 teams; another actually arrived in Denver from the east and "everyone crossed the street to get a sight of this newfangled frigate."

Colorful Language of The Old West

No other American figure produced so rich and muscular a body of speech as the cowboy. He had to develop humor to survive the hard life he led; he loved the freedom of range life and it loosened up his language; he was sharply observant of human foibles and had a talent for exaggeration.

When his stomach was empty he felt "hungrier 'n a woodpecker with the headache." He called his bottle of whiskey "Kansas sheep dip," and sometimes he got "so drunk he couldn't hit the ground with his hat in three throws…" but he might "fight you till hell freezes over, then skate with you on the ice."

When he rolled dice and eight was the point, it was "Ada from Decatur"; when the point was nine, it was "Nina from Carolina." At poker a "dead man's hand" was the eights and aces Wild Bill Hickok held when he was shot.

Out on the range the cowhand might be caught in an "Oklahoma rain," a dust storm; or it might be the equally treacherous "blue northers," the deadly, rolling winds that could drop the thermometer 50 degrees in one day.

A puncher's main job, of course, was tending his "cows" as he called all his cattle. Sometimes he called them "critters" or just "beef." To "beef" also means to kill a cow for food. Cattle in a group were a "bunch"; a herd of horses was a "band." An orphan calf was a "leppy," a weak calf was a "dogie."

Among the varmints that preyed on cattle were rustlers. These men turned cow stealing into a fine art. They were adept at changing a ranch's brand with a "running iron." Most rustlers, or "brand artists," started as cowpokes who figured they were as smart as their bosses and found it easy to pick up a few "mavericks" and strays here and there. Some did into "swinging a wide loop" over branded cattle. There were ranchers who got their start this way.

Cattle were gathered up twice a year at roundup time. The "wagon boss" gave the boys their "powders" or orders and the "lead drive men," those whose circuits carried them to the farthest reaches of the ranch, moved out first.

Some cowboy ballads originated as a means of quieting stampede-prone cattle at night. Composed impromptu by cowhands riding around the herds, the often atonal songs took their rhythm from a horse's gait. Sometimes they were simply mournful tones without words and were called "Texas lullabies."

Striking it Rich

Much of the West was settled quickly because men went to inhospitable places to search for gold and silver. Many great strikes were made through pure luck. Marshall, who started it all at Sutter's Mill, happened to notice some yellow flakes in a millrace. One newcomer on Tuolumne River in California panned 43 ounces of gold on his first day. Robert Womack, a cowhand in Colorado, spied a likely looking outcropping of rock at Cripple Creek. He staked a claim and a sample assayed at $250 a ton; delighted, Womack sold out for $500. Subsequently, the claim yielded $5 million. In Arizona, Henry Wickenburg found rich ore when he stooped down to pick up a culture he had shot. In Nevada in 1859, J. F. Stone, a veteran of the California gold fields, found miners cussing a troublesome blue sand that impeded their operations. Stone had the sand tested and the dumfounded assayer reported that the "blue stuff" was worth $4,700 a ton—one-fourth gold, three-fourths silver.

"What Was Your Name in the States?"

*Oh, what was your name in the States?
Was it Thompson or Johnson or Bates?
Did you murder your wife and fly for your life?
Say, what was your name in the States?
favorite ditty of the Forty-Niners*

Kansas Wedding Ceremony

Marrying Squire: Have him?
Bride: Yes.
Marrying Squire: Have her?
Groom: Kinder.
Marrying Squire: Done. One Dollar.

RED CLOUD, greatest of the Oglala Sioux warriors, was not only the best military tactician and strategist among western Indians, but he was also a brilliant diplomat. He was sufficiently skilled to cause the commissioners of the United States to capitulate to his terms in 1868 in the treaty of Laramie.

JIM BRIDGER answered an ad in 1822 for "enterprising young men" to trap furs near the sources of the Missouri. For the next 46 years he trapped, explored, guided expeditions and established Fort Bridger on the Oregon Trail. He had three Indian wives and knew the West as well as any man.

"A Brand's Something That Won't Come Off in the Wash"

Cattle brands in the Old West were a language all their own. When a mark was burned into a cow's hide, it told everyone—rustlers and others—who the cow's owner was. Brands were registered just as trademarks are today; by 1885 Colorado had 50,000 cattle brands on file. Branding traces its origins to antiquity; some brands have their origins in humor, romance and orneriness.

This is the Hell Bar brand from Culberson County, Texas. And this, a stylized andiron, was the brand of the most famous cowboy of all, Will Rogers. Some brands evolved with the years. Don Miguel Peralta started his big spread with this brand. A son, Carlos, was born, and Don Miguel added the "C" to the brand. Then Luis was born, and the brand grew. When José came along, the brand became. Finally Mario arrived and the final curves were added. A wanted man came West with nothing but two .45s which he sold to start his herd. This is his brand. One of the most popular motifs was some version of the dollar sign, such as. One fellow used this brand at first. When he lost money he changed the brand to a Double Zero. A Mr. Daniels, of considerable girth, used this mark. Some other brands used out West are the Bar Nothing, the Lazy Y 4, the Drunken T, the Cloudy Moon.

The Diamond Hoax

One foggy morning in 1872, a pair of prospectors, named Philip Arnold and John Slack, pounded on the door of a San Francisco bank and asked to deposit a leather pouch in the vault. They refused to disclose what was in the pouch. Finally, they were prevailed upon to open it. Out spilled the glittering contents, which they identified as uncut diamonds. With this, the two miners vanished back into the fog.

Their appearance resulted in a diamond boom. William C. Ralston, a prominent banker, formed a mining corporation. Arnold and Slack permitted themselves to be found. They were cut into the company as shareholders and then allowed themselves to be bought over for $300,000 each (they were not greedy, they said).

To allay fears, the stones were sent to Tiffany in New York and were pronounced genuine. But before receiving their payoff, Arnold and Slack were urged to reveal the location of the diamond field. They agreed to let a mining expert, Henry Janin, go with them to the field. After traveling 36 hours aboard a train and two more days aboard a pack mule, blindfolded all the way, Janin returned to San Francisco with few specifics, except another sack of gems that he had personally thumbed out of the gravel. The news kept the boom going.

It was not to last much longer. A well-known geologist, Clarence King, along with two colleagues, decided to go out and find the field. After taking a train to a small Union Pacific Station and riding horseback into the countryside, they reached a mesa about 15 miles southeast of the conjunction of Wyoming, Utah and Colorado. As experts, it didn't take them long to realize that the diamond field was a fraud and that the "mine" had been "salted." The dead giveaway was one superb stone that had been partially cut and polished and was found lying in the open atop a boulder, where any rain storm would have washed it away. Other gems turned up only at the bottom of holes in anthills where either provident ants had buried them or somebody had poked them in with a stick.

Finally the details of the swindle came to light. The two frontier bumpkins, Arnold and Slack, had gone to Amsterdam and bought $25,000 worth of flawed rejects from the city's gem merchants. Arnold presumably repaid the $300,000 he had received; Slack was never caught.

The 1,200-mile journey to market. To the cowboy of the Old West, nothing was more challenging and grueling than the long drive. Usually originating in southern Texas and ending at a railhead like Abilene, Denver or Cheyenne, the drive was organized like a military maneuver. From the first bellowed command of "Ho cattle, ho ho ho ho" to the epic sight of a pair of canny longhorns walking like drill sergeants at the head of a drove of some 2,500 cattle, every step could mean some unforeseen mishap.

Exhibit 119. Inside spread of brochure.

The 9 × 12 full-color envelope featured two strong action illustrations. The mailing side reproduced a cattle drive painting by Frederic Remington. Teaser copy said: "Thundering out of The Old West . . . The Cowboys." "And The Indians" continued the copy on the back side, accompanied by a striking silhouette photograph of an Indian war party (see Exhibit 121).

The order card measured 5½ × 11⅛. As an involvement device, it used a reproduction of an old-style poker chip. The chip was to be punched out of the stub area and affixed to the reply portion of the card (see Exhibit 122).

The so-called publisher's letter was being used in most book mailings at the time to highlight the offer. The letter usually took the form of a memo-size message which folded over with teaser copy on the outside. Time-Life Books went a step further and put the publisher's letter in a small sealed envelope with teaser copy done in the style of a "Wanted" poster (see Exhibit 123).

The mailing plan and results

The award-winning mailing had a production budget of $1,300,000. It included 10 million pieces at a cost of about $130 per thousand with the majority of pieces going

Exhibit 120. Front of four-page letter.

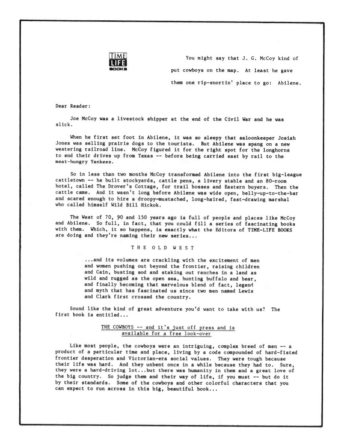

to Time-Life's own lists of book buyers and magazine subscribers. The mailing was released the last week in December 1972.

A small test earlier the same year had been used to establish the viability of the promotion and set the result quota for the big mailing. Among other things, the test had indicated that the series had strong appeal throughout the United States; it wasn't just limited to the western states. And the poker chip order card had been tested against a standard book token and showed a 10 percent result improvement.

But this was the only testing that had been done before the big drop. And Time-Life Books' management decided to make a couple of other changes in the package—changes that they hoped would improve results. But they didn't have time for prior testing. One of these was a change to the outer envelope described earlier which replaced the test envelope that had run into a rights and permissions snafu. Another important change was putting the publisher's letter in a sealed envelope. The results confirmed the judgment. Total response came in 30 percent over the result quota that had been established. On a 10 million-piece mailing, that obviously meant selling a lot of additional volumes!

Exhibit 121. Full-color envelope featuring action illustrations.

The Old West TV campaign

Based on its success in the mail, Time-Life Books naturally began testing other media for *The Old West* series. The media mix included television, which was producing good results on their other books. For its initial test, the firm did a 120-second TV commercial built around "The Cowboys" as the lead book. While not as successful as its direct mail program had been, the spot nevertheless indicated there was potential value for this series in television.

In the meantime, the lead book on the series had been changed to "The Gunfighters." People who have studied the marketing strategy of Time-Life Books know that the company does a lot of testing on its lead books. Sometimes to find the strongest lead book before a series is launched. But also to replace a lead book that is wearing out. It's a very effective strategy because the company can promote a series heavily with one lead book. Then a year or two later, the company can come back with a different lead book that can give ads and mailings a fresh appeal and thus attract a whole new batch of readers.

Exhibit 122. Order card with involvement device.

Exhibit 123. Publisher's letter in envelope with teaser copy.

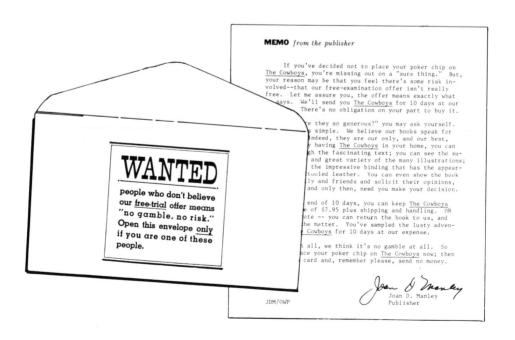

When the decision was made to switch the lead book on *The Old West*, it naturally required a change in the TV spot. Rather than merely update the old spot, the firm decided to do an entire new spot that could do a better job of capturing the flavor and excitement of the product.

TV script packed with action

A continuity book series poses some difficult challenges when it comes to television selling. Even with a two-minute spot, much of the time has to be devoted to explaining the offer—the 10-day free examination on the lead book and the fact that future volumes will be shipped automatically.

Recognizing this problem, Time-Life created a spot that made maximum use of short phrases and a rapid series of illustrations so as much as possible could be crowded into the limited time available.

The announcer was dressed in a western costume. The set was a sheriff's office complete with enough props to establish the Old West atmosphere (see Exhibit 124). Sound effects included gunshots, galloping horses, whooping Indians, locomotives, and banjo music.

As you can see from the following script, the spot started out talking about the volumes on cowboys, Indians, railroaders, and soldiers to establish the breadth of the series. The spot then focused on "The Gunfighters" and the lead book offer.

Video	**Announcer**
1. *Open on full screen of Time-Life Books logo.*	Out of the Old West come . . .
2. *Circle wipe to close-up (CU) of riding rifleman from The Cowboys. Zoom out to reveal entire group of riders. Sound effects (SFX): gunshots, shouts, galloping.*	the cowboys . . .
3. *Cut to cover of The Cowboys.*	
4. *Full screen of book spread.*	
5. *Cut to cover of The Indians.*	the Indians . . .
6. *Full screen of Indian reservation from The Indians. SFX: whooping, drums.*	
7. *Cut to cover of The Railroaders.*	the railroaders . . .
8. *Full screen of locomotive across prairie. SFX: engine, whistle*	
9. *Cut to cover of The Soldiers*	the soldiers . . .
10. *Full screen of soldiers battling Indians. SFX:shouting, gunshots, arrows.*	
11. *Cut to Old West setting: a sheriff's office with rifle rack, desk, potbellied stove, etc. Annnouncer sits behind the desk, beside a display of The Old West series. The Announcer holds up The Cowboys book. Zoom in for a close-up. Super series title.*	and they're all headin' your way in a rip-roarin' series from Time-Life Books called The Old West. These big books have covers that look and feel like real hand-tooled leather.

Video	**Announcer**
12. *Cut to slow pan of book spreads.*	The books are packed with more than 235 pages of rare photographs and authentic paintings by artists like Russell and Remington. True stories and eyewitness accounts that tell you what the lusty days of the Old West were really like.
13. *Cut to CU of narrator with The Gunfighters.*	Begin with The Gunfighters, yours for a ten-day free examination.
14. *Cut to picture of Jesse James. Super: The Gunfighters. SFX: banjo music.*	Meet Jesse James . . .
15. *Cut to Billy the Kid pic.*	Billy the Kid . . .
16. *Pat Garrett*	and Sheriff Pat Garrett . . .
17. *Belle Starr*	Belle Starr . . .
18. *Hardin*	John Wesley Hardin, who was so mean he once shot a man for snoring . . .
19. *Cassidy*	Butch Cassidy and his wild bunch . . .
20. *Bean*	Judge Roy Bean . . .
21. *Bean courthouse*	and all the rest.
22. *Gunfighters book weapons spread.*	You'll see the weapons the gunfighters used,
23. *Gunfighters book town spread with pistol in foreground.*	the wide open towns they fought over . . .
24. *Gunfighters book saloon spread.*	the saloons where they gambled . . .
25. *Gunfighters book hanging spread. SFX: gallows, wind.*	and the gallows that ended many a gunfighter's career.
26. *Cut to Announcer CU.*	Enjoy The Gunfighters for 10 days free.
27. *Back away from Announcer holding Gunfighters. Super price and 10 days free.*	If it's not as exciting as we say it is, return it without further obligation. If you decide to
28. *Cut to book montage, CU The Gunfighters.*	keep it, pay only $7.95 plus shipping and handling. Then, once every other month,
29. *Cut to full screen montage of six books.*	we'll send you future volumes in The Old West. Keep only the books you want, and
30. *Cut to CU of Announcer holding The Gunfighters.*	you can cancel your subscription at any time simply by notifying us.
31. *Zoom up on Announcer and hold.*	These big handsome books bring The Old West right into your living room. Send for The Gunfighters for a free 10-day examination and step back into The Old West. To order, here's all you have to do:

Of course, a local tag was added for each market with ordering instructions. The over-all result was a fast-moving spot with a complex series of fades, pans, and fast cuts that's hard to appreciate from just reading the script.

The new spot first appeared in March 1975. Its performance was 15 percent better than the original spot. This sales improvement was substantial enough to make a number of marginal TV stations pay out. And Time-Life Books soon was awarded another Silver Mailbox.

Exhibit 124. Frame from TV commercial showing Old West atmosphere.

Other media promotions

Space advertising was also an important part of the promotion mix for *The Old West.* Newspaper inserts were used in selected markets. Ads appeared not only in Time-Life's own magazines, but a variety of other publications including *Playboy, Field & Stream, Parade,* and *Family Weekly.*

Typical of the ads is the two-page insert that appeared in a fall 1976 magazine (see Exhibit 125). It offers "The Gunfighters" as the lead book and features photographs of six well-known gunslingers.

Telephone selling has also been used extensively on the series and produced excellent results. The company has 14 regional telephone sales offices spread across the country and has acquired considerable expertise with this selling medium.

Exhibit 125. Front side of magazine insert offering "The Gunfighters."

Over-all results

Perhaps the only disappointment for Time-Life Books with *The Old West* series has been foreign sales. Because of the domestic subject matter, the series doesn't have the broad appeal in other countries that some of Time-Life Books' other series enjoy.

But inside the United States, the series has been tremendously successful. One Time-Life Books executive, in a speech at the Second International Direct Mail/Marketing Conference in June 1975, described it as "our best selling library in terms of orders and profits in the United States."

If you want to see how successful the series has been, just do some quick arithmetic. As pointed out earlier, there have been over 750,000 starters for the series. Assume the average starter buys about $50.00 worth of books or, roughly, six selections at $7.95 each. This represents total mail order sales of over $35 million. And the series is still being actively promoted.

Granted, Time-Life has an extensive house list—about 24 million magazine subscribers and book buyers—that other publishers may not have. But in my opinion, this success story is more a result of a combination that's hard to beat—an outstanding product combined with an outstanding and award-winning promotion effort.

An insider's viewpoint

The following comments about *The Old West* marketing program were provided by Paul Stewart. Stewart is a vice-president of Time-Life Books, Inc., in charge of promotion for the company.

> It takes a lot of time, attention to detail, and dedicated people to make a promotion like this a big winner. A copywriter named Charlie Hollis, for example, spent three to four months researching and writing the newspaper brochure. It was his concept and he worked damn hard to make it come off.

> Or take the amount of thought that went into the mailing envelope. Over-all, we wanted an exciting envelope, one with both four-color and black-and-white illustrations. This represents the mix of color and black-and-white photographs in the books. (We adhere to this formula as it makes the reader's expectations more accurate when he receives the first book.) The envelope also advertises material from *two* books. The concept of Cowboys art on the front and Indians art on the back helps in creating the idea of a series.

> The poker chip token on the order card and the publisher's "Wanted" memo were two beliefs of mine that *The Old West* mailing should be fun and full of nostalgia. Over the years, we have made the brochure bigger to show more books and more material from the series. The more books shown in a mailing piece, the better the back-end performance of a subscriber (which is really where your profits are).

> Television turned out to be a tremendous triumph for us. Traditional direct response spots had no sound effects, no music, no razzamatazz—on the philosophy that such shenanigans lowered response. But we added them to our Gunfighters spot and it beat the original spot hands-down.

> Space advertising and telephone sales have also been very successful. I have no doubt that our direct mail, TV promotion, magazine ads, and newspaper inserts have all helped pave the way for telephone sales.

Most important of all, you need great books to generate a successful campaign. For our promotion efforts are merely designed to show *The Old West* for what it is—a downright fascinating series of books.

Appendix

The mathematics of planning profitable mailings

by Virgil D. Angerman, former Sales Promotion Manager, Boise Cascade Envelope Division

One of the questions asked frequently at direct mail meetings is, "How many orders per thousand can I expect?" Obviously, no one can give an accurate answer to that question; there are too many variables involved.

The response from a mailing depends upon the nature of the proposition offered; the copy used; the offer—whether cash, billed, or sold on time payments; the mailing list used; the appearance of the envelope; whether you use first or third class postage; the date of mailing; and the general economic condition of the country at the time of mailing.

Any one of these factors or variables can influence the pull of a mailing. It's not a question of how many orders per thousand can I expect, but how many orders per thousand *must I get* to breakeven.

To determine the breakeven point, you must know the actual cost of obtaining and filling an order. We have prepared a worksheet to show you how to do it. The figures used in the worksheet example are those experienced by several mailers of the offer.

Once you know the breakeven figure, you can proceed with your tests. The following worksheets show you how to calculate your breakeven point. (See Exhibits 126 through 130.)

[Editor's Note: These worksheets are presented with the original figures used by Virgil Angerman. Today it is difficult to make a mailing for $100 per thousand. But you can use the blank worksheet provided to figure your breakeven point using current costs. See Exhibit 131.]

Exhibit 126.

WORKSHEET FOR PLANNING PROFITABLE MAILINGS

Date: _Date_

PROPOSITION _4-Vol. Set "Practical Mathematics"_ KEY _64_

1 - Selling Price of Merchandise or Service	**$ 25.00**	
2 - Cost of Filling the Order		
a) Merchandise or Service	6.00	
b) Royalty	none	
c) Handling Expense (Drop Shipping & Order Processing)	.95	
d) Postage and Shipping Expense	.60	
e) Premium, including Handling and Postage	.30	
f) Use Tax, if any (1 x _3_ %)	.75	
TOTAL COST OF FILLING THE ORDER		8.60
3 - Administrative Overhead		
a) Rent, Light, Heat, Maintenance, Credit Checking, Collections, etc. (_10_ % of # 1)	2.50	
TOTAL ADMINISTRATIVE COST		2.50
4 - Estimated Percentage of Returns, Refunds or Cancellations	10%	
5 - Expense in Handling Returns		
a) Return Postage and Handling (2c plus 2d)	1.55	
b) Refurbishing Returned Merchandise (_10_ % of # 2a)	.60	
TOTAL COST OF HANDLING RETURNS	2.15	
6 - Chargeable Cost of Returns (_10_ % of $2.15)		.21
7 - Estimated Bad Debt Percentage	10%	
8 - Chargeable Cost of Bad Debts (# 1 x # 7)		2.50
9 - Total Variable Costs (# 2 plus # 3, # 6, and # 8)		13.81
10 - Unit Profit after Deducting Variable Costs (# 1 less # 9)		11.19
11 - Return Factor (100% less # 4)	90%	
12 - Unit Profit Per Order (# 10 x # 11)		10.07
13 - Credit for Returned Merchandise (_10_ % of # 2a)		.60
14 - Net Profit Per Order (# 12 plus # 13)		10.67
15 - Cost of Mailing per 1,000	100.50	
16 - NUMBER OF ORDERS PER 1,000 NEEDED TO BREAK EVEN		10.6

For additional copies of this form, contact Marketing Services Manager,
Boise Cascade Envelope Division, 313 Rohlwing Rd., Addison, IL 60101 - Tel. 312, 629-5000

Form No. 8-1

Exhibit 127.

HOW TO USE THE WORKSHEET

Let's take a hypothetical mail-order proposition and go through the various steps to see what costs must be included to determine how many orders per thousand you must get to break even. First, the Worksheet should carry the date, name of proposition, and the key or code for that particular mailing. You need this for future reference.

Date: _Date_

PROPOSITION _4-Vol Set "Practical Mathematics"_   KEY _64_

ITEM #1. Now, we start with Item #1, the retail selling price of the merchandise or service. In this case, let's say we are selling a 4-Volume set of books, "Practical Mathematics", for $25.00 on 10 days' free examination with a premium, a Calculating Chart, included as a "look-see" introduction. The customer keeps the chart whether he buys or returns the books. Post $25.00 in the panel opposite Item #1.

1 - Selling Price of Merchandise or Service	**$ 25.00**

ITEM #2. Under Item #2, we enter: 2-a, your cost of the books, including shipping carton, which is $6.00. This gives over a 4-to-1 mark-up which is an ideal selling margin.

Next consideration is Royalty, 2-b. If you are publishing a book or selling an item on which a royalty is paid to the author, manufacturer or inventor, this expense should be included as a part of the total cost of the merchandise or service. The author's royalty on books sold by mail is usually only 5% of the retail price because of the high promotional expense. Books sold through the retail trade, as a rule, carry a 10% royalty based on the retail price. Royalties to manufacturers and inventors vary from 1% to 5%, depending upon the market possibilities and the retail price of the item. In this hypothetical case there is no royalty, as the books are purchased from another publisher.

The Handling Expense (2-c) which includes the opening of the mail and processing the order for fulfillment amounts to 95¢. Postage and shipping expense (2-d) is 60¢. As we included a "look-see" premium in this offer, (Calculating Chart 2-e), we must add this item (30¢ cost) as a part of the expense of filling the order. If your State has a Use Tax (2-f), this must be added, also. Let's take 3% as an example. Multiply Item #1 by 3% and you have 75¢ tax. Adding all the expenses under #2, it costs $8.60 to fill an order.

2 - Cost of Filling the Order

a) Merchandise or Service	6.00
b) Royalty	none
c) Handling Expense (Drop Shipping & Order Processing)	.95
d) Postage and Shipping Expense	.60
e) Premium, including Handling and Postage	.30
f) Use Tax, if any (1 x _3_ %)	.75
TOTAL COST OF FILLING THE ORDER	8.60

Exhibit 128.

ITEM #3. But there are other costs that must be included. How about administrative costs which include rent, light, heat, use of equipment, maintenance, expense of checking credit, collection follow-up, office supplies, etc.? Many firms make a flat charge of 10% to 20% of the Retail Price (#1) to cover these expenses. Let's use 10% of $25.00 or $2.50, and enter this under #3-a as the total administrative cost.

3 - Administrative Overhead

    a) Rent, Light, Heat, Maintenance, Credit Checking, Collections, etc. (10 % of # 1)------------------------------ **2.50**

    TOTAL ADMINISTRATIVE COST-- **2.50**

ITEM #4. The next question is what percentage of your customers will return the merchandise if sold on a free examination offer? Suppose we take 10% as an average and post this under Item #4.

4 - Estimated Percentage of Returns, Refunds or Cancellations ------------------ **10%**

ITEM #5. How much does it cost to handle returns? It certainly costs as much as it did to ship the books. So let's charge $1.55 (2-c plus 2-d) for this item. Of course, some customers will prepay returned merchandise but let's not count on it. Some of the books may be damaged in shipping, so allow 10% of the cost of the set (10% of $6.00 (2-a) or 60¢ for refurbishing (5-b). This brings the Total Cost of Handling Returns (Item #5) to $2.15 per order.

5 - Expense in Handling Returns

    a) Return Postage and Handling (2c plus 2d) ----------------------- **1.55**

    b) Refurbishing Returned Merchandise (10 % of # 2a)-------------- **.60**

    TOTAL COST OF HANDLING RETURNS -------------------------------- **2.15**

ITEM #6. As we are figuring that 10% of the orders will be returns, refunds or cancellations (Item #4), the Total Cost of Handling Returns will be 10% of $2.15 (Item #5), 21.5 cents per order. Let's say 21¢.

6 - Chargeable Cost of Returns (10 % of $2.15)----------------------------- **.21**

ITEM #7. Bad debts are another expense that must be considered. This percentage will vary from about 5% to 25%, depending upon the proposition, the way the offer is presented and the list used. Let's take 10% as an average figure and enter it in Item #7.

7 - Estimated Bad Debt Percentage -- **10%**

ITEM #8. The Chargeable Cost of Bad Debts is 10% (Item #7) times $25.00 (Item #1). This amounts to $2.50 that must be allowed for the cost of bad debts. Enter $2.50 opposite Item #8.

8 - Chargeable Cost of Bad Debts (# 1 x # 7) ------------------------------------- **2.50**

Exhibit 129.

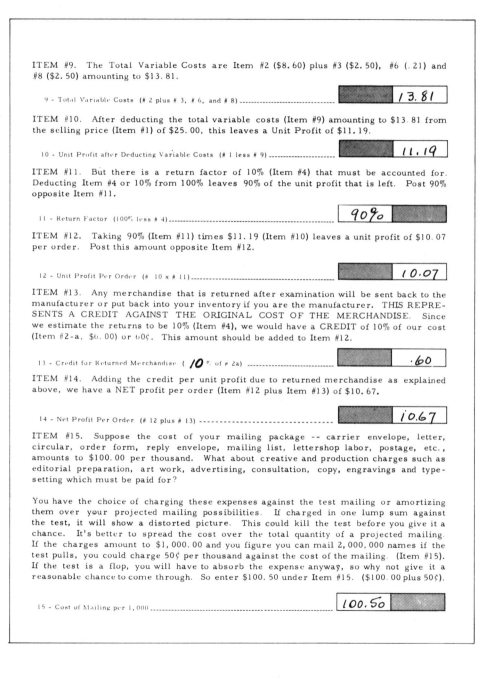

ITEM #9. The Total Variable Costs are Item #2 ($8.60) plus #3 ($2.50), #6 (.21) and #8 ($2.50) amounting to $13.81.

9 - Total Variable Costs (# 2 plus # 3, # 6, and # 8) ------------------------------ 13.81

ITEM #10. After deducting the total variable costs (Item #9) amounting to $13.81 from the selling price (Item #1) of $25.00, this leaves a Unit Profit of $11.19.

10 - Unit Profit after Deducting Variable Costs (# 1 less # 9) ---------------------- 11.19

ITEM #11. But there is a return factor of 10% (Item #4) that must be accounted for. Deducting Item #4 or 10% from 100% leaves 90% of the unit profit that is left. Post 90% opposite Item #11.

11 - Return Factor (100% less # 4) --- 90%

ITEM #12. Taking 90% (Item #11) times $11.19 (Item #10) leaves a unit profit of $10.07 per order. Post this amount opposite Item #12.

12 - Unit Profit Per Order (# 10 x # 11)------------------------------------- 10.07

ITEM #13. Any merchandise that is returned after examination will be sent back to the manufacturer or put back into your inventory if you are the manufacturer. THIS REPRESENTS A CREDIT AGAINST THE ORIGINAL COST OF THE MERCHANDISE. Since we estimate the returns to be 10% (Item #4), we would have a CREDIT of 10% of our cost (Item #2-a, $6.00) or 60¢. This amount should be added to Item #12.

13 - Credit for Returned Merchandise (10 % of # 2a) --------------------------- .60

ITEM #14. Adding the credit per unit profit due to returned merchandise as explained above, we have a NET profit per order (Item #12 plus Item #13) of $10.67.

14 - Net Profit Per Order (# 12 plus # 13) ------------------------------- 10.67

ITEM #15. Suppose the cost of your mailing package -- carrier envelope, letter, circular, order form, reply envelope, mailing list, lettershop labor, postage, etc., amounts to $100.00 per thousand. What about creative and production charges such as editorial preparation, art work, advertising, consultation, copy, engravings and type-setting which must be paid for?

You have the choice of charging these expenses against the test mailing or amortizing them over your projected mailing possibilities. If charged in one lump sum against the test, it will show a distorted picture. This could kill the test before you give it a chance. It's better to spread the cost over the total quantity of a projected mailing. If the charges amount to $1,000.00 and you figure you can mail 2,000,000 names if the test pulls, you could charge 50¢ per thousand against the cost of the mailing. (Item #15). If the test is a flop, you will have to absorb the expense anyway, so why not give it a reasonable chance to come through. So enter $100.50 under Item #15. ($100.00 plus 50¢).

15 - Cost of Mailing per 1,000 -- 100.50

Exhibit 130.

ITEM #16. If you have a Net Profit Per Order of $10.67 (#14) and the cost of mailing 1,000 letters is $100.50, divide $10.67 into $100.50 and you need 10.6 orders, or 1.06% per thousand to break even.

16 - NUMBER OF ORDERS PER 1,000 NEEDED TO BREAK EVEN------------------ | | 10.6

Suppose your breakeven point on a test mailing is 10.6 orders (1.06%) per thousand letters mailed. How many orders more than 10.6 per thousand should you get to justify going ahead with a large mailing? It is generally considered safe if you get 33-1/3% (1/3) more orders. In this analysis, 1/3 more than 10.6 would give us a total of 14.1 orders per thousand or 3.5 orders more than the breakeven point.

If the final mailing pulled 14.1 orders per thousand, 3.5 orders more than the breakeven point, and the unit profit is $10.67 per order, the net profit would be $37.335 per thousand. (3.5 x $10.67). On a 100,000 mailing, the net profit would be $3,733.50; on 500,000, it would be $18,667.50; on one million $37,335.00.

A word of Caution! The time elapsing between the date of the test and the date of the final mailing may affect results. For example, a test made in January that pulls 14.1 orders per thousand might pull only 10.6 or less if mailed in June. So test in the poor months, if possible, and mail in the good months to eliminate unprofitable mailings.

Exhibit 131.

WORKSHEET FOR PLANNING PROFITABLE MAILINGS

Date: _____

PROPOSITION _____ KEY _____

1 - Selling Price of Merchandise or Service ----------------------------------

2 - Cost of Filling the Order

    a) Merchandise or Service -----------------------------

    b) Royalty ---

    c) Handling Expense (Drop Shipping & Order Processing)----------------

    d) Postage and Shipping Expense----------------------------------

    e) Premium, including Handling and Postage----------------------------

    f) Use Tax, if any (1 x _____ %) -----------------------------------

    TOTAL COST OF FILLING THE ORDER----------------------------

3 - Administrative Overhead

    a) Rent, Light, Heat, Maintenance, Credit Checking,
       Collections, etc. (_____ % of # 1)---------------------

    TOTAL ADMINISTRATIVE COST----------------------------------

4 - Estimated Percentage of Returns, Refunds or Cancellations ---------------------

5 - Expense in Handling Returns

    a) Return Postage and Handling (2c plus 2d) ----------------------------

    b) Refurbishing Returned Merchandise (_____ % of # 2a)---------------

    TOTAL COST OF HANDLING RETURNS -----------------------------------

6 - Chargeable Cost of Returns (_____ % of $ _____)----------------------------

7 - Estimated Bad Debt Percentage ------------------------------------

8 - Chargeable Cost of Bad Debts (# 1 x # 7) ----------------------------

9 - Total Variable Costs (# 2 plus # 3, # 6, and # 8) ------------------------

10 - Unit Profit after Deducting Variable Costs (# 1 less # 9) --------------------

11 - Return Factor (100% less # 4) ------------------------------------

12 - Unit Profit Per Order (# 10 x # 11)------------------------------------

13 - Credit for Returned Merchandise (_____ % of # 2a) --------------------

14 - Net Profit Per Order (# 12 plus # 13) -----------------------------

15 - Cost of Mailing per 1,000 ---

16 - NUMBER OF ORDERS PER 1,000 NEEDED TO BREAK EVEN ----------------

For additional copies of this form, contact Marketing Services Manager,
Boise Cascade Envelopes Division, 313 Rohlwing Rd., Addison, IL 60101 - Tel. 312, 629-5000

Form No. 8.9

Kobs' 99 proven direct response offers

A review of tested, successful propositions that can improve your results.

Basic offers

1. *Right price.* The starting point for any product or service being sold by mail. Consider your market and what's being charged for competitive products. And make sure you have sufficient margin for your offer to be profitable. Most products sold by mail require at least a three-time markup.

2. *Free trial.* If mail order advertisers suddenly had to standardize all their efforts on one offer, this would no doubt be the choice. Widely used for book and merchandise promotions. Viewed from the standpoint of a consumer, the free trial relieves the fear that you might get stuck buying by mail, because the advertiser is willing to let you try *his* product before he gets *your* money. Most free trial periods are 10 or 15 days. But the length of the trial period should fit the type of product or service being offered.

3. *Money-back guarantee.* If for some good reason you can't use a free-trial offer, this is the next best thing. The main difference is that you ask the customer to pay part or all of the purchase price *before* you let him or her try your product. This puts inertia on your side. The customer is unlikely to take the time and effort to send a product back unless he or she is really unhappy with it.

4. *Cash with order.* This is the basic payment option used with a money-back guarantee. It's also offered with a choice of other payment options. Incentives (such as paying the postage and handling charge) are often used to encourage the customer to send his or her check or money order when the order is placed.

5. *Bill me later.* This is the basic payment option used with free-trial offers. The bill is usually enclosed with the merchandise or follows a few days later. And it calls for a single payment. Because no front-end payment is required by the customer, the response can be as much as double that of a cash offer.

6. *Installment terms.* This payment option works like the one above, except that it usually involves a bigger sale price with installment terms set up to keep the payments around $10.00 to $20.00 per month. Usually this is a necessity in selling big-ticket items by mail to the consumer.

7. *Charge card privileges.* Offers the same advantages of "bill me later" and installment plans but the seller doesn't have to carry the paper. Can be used with bank charge cards, travel and entertainment cards, and specialized cards (like those issued by the oil companies).

8. *C.O.D.* This is the U.S. Postal Service acronym for Cash-On-Delivery. The mailcarrier collects when he or she delivers the package. Not widely used today because of the added cost and effort required to handle C.O.D. orders.

Free gift offers

9. *Free gift for an inquiry.* Provides an incentive to request more information about a product or service. Usually increases inquiries, though they become somewhat less qualified.

10. *Free gift for a trial order.* Commonly called a "keeper" gift, because the customer gets to keep the gift just for agreeing to try the product.

11. *Free gift for buying.* Similar to the above, except the customer only gets to keep the gift if he or she buys the product or service. The gift can be given free with any order, tied to a minimum purchase, or used as a self-liquidator.

12. *Multiple free gifts with a single order.* If one gift pays out for you, consider offering two or more. You may even be able to offer two inexpensive gifts and spend the same amount as one more expensive item. Biggest user of multiple gifts is Fingerhut Corporation. At last count, they were up to four free gifts for a single order!

13. *Your choice of free gifts.* Can be a quick way to test the relative appeal of different gift items. But will seldom work as well as the best gift offered on its own. The choice probably leads to indecision on the consumer's part.

14. *Free gifts based on size of order.* Often used with catalogs or merchandise suitable for a quantity purchase. You can offer an inexpensive gift for orders under $10.00, a better gift for orders running between $10.00 and $25.00, and a deluxe gift for orders over $25.00.

15. *Two-step gift offer.* Offers an inexpensive gift if the customer takes the first step, a better gift for taking the second step. Such as a free record album for trying a new stereo set, and a deluxe headset if you elect to buy it.

16. *Continuing incentive gifts.* Used to get customers to keep coming back. Book clubs often give bonus coupons to save up for additional books. Also suitable is silverware where you give one place setting per order. Or trading stamps, like S&H Green Stamps.

17. *Mystery gift offer.* Sometimes works better than offering a specific gift. It helps if you can give some indication of the item's retail value.

Other free offers

18. *Free information.* Certainly an inexpensive offer, and a very flexible one. The type of information you provide can range from a simple product catalog sheet to a full-blown series of mailings. If the information is not going to be delivered by a salesperson, this should be played up.

19. *Free catalog.* Can be an attractive offer for both the consumer and the business market. In the business field, catalogs are often used as buying guides and saved for future reference. In the consumer field, you can often attach a nominal charge for postage and handling or offer a full year's catalog subscription.

20. *Free booklet.* Helps establish your company's expertise and know-how about the specific problems of your industry. Especially if the booklet contains helpful editorial material, not just a commercial for your product or service. The booklet should have an appealing title, like "How to Save Money on Heating Costs" or "29 Ways to Improve Your Quality Control System."

21. *Free fact kit.* Sometimes called an Idea Kit. It's usually put together in an attractive file folder or presentation cover. You can include a variety of enclosures from booklets to trade paper articles to ad reprints.

22. *Send me a salesman.* This one is included here because the offer is actually a free sales call with wording like "have your representative phone me for an

appointment." Normally produces more qualified inquiries than a free booklet or fact kit. Those who respond are probably ready to order or seriously considering it.

23. *Free demonstration.* Important for things like business equipment that has to be demonstrated to be fully appreciated. If the equipment is small enough, it can be brought into the prospect's plant or office. If not, the prospect might be invited to a private showing or group demonstration at the manufacturer's facilities.

24. *Free "survey of your needs."* Ideal for some industrial products or services. Like a company that sells chemicals for various water treatment problems. Offering a free survey by a sales representative or technical expert is appealing and gives you the opportunity to qualify a prospect and see if your product or service really fits his or her needs.

25. *Free cost estimate.* Many large industrial sales are only made after considerable study and cost analysis. The offer of a free estimate can be the first step in triggering such a sale.

26. *Free dinner.* Like the rest of the offers that follow in this section, this one is particularly suited to certain types of direct marketing companies. It's widely used by real estate or land companies that offer a free dinner at a nearby restaurant. Persons who attend also get a sales presentation on the property.

27. *Free film offer.* Many mail order film processing companies have been built with some variation of this offer. Either the customer gets a new roll of film when he or she sends one in for processing, or the first roll is offered free in hopes that it will be sent back to the same company later for processing.

28. *Free house organ subscription.* Many industrial companies put out elaborate house organs for customers and prospects which contain a good deal of helpful editorial material. You can offer a free sample issue. Or better yet, a year's subscription.

29. *Free talent test.* Popular with home-study schools. Especially those that offer a skilled course, such as writing or painting. Legal restrictions require that any such test be used to measure real talent or ability, not just as a door opener for the salesperson.

30. *Gift shipment service.* This is one of the basic appeals of offers used by virtually all mail order cheese and gift-food firms. You send them your gift list, and they ship direct to the recipients at no extra cost.

Discount offers

31. *Cash discount.* This is the basic type of discount. It's often dramatized by including a discount certificate in the ad or mailing. However, it should be tested carefully. In most cases, a discount offer will not do as well as an attractive free gift of the same value.

32. *Short-term introductory offer.* A popular type of discount used to let somebody try the product for a short period at a reduced price. Examples include "Try 10 weeks of the *Wall Street Journal* for only $5.97" and "30 days of accident insurance for only 25¢." It's important to be able to convert respondents to long-term subscribers or policyholders.

33. *Refund certificate.* Technically, it's a delayed discount. You might ask somebody to send $1.00 for your catalog and include a $1.00 refund certificate good

on a first order. The certificate is like an uncashed check—it's difficult to resist the urge to cash it.

34. *Introductory order discount.* A special discount used to bring in new customers. Can sometimes cause complaints from old customers if they're not offered the same discount.

35. *Trade discount.* Usually extended to certain clubs, institutions, or particular types of businesses.

36. *Early-bird discount.* Designed to get customers to stock up before the normal buying season. Many Christmas cards and gifts have been sold by mail with this offer.

37. *Quantity discount.* This discount is tied to a certain quantity or order volume. The long-term subscriptions offered by magazines are really a quantity discount.The cost per copy is usually lower on a two-year subscription because it represents a quantity purchase—say, 24 issues instead of 12.

38. *Sliding-scale discount.* In this case, the amount of the discount depends on the date somebody orders or the size of the order. Such as a 2 percent discount for orders up to $50.00, a 5 percent discount for orders over $50.00, and a 10 percent discount for orders over $100.

39. *Selected discounts.* These are often sprinkled throughout a catalog to emphasize certain items the advertiser wants to push or give the appearance that everything is on sale.

Sale offers

40. *Seasonal sales.* Such as a pre-Christmas sale or a summer vacation sale. If successful, they are often repeated every year at the same time.

41. *Reason-why sales.* This category includes inventory reduction, clearance sales, and similar titles. These explanatory terms help give the sale a reason-for-being and make it more believable to the prospect.

42. *Price-increase notice.* A special type of offer that's like a limited-time sale. Gives customers a last chance to order at the old prices before increases become effective.

43. *Auction-by-mail.* An unusual type of sale. Has been used to sell such items as lithographs and electronic calculators when their quantities were limited. Customers send in a "sealed bid" with merchandise usually going to the highest bidder.

Sample offers

44. *Free sample.* If your product lends itself to sampling, this is a strong offer. Sometimes you can offer a sample made *with* or *by* your product. Such as a steel company who uses take-apart puzzles made from their steel wire. Or a printer who offers samples of helpful printed material it has produced for other customers.

45. *Nominal charge samples.* In many cases, making a nominal charge for a sample—like 10¢, 25¢ or $1.00—will pull better than a free-sample offer. The charge helps establish the value of the item and screens out some of the curiosity seekers.

46. *Sample offer with tentative commitment.* This is also known as the "complimentary copy" offer used by many magazines. In requesting the sample, the prospect is also making a tentative commitment for a subscription. But if the prospect doesn't like the first issue, he or she just writes "cancel" on the bill and sends it back.

47. *Quantity sample offer.* A specialized offer that has worked for business services and newsletters. Like a sales training bulletin where the sales manager is told to "just tell us how many salespeople you have, and we'll send a free sample bulletin for each one."

48. *Free sample lesson.* This has been widely used by home study schools who offer a sample lesson to demonstrate the scope and content of their course.

Time limit offers

49. *Limited-time offers.* Any limited-time offer tends to force a quick decision and avoid procrastination. It's usually best to mention a specific date, such as "This special offer expires November 20" rather than "This offer expires in 10 days."

50. *Enrollment periods.* Have been widely used by mail order insurance companies who include a specific cutoff date for the enrollment period. It implies that there are savings involved by processing an entire group of enrollments at one time.

51. *Prepublication offer.* Long a favorite with publishers who offer a special discount or savings before the official publication date of a new book. The rationale is that it helps them plan their printing quantity more accurately.

52. *Charter membership (or subscription) offer.* Ideal for introducing new clubs, publications, and other subscription services. Usually includes a special price, gift, or other incentive for charter members or subscribers. And it appeals to those who like to be among the first to try new things.

53. *Limited edition offer.* A relatively new direct response offer. But a proven way to go for selling coins, art prints, and other collectible items.

Guarantee offers

54. *Extended guarantee.* Such as letting the customer return a book up to a year later. Or with a magazine, offering to refund the unexpired portion of a subscription any time before it runs out.

55. *Double-your-money-back guarantee.* Really dramatizes your confidence in the product. But it better live up to advertising claims if you make an offer like this.

56. *Guaranteed buy-back agreement.* While it's similar to the extended guarantee, this specialized version is often used with limited edition offers on coins and art objects. To convince the prospect of their value, the advertiser offers to buy them back at the full price during a specified period that may last as long as five years.

57. *Guaranteed acceptance offer.* This specialized offer is used by insurance firms with certain types of policies that require no health questions or underwriting. It's especially appealing to those with health problems who might not otherwise qualify.

Build-up-the-sale offers

58. *Multi-product offers.* Two or more products or services are featured in the same ad or mailing. Maybe you've never thought about it this way, but the best-known type of multiproduct offer is a catalog, which can feature a hundred or more items.

59. *Piggyback offers.* Similar to a multiproduct offer, except that one product is strongly featured. The other items just kind of ride along or "piggyback" in the hope of picking up additional sales.

60. *The deluxe offer.* A publisher might offer a book in standard binding at $9.95. The order form gives the customer the option of ordering a deluxe edition for only $2.00 more. And it's not unusual for 10 percent or more of those ordering to select the deluxe alternative.

61. *Good-better-best offer.* This one goes a step further by offering three choices. The mail order mints, for example, sometimes offer their medals in a choice of bronze, sterling silver, or 24K gold.

62. *Add-on offer.* A low-cost item related to the featured product can be great for impulse orders. Such as offering a wallet for $7.95 with a matching key case offered for only $1.00 extra.

63. *Write-your-own-ticket offer.* Some magazines have used this with good success to build up the sale. Instead of offering 17 weeks for $4.93, which is 29¢ per issue, they give the subscriber the 29¢-an-issue price and let him or her fill in the number of weeks he or she wants the subscription to run.

64. *Bounce-back offer.* This approach tries to build on the original sale by enclosing an additional offer with the product shipment or invoice.

65. *Increase and extension offers.* These are also follow-ups to the original sale. Mail order insurance firms often give policyholders a chance to get increased coverage with a higher-priced version of the same policy. Magazines often use an advance renewal offer to get subscribers to extend their present subscription.

Sweepstakes offers

66. *Drawing-type sweepstakes.* The majority of sweepstakes contests are set up this way. The prospect gets one or more chances to win. But all winners are selected by a random drawing.

67. *Lucky number sweepstakes.* With this type of contest, winning numbers are preselected before the mailing is made or an ad is run. Copy strategy emphasizes "You may have already won." And for those winning numbers that are not actually entered or returned, a drawing is held for the unclaimed prizes.

68. *"Everybody wins" sweepstakes.* No longer widely used, but a real bonanza when this offer was first introduced. The prize structure is set up so the bottom or low-end prize is a very inexpensive or nominal one. And it's awarded to everyone who enters and doesn't win one of the bigger prizes.

69. *Involvement sweepstakes.* This type requires the prospect to open a mystery envelope, play a game, or match his or her number against an eligible number list. In doing so, the prospect determines the value of the grand prize he or she wins *if* that entry is drawn as the winner. Some of these involvement devices have been highly effective in boosting results.

70. *Talent contests.* Not really a sweepstakes, but effective for some types of direct marketing situations. Such as the mail order puzzle clubs and the "draw me" ad which offers a free scholarship from a home-study art school.

Club and continuity offers

71. *Positive option.* You join a club and are notified monthly of new selections. To order, you must take some positive action, such as sending back an order.

72. *Negative option.* You are still notified in advance of new selections. But under the terms you agreed to when joining, the new selection is shipped *unless* you return a rejection card by a specific date.

73. *Automatic shipments.* This variation eliminates the advance notice of new selections. When you sign up, you give the publisher permission to ship each selection automatically until you tell him or her to stop. It's commonly called a "Till Forbid" offer.

74. *Continuity load-up offer.* Usually used for a continuity book series, like a 20-volume encyclopedia. The first book is offered free. But after you receive and pay for the next couple of monthly volumes, the balance of the series is sent in one load-up shipment. However, you can continue to pay at the rate of one volume per month.

75. *Front-end load-ups.* This is where a record club gives you four records for $1.00, if you agree to sign up and accept at least four more selections during the next year. The attractive front-end offer persuades you to make a minimum purchase commitment. And the commitment usually has a fixed time period for buying your remaining selections.

76. *Open-ended commitment.* Like the front-end load-up, except that there is no time limit for purchasing your four additional selections.

77. *"No-strings-attached" commitment.* Like the above two offers, except it's more generous because you are not committed to any future purchases. The publisher gambles that you will find future selections interesting enough to make a certain number of purchases.

78. *Lifetime membership fee.* You pay a one-time fee to join—usually $5.00 or $10.00—and get a monthly announcement of new selections. But there's no minimum commitment, and all ordering is done on a positive-option basis.

79. *Annual membership fee.* Here you pay an annual fee for club membership. It's often used for travel clubs where you get a whole range of benefits, including travel insurance. Also used for fund-raising, where a choice of membership levels is often effective.

Specialized offers

80. *The philanthropic privilege.* This is the basis of all fund-raising offers. The donor's contribution usually brings nothing tangible in return but helps make the world a better place in which to live. Sometimes enhanced by giving gummed stamps, a membership card, or other tokens of appreciation.

81. *Blank check offer.* First used in the McGovern fund-raising campaign. Supporters could fill out blank, post-dated checks which were cashed one-a-month to provide installment contributions. Later adapted for extending credit to bank charge card customers.

82. *Executive preview charge.* A successful offer for such things as sales training films. Executive agrees to pay $25.00 to screen or preview the film. But if he decides to buy or rent it, the preview price is credited against the full price.

83. *Yes/no offers.* Asks the prospect to let you know his or her decision either way. In most cases the negative responses have little or no value. But by forcing a decision, you often end up with more "yes" responses.

84. *Self-qualification offer.* Uses a choice of options to get the prospect to indicate a degree of interest in your product or service. Such as offering a free booklet or a free demonstration. Those who request the latter qualify themselves as serious prospects and should get more immediate attention.

85. *Exclusive rights for your trading area.* Ideal for selling some business services to firms who are in a competitive business. Such as a syndicated newsletter that a bank buys and sends to its customers. You give the first bank that responds an exclusive for its trading area. The percentages that order are such that you seldom have to turn anybody down.

86. *The super-dramatic offer.* Sometimes very effective. Such as the offer to "Smoke my new kind of pipe for 30 days. If you don't like it, smash it up with a hammer and send back the pieces."

87. *Trade-in offer.* An offer like "We'll give you $10.00 for your old slide rule when you buy a new electronic calculator" can be very appealing.

88. *Third-party referral offer.* Instead of renting somebody's list, you get the list owner to make a mailing for you—over his or her name—and recommend your product or service. Usually works better than your own promotion because of the rapport a company has with its own customers.

89. *Member-get-a-member offer.* Often used to get customers to send in the names of friends who might be interested. Widely used by book and record clubs who give their member a free gift if he or she gets a new member to sign up.

90. *Name-getter offers.* Usually designed for building a prospect list. A firm can offer a low-cost premium at an attractive self-liquidating price.

91. *Purchase-with-purchase.* Widely used by cosmetic firms and department stores. An attractive gift set is offered at a special price with a regular purchase.

92. *Delayed billing offer.* The appeal is "Order now and we won't bill you until next month." Especially effective before holidays when people have other expenses.

93. *Reduced down payment.* Frequently used as a follow-up in an extended mailing series. If customer does not respond to the regular offer in previous mailings, you reduce the down payment to make it easier for the customer to get started.

94. *Stripped-down products.* Also used in an extended mailing series. A home-study school, for example, which doesn't get the prospect to order the full course will come back with a starter course at a lower price.

95. *Secret bonus gift.* Usually used with TV support. The commercial offers an extra bonus gift not mentioned in the ad or mailing being supported, such as offering a bonus record if you write the album number in the "secret gold box" on the order form.

96. *Rush shipping service.* An appealing offer for things like seasonal gifts and film processing. Customers are often asked to pay an extra charge for this service.

97. *The competitive offer.* Can be a strong way to dramatize your selling story. Like Diner's Club offering prospects $5.00 to turn in their American Express card.

98. *The nominal reimbursement offer.* Used for research mailings. A token payment is offered to get somebody to fill out and return a questionnaire.

99. *Establish-the-value offer.* With an attractive free gift, you can build its value and establish credibility by offering an extra one for a friend at the regular price.

Bibliography

Most of these publications can be ordered directly from Crain Books (Chicago) or the Direct Mail Marketing Association. Many are also available in the business reference sections of public libraries. Naturally, these prices are subject to change.

Direct Mail and Mail Order Handbook
by Richard S. Hodgson
2nd edition
Dartnell
4660 Ravenswood Avenue
Chicago, IL 60640
$39.50

Direct Mail List Rates and Data
Standard Rate and Data Service
5201 Old Orchard Road
Skokie, IL 60076
$55.00 semiannually

Direct Marketing Magazine
Hoke Communications, Inc.
224 Seventh Street
Garden City, NY 11530
$20.00 annually

Fact Book on Direct Response Marketing
Direct Mail Marketing Association
6 E. 43rd Street
New York, NY 10017
$19.97

Friday Report—Newsletter
Hoke Communications, Inc.
224 Seventh Street
Garden City, NY 11530
$60.00 per year—published weekly

Handbook of Industrial Direct Mail Advertising
edited by Edward N. Mayer, Jr., and Roy Ljungren
Business/Professional Advertising Association
205 E. 42nd Street
New York, NY 10017
$10.00

How to Build Your Business by Telephone
by Murray Roman
McGraw-Hill Book Company
1221 Avenue of the Americas
New York, NY 10020
$16.50

How to Start and Operate a Mail Order Business
by Julian L. Simon
2nd edition
McGraw-Hill Book Company
1221 Avenue of the Americas
New York, NY 10020
$14.50

Instant Art for Mail Order Operators
Career Publishing Corporation
P.O. Box 19905
Dallas, TX 75219
$15.00

Keep Your Customers (And Keep Them Happy)
by Stanley J. Fenvessy
Dow Jones-Irwin
1818 Ridge Road
Homewood, IL 60430
$11.95

The Mailer's Guide to Postal Regulations
Lyle Stuart, Inc.
120 Enterprise Avenue
Secaucus, NJ 07094
$40.00

Memo to Mailers—Eight-page Newsletter
United States Postal Service
P.O. Box 6400
Arlington, VA 22206
Available free to firms generating large quantities of mail. Published monthly

My First 65 Years in Advertising
by Maxwell Sackheim
Tab Books
Blue Ridge Summit, PA 17214
$5.95

Planning and Creating Better Direct Mail
by John D. Yeck and John T.Maguire
McGraw-Hill Book Company
1221 Avenue of the Americas
New York, NY 10020
$12.00

Robert Collier Letter Book: How to Write Successful Direct Mail Letters
by Robert Collier
6th edition
Prentice-Hall, Inc.
Route 9W
Englewood Cliffs, NJ 07632
$14.95

Successful Direct Marketing Methods
by Bob Stone
2nd edition
Crain Books
740 Rush Street
Chicago, IL 60611
$24.95

Tested Advertising Methods
by John Caples
4th edition
Prentice-Hall, Inc.
Route 9W
Englewood Cliffs, NJ 07632
$11.95

United States Postal Manual
Superintendent of Documents
Government Printing Office
Washington, DC 20402
$10.00 annually each for domestic and foreign. Includes regular updates.

Where to get more information

In addition to the sources listed in the bibliography, a wealth of other direct marketing information is available from various organizations. The two best sources are:

1. Direct Mail Marketing Association
   6 East 43rd Street
   New York, NY 10017
   (212) 689-4977

The leading trade association in the field. Has 1,800 member firms. Sponsors an annual conference and trade show plus numerous workshops, seminars, and institutes. Has an annual awards competition and a library of over 2,000 successful case histories. Maintains an information center service. Represents direct marketers in legislative and governmental affairs.

2. *Direct Marketing* Magazine
   224 Seventh Street
   Garden City, NY 11530
   (516) 746-6700

This monthly publication provides articles and case histories on all aspects of direct marketing. Each issue also contains an extensive directory of supplier listings. The publisher, Hoke Communications, also publishes *Friday Report*, a weekly newsletter, and offers recordings of many seminars and conferences. Its annual catalog of *Ideas in Sound* is available upon request.

Associations

The following organizations represent various aspects of the direct marketing industry:

Associated Third Class Mail Users
1725 K Street, N.W., Washington, DC 20006   (202) 296-5232

Asociacion Mexicana de Mercadotecnia
c/o Libros de Time-Life Paseo De La Reforma,
Mexico 5, D.F., Mexico   (905) 527-0398

Associaton of Direct Marketing Agencies
111 Presidential Blvd., Bala Cynwyd, PA 19004   (215) 667-9600

Australian Direct Marketing Association
32 Buckingham St., Surrey Hills, N.S.W., 2010, Australia   (2) 699-7955

British Direct Mail Marketing Association
1 New Burlington St., London, W1X 1FD, England   (01) 437-4485

Canadian Direct Mail Association
130 Merton St., Toronto, M4S 1A4   (416) 484-8554

Direct Marketing Writers Guild
516 Fifth Avenue, New York, NY 10016   (212) 972-9000

EDMA/European Direct Mail Association
P.O. Box 14, Baechelacherstr, 12, Ch-8128 Hinteregg,
Zurich, Switzerland

Envelope Manufacturers Association
1 Rockefeller Plaza, New York, NY 10020   (212) CI-5-5885

Fulfillment Management Association
755 2nd Avenue, New York, NY 10017   (212) 986-4600

Japan Direct Mail Association
Masuda Bldg., 3-2-12 Kyobaschi, Chuo-Ku, Tokyo 104 Japan   (03) 278-1592

MASA International
7315 Wisconsin Avenue, Washington, DC 20014   (301) 654-7030

Parcel Shippers Association
1211 Connecticut Avenue, N.W., Washington, DC 20036   (202) 296-3690

Local direct marketing clubs

Most of the following clubs sponsor monthly luncheon meetings with guest speakers, plus an annual Direct Marketing Day seminar. Addresses and phone numbers are not included because club officers are usually changed annually, but a current list appears monthly in *Direct Marketing* magazine.

Chicago Association of Direct Marketing
Direct Marketing Association of Southwestern Ontario
Direct Marketing Club of Des Moines
Direct Marketing Club of Kansas City
Direct Marketing Club of St. Louis
Direct Marketing Club of North Texas
Direct Marketing Club of Southern California (Los Angeles)
Direct Marketing Club of Washington, DC
Florida Mail Marketing Association
Houston Direct Marketing Club
Hundred Million Club of New York
Long Island Direct Marketing Association
Mail Marketing Club of Detroit
Mail Marketing Club of New England
Midwest Mail Marketing Association (Minneapolis/St. Paul)
Ohio Valley Direct Marketing Club (Cincinnati)
Philadelphia Direct Marketing Club
School of Direct Marketing of the Cleveland Ad Club

Universities

A number of leading universities offer courses in direct marketing. Roosevelt University in Chicago offers not only an undergraduate course on direct marketing, but a complete master's degree program.

Index